W0112027

Management for Professionals

For further volumes:
http://www.springer.com/series/10101

Ferri Abolhassan
Editor

The Road to a Modern IT Factory

Industrialization – Automation – Optimization

Editor
Dr. Ferri Abolhassan
T-Systems International GmbH
Saarbrücken
Germany

ISSN 2192-8096 ISSN 2192-810X (electronic)
ISBN 978-3-642-40218-0 ISBN 978-3-642-40219-7 (eBook)
DOI 10.1007/978-3-642-40219-7
Springer Heidelberg New York Dordrecht London

Library of Congress Control Number: 2014936634

Printed on acid-free paper

Springer is part of Springer Science+Business Media (www.springer.com)

Contents

List of Contributors

Dr. Ferri Abolhassan is a Director of T-Systems International GmbH, where he manages the Delivery unit. He began his professional career in 1987 at Siemens' research and development division in Munich. Following a period at IBM in the United States, he held a range of executive positions at SAP from 1992 to 2001, including that of Senior Vice President of the global Retail and Consumer Products business unit. This was followed by a period at the helm of IDS Scheer AG in the role of CEO and Co-Chairman. Beginning in 2005, Dr. Abolhassan returned to work within SAP top management, with his last position there being Executive Vice President EMEA.

In 2008, he took over the Systems Integration division at T-Systems and joined the company's Management Board. Responsible for managing Production at T-Systems since late 2010, Dr. Abolhassan assumed the leadership of the company's overall Delivery unit with effect from 1 January 2013.

Gregor Altmann is Vice President Projects & Transition Management at T-Systems International GmbH. He has held a range of executive positions at subsidiaries of Deutsche Telekom and works in the field of telecommunications networks operations and optimization.

Henryk Biesiada is T-System's Vice President Global Production Strategy & Design, and responsible for developing the conceptual rationale behind the company's global IT production strategies. After completing his computer science degree, he worked at the University of Kaiserslautern from 1987 to 1989, before moving into business. At Tecmath GmbH, he was given executive responsibility for the firm's Measurement Data Processing unit. From 1997 to 2001, Henryk Biesiada was in charge of application development at the Tengelmann retail group. In September 2001, he joined T-Systems International GmbH, where he has held a number of high-profile management positions.

He is a frequent speaker at international symposia and a prolific author in renowned industry journals, in addition to having authored and co-authored six books and monographs.

Prof. Dr. oec. Walter Brenner was appointed as Professor of Information Management at the University of St. Gallen (HSG) on 1 April 2001 and is Executive Director of the Institute of Information Management. In his academic career, Dr. Brenner has held professorships at the University of Essen and the TU Bergakademie Freiberg. His research activities focus on the industrialization of information management, the management of IT service providers, customer relationship management, the integration of new technologies, and design thinking. He is a freelance consultant on questions of information management, and prepares companies for the digital and interconnected world of tomorrow.

Dr. Stefan Bucher has held the position of Senior Vice President Solutions & Projects at T-Systems' Delivery unit since 2013. He has global responsibility for transition and transformation projects, also covering solution design in the deal process. Prior to this assignment, he held various executive positions at T-Systems, including Head of Computing Services & Solutions and Global Delivery Management for Royal Dutch Shell. Dr. Bucher joined T-Systems in 1997. He holds a Ph.D. in physics from Ludwig-Maximilian University (LMU), Munich.

Bernd Debus is Vice President Capacity Management, Efficiency and Six Sigma at T-Systems International GmbH. He has held a range of executive appointments at T-Systems. In addition to previous roles in service and sales support, he has been in charge of introducing lean production methods in the organization's domestic and international production units. In his current role, he is actively involved with the standardization of portfolios and their implications for the introduction of lean IT production.

Dr. Stefan Diefenbach is Vice President Strategy & Program Management at T-Systems, where he is responsible for identifying and quantifying internal efficiency improvements and their practical realization in real-world projects. He is also in charge of tracking relevant trends in the global ICT business and integrating these into a holistic portfolio strategy. After receiving his doctorate in physics from Ruhr University Bochum and a number of years at the German Aerospace Center, he moved to Deutsche Telekom in 2000, where he held a number of strategic positions.

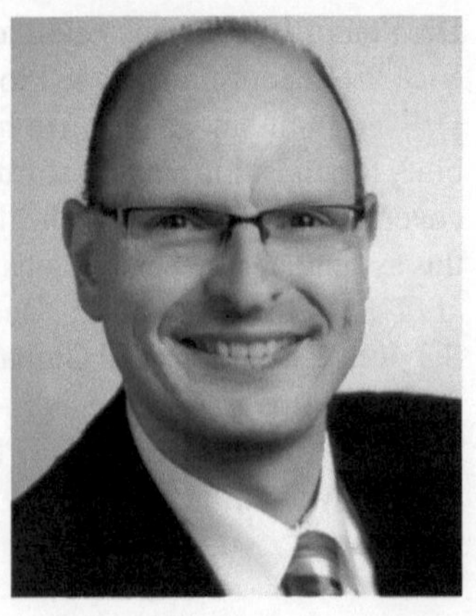

Holger Dörnemann is Senior Manager Systems Engineering at VMware Global Inc., where he is responsible for technical customer service in VMware's German sales operations. With his team, he actively trials new technologies and solutions at clients. Before coming to VMware, he held technical responsibility for systems and service management at IBM's Tivoli Software, where he covered aspects of dynamic data centers and green IT initiatives. His work focuses on the standardization and automation of data center operations as the basis for cloud computing.

Christine Ebner-Um studied political sciences, sociology, and modern history at the University of Duisburg-Essen. She spent a number of years as co-partner at a leading consultancy firm, where she covered a diverse range of projects for clients from a broad range of industries and led an account cluster of consultants tackling questions of IT security and the global workplace. Christine Ebner-Um also oversaw a major organizational development program for a fast-growing IT unit in the Chinese operations of a leading German carmaker. In late 2012, she joined the Strategy Unit in the Delivery Division at T-Systems International GmbH. Here, she works on the global transformation of Delivery in the direction of industrialized IT.

Thomas Ehrlich is Vice President Partners & Pathways EMEA at NetApp, where he has responsibility for channel organization, system integration, and business alliances in the EMEA business at the storage solutions provider. His work covers aspects of solution integration, cloud business, and big data. After moving to NetApp from sgi in 1999, Thomas Ehrlich has held a range of executive positions at the company.

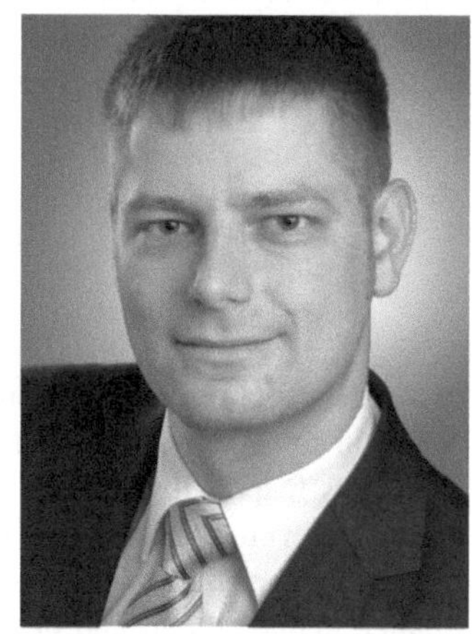

Björn Froese works as a management consultant at Detecon International, where he focuses on aspects of strategy and innovation. After graduating in industrial engineering and management from Berlin and Berkeley, he now advises ICT organizations on matters of corporate finance. In his financial management work, he has successfully established the strategic innovation unit "Education".

To round off his professional expertise, he completed his Master of Commercial Law at Saarland University, where he majored in contract management.

Carsten Glohr is a Managing partner of Detecon International, with responsibility for T-Systems sector with significant consultant budgets. He is responsible for Detecon's IT outsourcing, IT benchmarking, and IT performance measurement activities. In his consulting projects, he has overseen around 40 outsourcing transactions (including three highly complex projects with total budgets exceeding €1 billion and a range of next-generation outsourcing projects).

Dr. Katharina Grimme is Principal Consultant Outsourcing & BPO Markets at the Pierre Audoin Consultants (PAC) market analysis and consultancy firm, where she advises executives at leading companies on market trends, technological developments, and strategic decisions concerning outsourcing and IT services. Her extensive expertise and profound knowledge of the market make her an internationally respected specialist for outsourcing, BPO, and cloud computing. Before joining PAC, Dr. Grimme worked at NelsonHall and Ovum, where she was responsible for outsourcing research and consulting. She has a Ph.D. from the University of Sussex and an MBA from Birmingham Business School.

Dr. Marcus Hacke is T-Systems' Senior Vice President for Portfolio & Solution Design. In his role, he is responsible for defining and developing the service portfolio, standardizing the company's service elements, innovation and alliance management, and designing client solutions. Since joining the company in 2004, he has held various executive roles in Sales, Portfolio & Offering Management, and in the Service Line Computing & Desktop Services.

Before coming to T-Systems, Dr. Hacke spent seven years as a consultant at McKinsey & Company. After graduating in physics from Ruhr University Bochum, he completed his doctorate at RWTH Aachen University.

Dr.-Ing. Tom In der Rieden is Vice President Global Business Operations at T-Systems, where he works in the company's Computing Services & Solutions (CSS) service line.

Before joining T-Systems in 2010, he contributed substantially to establishing and managing Saarland University's computer science excellence cluster, one of the first of its type in Germany.

In his previous career, he has overseen international research projects with a focus on zero-error computing systems for the Federal Ministry of Education and Research.

In his research work, he has worked closely with Microsoft Research and the development teams of Audi, Bosch, BMW, and Infineon.

Stephan Kasulke is a Senior Vice President at T-Systems International GmbH with responsibility for Global Quality, Processes, and Tools. In this function, he oversees the implementation of the Zero Outage program for higher-quality operations.

Jörn Kellermann can look back on about 20 years in the IT industry. Following freelance work, he joined debis Systemhaus (now T-Systems) in 1999. At T-Systems, he has held a variety of positions in sales, consulting, and IT service delivery. His most recent work focused on managing global dynamic platform operations. Jörn Kellermann currently has overall responsibility for Computing Services supplied to T-Systems' clients, including the delivery and operation of IP networks and data centers down to the level of individual applications.

Jörn Kellermann holds degrees in computer science and business management.

Peter Kreutter is Director of the WHU Foundation in Vallendar and Executive Director of the WHU's Strategy Research Network (SRN). After initially training in banking, he went on to complete degrees in economics and political science at Friedrich Alexander University Erlangen-Nuremberg (FAU) and Trinity College Dublin. Following this, he worked for Deutsche Bank, Sal. Oppenheim jr. & Cie. and others. He focuses his research efforts on the long-term evolution of industries and strategic options for high-companies. Springer published Kreutter's most recent book on the "Globalization of Professional Services" in 2012.

Dr. Markus Löffler is a Director (Senior Partner) at McKinsey & Company and Co-Head of Global IT Performance Management Practice. He is responsible for strategic projects that focus on IT Strategy, IT Enablement and IT Efficiency, focusing especially on clients in the financial services and high-tech/telecommunications sectors.

Dr. Felix Reinshagen is a Junior Partner at McKinsey & Company and a member of the Leadership Team at the Business Technology Office in Germany. He is responsible for strategic projects that focus on IT Strategy, IT Enablement and IT Performance Management, with a particular emphasis on clients in the high-tech/telecommunications and financial services sectors.

Michael Rubas studied social science at the Universities of Konstanz and Bath. He has been Senior Vice President at T-Systems International GmbH since September 2008, where he is in charge of HR Business Partners for the 35,000 people working in the Delivery unit. Before taking on these responsibilities, he was a member of the executive board of T-Systems Switzerland, with responsibility for planning, implementation, data center operations, desktops, and network infrastructure, as well as overseeing organizational development at Mercedes-Benz AG.

Peter Schnitzenbaumer is a Vice President at T-Systems International GmbH, where, within the TSS (Telecommunication Services & Solutions) service line, he oversees the corporate Global Business Operations (GBO) unit, whose 150 people handle budgets totaling some €65 million.

Before joining T-Systems, he held executive positions at BT (Germany) GmbH/Viag Interkom GmbH, with his last position being Head of Business Consultancy Germany in BT's Global Services—Service Operations unit.

Petra Trost-Gürtner is a Senior Vice President at T-Systems International GmbH, where she manages the TSS (Telecommunication Services & Solutions) service line. With its global workforce of 3,000 people and budget of €800 million, the TSS is responsible for the provisioning and operation of products, platforms, services, and solutions for domestic and international ICT clients. Before T-Systems, she held executive positions at Hewlett Packard and Viag Interkom, with her last role being BT's Head of Business Transformation Germany.

Prof. Dr. oec. Falk Uebernickel is Assistant Professor for Information Management at the University of St. Gallen (HSG) and Managing Partner of the ITMP St. Gallen AG consultancy, having joined the firm from an international consultancy company. His current consulting and research interests focus on IT management and innovation management for global businesses and IT organizations.

Dr.-Ing. Hans-Rüdiger Vogel is a Managing Consultant for Detecon International GmbH. As a holder of a degree in geophysics and a doctorate in mining engineering, a holistic and interdisciplinary outlook has become a mainstay of his work in more than 18 years of IT consulting, taking him from Computacenter, Avinci, and Logica to Detecon in 2009. As part of the company's commitment to green IT, he has overseen projects such as the development of a green enterprise data center strategy for one of China's major mobile communications providers.

Birgit Wahl is a Senior Vice President at T-Systems, in charge of the company's near- and offshore locations. These include the global network of offices across Europe, Asia, and the Americas. She has overseen the constant expansion of these locations and introduced efficiency measures for the continuous improvement of productivity. During her activities there, she gained experience both in Production and Systems Integration business.

Dr. Rainer Weidmann is a Managing Consultant at Detecon International GmbH. After completing his physics degree and a period in teaching and research, Dr. Weidmann joined debis Systemhaus. Since 1999, he has covered a range of executive management functions, with complete operational responsibility (plan—build—run) for a number of data centers across Germany. He continued his work in this area at T-Systems until 2007.

Between 2007 and 2011, Dr. Weidmann established the Datacenter Engineering unit with a focus on datacenter architecture and innovation at T-Systems. In this role, he introduced the world's first "fuel cell technology in data center operations" project in 2008 and cooperated with Intel on the "Data Center 2020—Energy efficiency in data centers" project in 2009. He is in demand as a speaker and data center expert at domestic and international conferences and has co-authored numerous publications in the field.

Dirk Wellershaus is a Senior Manager in T-System's Strategy & Program Management division, with responsibility for conceptual issues in portfolio management, as well as the direction of strategic projects for organizational development and the enhancement of specific portfolio solutions in strategic partnerships. After completing his business engineering degree at Darmstadt, Eindhoven, and Vienna, he joined Deutsche Telekom as a trainee in 2004, where he occupied a number of positions, most with a strong strategic focus.

Marc Wilczek works in T-Systems' Computing Service Division as Vice President for Portfolio, Innovation and Architecture. In this role, he is responsible for driving business transformation towards higher cloud adoption and standardization throughout the IT stack (IaaS, PaaS, SaaS)—from blueprint to Go-2-Market. Before joining T-Systems, he was Senior Vice President and Member of the Group Executive Committee at CompuGroup Medical AG, where he oversaw all field operations across the Asia Pacific, Latin America, Middle East and Africa geography. Prior to this, he held various leadership roles at IT security provider Sophos, and most recently served as Managing Director for the Asia Pacific region. He holds master's degrees in business administration from FOM Graduate School for Economics & Management in Frankfurt/Main and the London Business School, and also attended New York's Columbia University on academic exchange.

Thomas Wind is Vice President Capacity Management at T-Systems International GmbH. He can look back on 15 years in strategic and organizational consulting, with particular emphasis on business development, sales, and customer service, most recently as the Managing Director of TellSell Consulting GmbH in Frankfurt/Main. He began his professional career at the public Treuhandanstalt, followed by appointments at the Gesellschaft für Wirtschaftsförderung Saar mbH and various ICT consultancy firms.

Introduction 1

Ferri Abolhassan

Businesses need efficient processes. This is and remains a real and obvious challenge. Obvious, because there is general consensus about this fact; a challenge, because it is still no everyday reality at most companies. When asked "How well are your processes working", the respondents of many staff, partner, or even management surveys will give a disarmingly honest answer: The optimization and continuous improvement or even the simple monitoring of processes is often neglected. Very few companies have allocated the topics a dedicated place among the directorial responsibilities of their executive managers.

A more encouraging picture appears when it comes to the recognition that information and communication technology is an essential and indispensable means for pursuing a company's mission or running its production or service delivery processes. Nonetheless, the lasting effectiveness and efficiency that companies are aspiring to will only be possible by considering processes and IT as one joint package. There is, happily, general agreement that most business processes would nowadays be unthinkable without the support of IT solutions. This applies to the manufacturing industry just as much as to the world of finance or the service sector. With the increasing relevance of IT, the requirements of users are also growing; users expect more and more in terms of efficiency, effectiveness, and quality.

Irrespective of whether it is handled by an in-house team or by an external provider, IT remains caught up in the tension between the functional and qualitative requirements of operational departments—essentially meaning the end user—and the pursuit of greater efficiency and optimized processes. The latter perspective considers quality and funtionality purely in terms of costs and economization. IT is often faced with mutually contradictory demands: On the one hand, people expect the shortest possible time-to-market and customized solutions at an acceptable

F. Abolhassan (✉)
T-Systems International GmbH, Mecklenburgring 25, 66121 Saarbrücken, Germany
e-mail: Ferri.Abolhassan@t-systems.com

F. Abolhassan (ed.), *The Road to a Modern IT Factory*, Management for Professionals,
DOI 10.1007/978-3-642-40219-7_1, © Springer-Verlag Berlin Heidelberg 2014

price; on the other hand, the laws of the market demand a very efficient and economical delivery of the products. Development of solutions that fulfill all of these expectations—from users and businesses alike—requires dedicated, concerted action from the operational departments and IT units or external IT service providers. At the same time, the evolution of IT continues to progress in leaps and bounds, leaving companies lacking the resources to keep pace with developments. Companies are rapidly finding themselves unequal to the task of handling a growing dependency on an ever-more complex IT landscape. The call for standards is a clear signal and a call for help, coming from companies trying to introduce some stability and order into these developments. In a sense, the IT industry needs to "automate and industrialize" itself.

This is the challenge that "The Road to a Modern IT Factory" intends to explore. A confrontation with the topic is inevitable, because one thing is clear: The IT sector is currently undergoing one of its most critical phases of transformation ever in its history. IT providers and IT service organizations need to achieve what can be called an industrial revolution in their production and service processes. Only if they manage to do that can they hope to fulfill the obvious requirements of specific business departments or businesses in general. The manufacturing industry can serve as a model, as it has managed the leap from cottage industry to modern just-in-time production powerhouses in the course of the previous century, that offer the highest standards of service and quality.

The path towards twenty first-century industrialized IT production and, in extension, truly efficient processes will be long. After all, IT industrialization can be considered to lag two decades behind the evolution of industrial production (cf. Institute of Information Management, University of St. Gallen). Some headway has already been made: The people in charge are beginning to apply a more systematic approach to process and efficiency improvements. They have come to understand that there will be no alternative option to IT industrialization. The challenge now lies on the side of effective implementation: IT departments and external providers need to join forces to establish standardized structures and process models on all levels—from data centers down to individual user queries. It does not stop there: They need to form an industrial culture and live the idea of industrial IT to make the leap from "cottage industry IT" to "IT factories" as their peers in manufacturing have done before. Isolated efforts or projects will lead nowhere in this groundbreaking transformation.

1.1 No Progress Without IT Industrialization

The conclusion is: IT industrialization is the precondition for efficient processes. What does this mean specifically? "*Production-line IT*" would be a too narrow definition, since service processes and infrastructures should not be neglected. IT industrialization, in the very sense of the word, means the application of the professional concepts and methods of traditional industrial manufacturing—such as those used in car making or mechanical engineering—to the IT sector

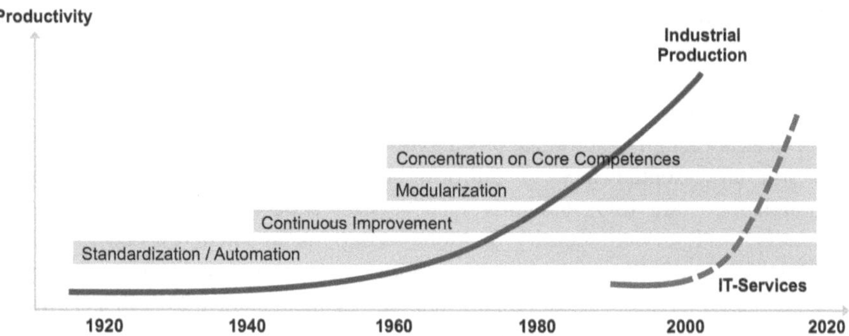

Fig. 1.1 The evolution of IT industrialization (Source: Univerity of St. Gallen, graphic: Computerwoche. Cf. Brenner et al. 2007)

(cf. Brenner et al. 2007). In practical terms, this primarily concerns IT hardware and software development, as well as the management of information and services.

At first sight, the term IT industrialization seems quite fuzzy, with few concrete footholds for its practitioners to go on. But a closer look makes it clear that this is not about inventing the wheel again. There are already many useful concepts available, such as automation and standardization (cf. Brenner et al. 2009). Henry Ford's legendary Model T is the archetype—in a sense the first true mass-market industrial scale product. Built to a single plan, sold in "any color, as long as it's black", and designed with simple functionality and easy maintenance in mind, the "Tin Lizzie" revolutionized the automotive industry (cf. Brenner et al. 2007). The key to its success: strictly standardized division of labor and assembly line production, which helped bring down the price of cars by more than half. The chart above illustrates other aspects of industrialization. It also shows how far IT services have come when compared to traditional industrial manufacturing (Fig. 1.1).

One step at a time: Only when areas like hardware and software production have been standardized and automated in line with their industrial role-models can IT service organizations be able to complete their transition into "IT factories". In IT, everything is connected to everything else. The value chain as a whole can only be perfected when the right foundations are in place.

Promising progress has been made on the hardware side, where virtually everything is produced to uniform industrial standards. Industrial software development has also come a long way, as can be seen in the standardization and automation concepts that are being applied in coding and test automation (cf. BITKOM 2010). However, the IT industry remains far removed from software 'engineering' in an industrial sense, i.e., using engineers' approaches that are common in mechanical engineering or similar fields. The key problem is the lack of an overall framework. For instance, there are many platform standards for development or runtime environments like Java or .NET, but the competition between the entities and committees in charge of standardization stand in the way of truly interchangeable and cross-usable components and methods that would be essential for software engineering.

The industrialization of IT services is an even more challenging task. The complex and dynamic interplay of people, processes, and technologies means that IT services are tough to automate or standardize (cf. Böhmann et al. 2008). There is also still an essential lack of uniform and universally applicable standards. Although there are ISO standards such as ISO 20000 to define the minimum standards for IT service, security, and relationship management (cf. Federal Ministry of the Interior 2006), some equally essential aspects, such as IT project management, are not addressed. What remains are only de facto standards such as ITIL (IT Infrastructure Library). This means that the IT industry is in urgent need of binding standards that the people in charge can trust and follow. After all, even the most robust and architecturally sophisticated building cannot be built without a firm foundation and a sound set of blueprints.

1.2 Cost-Efficient, but Tailor-Made

Another obstacle lies in the challenge of responding to the user's expectations with solutions that are as customized as possible, whilst staying as cost-efficient as necessary. The tension of this seeming contradiction in terms can be eased somewhat with the help of IT industrialization. How this can be done is readily visible in other industries, such as the car making sector: for instance, the *MQB modular transverse matrix* introduced by Volkswagen AG (cf. Goppelt 2012) provides many different models of the group's various brands with a set of similar components, such as axles, steering units, or entire engine-transmission assemblies. The equivalent of the automotive industry's MQB in IT production includes concepts such as service-oriented architectures (SOA) (cf. Banke et al. 2007). Modular designs allow IT processes and components to be realized in a much more efficient and effective manner.

1.3 Keep Going or Quit

What must not be forgotten is the never-ceasing evolution and improvement of processes based on set rules that all people in companies need to follow in their everyday work. A good example of such proactive improvement processes is the *Kaizen* concept, or "change for the better", introduced in Japanese manufacturing and perfected by Toyota (cf. Imai 1996). It means nothing more exotic than the constant improvement of process and product quality to achieve ground-breaking commercial successes. The IT industry is doing its best to establish similar optimization concepts, for instance by creating transparency about quality in *Service Level Agreements (SLA)* or *Operative Level Agreements (OLA)*. Despite this, measurable improvement in IT is and will remain a special challenge.

1.4 Creating More Value by Concentrating on Core Competencies

Whenever processes are optimized, attention also needs to be paid to quality when outsourcing individual tasks or production phases. Globalization and international competition have forced many companies to take a close look at their value chains and find ways to save costs. IT is no exception to this. Near- and off-shoring or outsourcing are now well-established responses but are often limited to processes that add little value. The question for the future is how it will be possible to procure even more complex services from outside partners, while keeping a consistent and acceptable level of quality.

Another important development that affects matters of effectiveness and efficiency is the commoditization of IT. Turning IT solutions into a mass-produced, easily replicable commodity is confronting IT service providers with the need to steer their way through the opposing forces of customer expectations, reliable operations, and dwindling profit margins. The reasons are simple: When products and services become cheaper and more readily available as a result of standardization and automation, they turn into a commodity, losing their luster in the eyes of the customer. Even highly complex solutions are expected as par for the course. There is also a risk that a copy and paste mentality will lead to less interest in innovation. With services being readily and consistently available to a large market, many providers are worried about losing their USPs in the market. However, this is only one side of the coin. In fact, well-established IT service providers now have an opportunity to become pioneers and market their self-developed products and services across markets and sectors of industry. Again, the precondition is proven superior quality and innovative prowess. And this is precisely where they can once again benefit from the toolkit of industrialization.

1.5 As Readily Available as Electricity from the Tap

All of the hard work that goes into improving efficiency, effectiveness, and quality has one mission: making IT as readily and easily available as electricity—in a sense, "*IT on tap*". Nothing could be easier to use for the end users in business. A brave new world: Just like households everywhere get their power around the clock from the local grid, storage or computing services can be sourced quickly and simply from centralized, cost-efficient IT networks, at the point of need. The magic word here is *cloud computing*. In future, other IT resources will also be much more easily accessible in other areas. With IT service providers taking charge of ensuring quality and availability, companies can concentrate on what they do best: developing, producing, and selling their products. By reliably providing storage and data processing capacities, software and customer applications, or product and platform environments, the IT industry is making the leap from a support to a core process that is simply always there—"*IT on tap*".

A look at how far industrialized IT has come shows us that the industry is still in the early stages of groundbreaking changes. This makes it absolutely essential for it to engage systematically with the issue it is facing. "The Road to a Modern IT Factory", is offered as a initial reference work that casts an interdisciplinary look at the status quo of applied research and IT practice in the area. It intends to give the decision makers in IT a readable and comprehensible introduction to the issue. Finally, IT experts in business as well as IT providers at large will get answers to the many unresolved questions they are facing. And the IT sector will find material to fuel the current debate in the industry. With this ambition in mind, this book introduces ways to transition isolated IT processes and standalone solutions into industrialized structures.

With the insights and contributions of authors drawn from many disciplines, the reader is given a 360° view of the current state of industrialization of IT. The first part of the book analyses the critical factors for success at a global IT service provider and, thereby illustrating the current set of challenges facing the IT sector. The second part examines the transformations under way in the IT industry and the change from a project focus to a product focus. Old isolated solutions are transferred into factory-like structures and standardized, automated product and platform offerings are being established with the advent of industrialized IT.

After surveying the current state and the internal and external conditions in the industry, the authors discuss the next steps on the way to the IT factory of the future. Part three of the book reviews tools for short-term optimizations and efficiency improvements in IT processes and infrastructures: Quality management, governance models, performance management, and reporting.

Building on this, the fourth part considers the medium- to long-term management of these transformations, paying particular attention to the structural changes that are needed. The vision of modern automated IT production is explained in detail, with a discussion of how this vision can be turned into reality by implementing its two essential pillars: Standardization and automation. IT service providers are facing major challenges in this respect, in particular in terms of the sustainable use of resources such as computing capacity or energy in cloud computing or other IT activities. The question of which core competencies to focus on also comes into effect here—raising the issues of outsourcing and near- or off-shoring.

Optimizing value chains with effective make-or-buy decisions will become ever more relevant for the competitiveness of IT businesses and their transition into the IT factories of the future. The expert authors also consider the people management during transformation, a central aspect that is too often neglected in the context of technological or structural progress. It is, however, just as decisive for the success of industrial IT to get employees on board for the transformation process, because they have the expertise that is needed to provide IT services and execute IT projects at clients. They need to get behind and speak up for the changes. To be able to do so, they need to be given opportunities to develop in the form of high-quality training and development. Certified courses ensure a consistently high level of expertise and thereby guarantee the best possible solutions for the client.

The fifth and final part of the book takes a look ahead at the future development of industrialized IT. The authors illustrate ways in which how IT can establish itself as an engine for innovation across the boundaries of industry. This relies on internal and external innovation campaigns and needs to consider the many forces that will influence the future of the industry, such as disruptive technologies that mature over decades and can shake up established markets or displace long-standing products. New trends like *crowd sourcing* will also have an impact on the IT industry. By contrast to regular outsourcing, crowd sourcing moves traditionally internal activities to internet volunteers, such as the testing of apps or web applications to improve their usability (cf. Howe 2006). This means that services are produced in collaboration with interactive experts who contribute their unique know-how and ideas in the most efficient way possible. Companies can benefit considerably from this.

The backbone of this book is formed from the many specialists who have contributed to it. Many experts from the world of applied research and academia have agreed to introduce and debate these often challenging issues, including researchers from the University of St. Gallen (HSG) and the WHU—Otto Beisheim School of Management. Representatives from IT market research, market analysis, and management consulting houses like PAC, McKinsey, and Detecon have also enriched this volume with their expertise. Their work is complemented by the insights of specialist practitioners from VMware, NetApp, and T-Systems. We thank all authors for agreeing to share their extensive experience and industry know-how in this publication.

1.6 The Future Starts Today

We began by saying that most business processes could not live without IT support. In the end, IT will provide a major contribution to encouraging businesses to make a serious attempt at tackling the long-postponed task of improving the efficiency of their processes. And, once again, IT industrialization forms the precondition for ensuring IT is fit for this purpose. It makes higher quality and efficiency as well as lower costs possible in the production of software as well as client applications as well as the provision of products and platform environments. There is a long way to go still, but the first steps have been taken. It is now upon us to push the discussion and give clients "*IT on tap*" solutions. The successful industrialization of IT can help establish IT as an important business enabler. In the end, the competitiveness of IT service providers will also depend on whether they are able to seize the many advantages of IT industrialization.

References

Banke, K., Krafzig, D., & Slama, D. (2007). *Enterprise SOA. Best Practices für Serviceorientierte Architekturen – Einführung, Umsetzung, Praxis*. Heidelberg: mitp.

BITKOM. (2010). *Industrielle Softwareentwicklung*. Berlin: Leitfaden und Orientierungshilfe.

Böhmann, T., Krcmar, H., & Walter, S. M. (2008). Grundlagen der IT-Industrialisierung. *Industrialisierung des Software Managements, 2008*, 19–30.

Brenner, W., Ebert, N., Hochstein, A., & Übernickel, F. (2007). IT-Industrialisierung – Was ist das? *Computerwoche, 15*, 5.

Brenner, W., Resch, A., & Schulz, V. (2009). *Die Zukunft der IT in Unternehmen*. Frankfurt/Main.

Competence center for the industrialization of information management at the University of St. Gallen. Retrieved December 11, 2012, from http://www.cciim.ch/

German Federal Ministry of the Interior, Koordinierungs- und Beratungsstelle der Bundesregierung für Informationstechnik in der Bundesverwaltung (KBSt). (2006). *ITIL und Standards für IT-Prozesse*. Version 1.0.1, Berlin.

Goppelt, G., Heise.de. Retrieved December 11, 2012, from http://www.heise.de/autos/artikel/Ist-der-modulare-Querbaukasten-von-Volkswagen-eine-Qualitaetsbremse-1318973.html

Howe, J. (2006). The rise of crowdsourcing. Retrieved December 11, 2012, from http://www.wired.com/wired/archive/14.06/crowds.html

Imai, M. (1996). *Kaizen. Der Schlüssel zum Erfolg der Japaner im Wettbewerb*. Berlin.

Part I

Critical Factors for Successful Global IT Service Organizations

The Challenges of Modern IT

2

Falk Uebernickel and Walter Brenner

2.1 Motivation

The world of information technology (IT) continues to undergo rapid change. The appearance of new technologies such as cloud computing, mobile communication, social media or big data is exerting a lasting effect on established industries and is even forging new industries and shaping society itself. Examples include companies like Zalando[1] or Car2Go,[2] which have successfully used IT to set up new business models and go head-to-head with established companies in the market. This progress requires agility (cf. Schaffry 2012) and customer focus, as well as efficiency, effectiveness and quality across the entire IT sector. Both the "clock speed" now required for product development and the pace of development for new application systems or mobile device applications are accelerating significantly. At the same time, requirements for these systems' operational stability, security and flexibility (in terms of scaling) are also growing. On the customer side, we observe a new, higher-quality kind of IT literacy. The "digital natives"[3] are demanding new, IT-based solutions for their daily tasks at home and in the office (cf. Brenner et al. 2011).

There is an obvious parallel to developments in traditional industries. As it matured over the last 100 years, industrial manufacturing passed a number of milestones, starting with standardization and the streamlining of process flows,

[1] Formed in Berlin in 2008, Zalando is now one of the most successful footwear and fashion stores online.

[2] Car2Go is a car-sharing business set up by the car maker Daimler and the car rental company Europcar.

[3] The term "digital natives" is used to refer to people born after 1980. Digital natives are characterized by the ease with which they interact with IT and technology.

F. Uebernickel (✉) • W. Brenner
Institute of Information Management, University of St. Gallen, Müller-Friedberg-Straße 8, 9000 St. Gallen, Switzerland
e-mail: Falk.Uebernickel@unisg.ch; Walter.Brenner@unisg.ch

F. Abolhassan (ed.), *The Road to a Modern IT Factory*, Management for Professionals, DOI 10.1007/978-3-642-40219-7_2, © Springer-Verlag Berlin Heidelberg 2014

continuing with the explicit assurance of quality, and culminating in an end-to-end customer focus in production. The entire IT sector faces similar challenges (cf. Zarnekow et al. 2005). On the one hand, there is both the compulsion and the necessity to focus on the customer, innovate and be agile; on the other hand, continuous improvements to effectiveness, efficiency and quality are also critical (cf. Bravo-Sànchez et al. 2005). These challenges and the process of change are affecting both in-house IT units (within companies or corporations) and IT service organizations (occasionally described as IT service providers), which, with outsourcing revenue totaling USD 246.6 billion in 2011 (cf. Gartner 2012),[4] are making a considerable contribution to IT value creation. At the end of the day, structural problems will be the fate of anyone resting on past laurels!

For this reason, we may ask which factors will be critical for the success of IT service organizations in the future. To be able to answer this question adequately, we will first take a look at the future positioning of the Chief Information Officer (CIO) in companies and corporations, so as to derive a corresponding scope of duties. Here, we will be drawing on 50 interviews conducted in 2012 with CIOs, senior IT management staff and Chief Executive Officers (CEOs), most of whom were working in DAX-listed companies at the time. From this standpoint, we then return to answer our main line of inquiry, namely the success factors for IT service organizations.

2.2 A World in Flux

Facing up to the need to change presents a major challenge to both companies and people alike. Change implies upheaval, and is equated with the abolishment of outdated—yet familiar and habitual—methods and mechanisms. The uncertainty of the future is associated with the fear of inadequacy and the fear of its consequences. Yet both change and upheaval also imply progress for a company, and for society at large. Change is the process that drives the exit and entry of companies from and into markets, while existing companies grasp change as a mechanism for adjusting to match new circumstances—which, in turn, are accompanied by new chances for growth. Within these processes of change, IT unarguably has a major role to play, both in the digital economy and in traditional product-oriented industries such as the automotive sector or retail. Directly associated with this is a change in the business role of the CIO and the positioning of IT service organizations within the market—both today and in the future. The era of the "Head of Data Center Operations" or the "IT Service Organization Manager" is most certainly over (cf. Brenner and Witte 2007). The nature and velocity of these changes require affected individuals and organizations to adapt the ways in which they think and act. The following section discusses examples of IT-driven change.

[4] From 2010 to 2011, growth in outsourcing revenue was an impressive 7.8 %.

2.2.1 Business Models Built on Information Technology

In recent years, trends such as networking, data integration, a massive increase in data processing capacities and others have created an environment where new business models can be generated by IT. In other areas, the consumer-driven need for solutions integrated into day-to-day life has also contributed to a new wave of company start-ups. Whether we look at existing industries or new ideas pursued by young entrepreneurs, the change driving and being driven by IT is a global phenomenon and only the initial phase of an enduring trend.

What are its implications? Keeping pace with this change requires fast turnarounds as well as a high degree of agility and flexibility. Customer requirements often "materialize" very rapidly and require a prompt response from industry players. While tried-and-tested business models and businesses have persisted for decades in some cases, modern development cycles are characterized by much shorter periods. One of the enabling factors here is an IT infrastructure increasingly based on standardized and modularized components and technologies. The deep integration of IT into machinery, day-to-day appliances and vehicles ("embedded systems") is also offering previously unavailable levels of accessibility to information. To adequately meet these challenges, companies are faced with the task of querying their established processes and organizational structures.

One example is Daimler, which teamed up with Europcar in 2012 to launch the company and eponymous car-sharing service "Car2Go". In contrast to traditional car rental business models, the customer is no longer tied to fixed rental locations for hiring and returning a vehicle. Instead, the vehicles are scattered throughout the urban area, and can be located and hired using a mobile application. Managed by in-vehicle sensor systems, all of the consumption and mobility data can be accessed and used to bill the transport service provided. To function, this business model is critically dependent on the calculation of the rental period to the nearest minute, the miles driven, the fuel consumption and other parameters. Implementing a business model of this type would be unthinkable without the extensive deployment of information technology. Similar models are now also being operated by BMW (DriveNow).

A further example of the integration of IT into traditional industry is shown by its utility for business applications (business to business, B2B). Back in the 1960s, Rolls-Royce's aircraft engine manufacturing unit was already offering its "Power by the Hour" service. At its heart, this service ensures preventive maintenance and upkeep for engines. The service portfolio has been considerably expanded since 2002. One addition is a real-time monitor, which deploys information and communication technology to enable the collection and evaluation of additional machinery-related data. This enables a permanent exchange of data between the engine, the aircraft and the manufacturer. This represents a fundamental change of the business model: instead of selling the customer an aircraft engine as an investment, the manufacturer offers the airline an engine that is always fully operational. The approach also aligns the business models of Rolls-Royce and the airline: Rolls-Royce generates income whenever an aircraft is airborne.

The market is also home to many start-ups, which are creating business potential or taking a revolutionary approach to existing models. As one example, Airbnb has used an internet platform to open up a new segment in the hotel sector. For residential property owners, Airbnb offers an easy way to compete with traditional accommodation providers by offering cheap overnight stays to tourists and business travelers. Since its launch in 2008, around 10 million overnight stays have been booked using the portal (cf. Airbnb 2012). In 2012, user numbers grew so sharply that an online booking was completed every 2 s.

Groupon provides us with another example. The Groupon website can be used by restaurants, cinemas, theaters, travel agents or product manufacturers and other service providers to offer their services for a limited time. Discounts and reductions are granted depending on the total number of buyers for a service or product, and are immediately visible to all participants. The company's business model sees Groupon taking a cut of the revenue generated. To date, the model has proved so successful that it has been copied in many other countries. One competing service in Switzerland, for example, is deindeal.ch.

2.2.2 New Competitors

Provider or customer? In terms of the IT service organization market, finding an answer to this question is no longer a simple matter. A few years ago, the situation was clear: providers such as IBM, HP or T-Systems were offering professional services for information technology on a global scale. On the opposite side were companies whose business focused on the sale of other kinds of products and services. This principle no longer holds true, however. Leading the charge into the market for new providers of infrastructure-like IT services is Amazon.com, whose "S3" cloud service product had almost an exabyte of storage space at the end of 2012, according to industry estimates[5] (cf. Rodriguez 2011). This makes Amazon.com about 20 times larger than the prominent storage provider Dropbox (estimated at 40 petabytes) and, in all likelihood, the largest professional storage provider.

In terms of IT services rendered directly to the customer, Google has conquered large portions of the market. Starting as a "humble" search engine provider, the company has progressed to professional IT service provision for email and office products—such as GoogleDocs and GoogleDrive. In mid-2012, Google announced that the number of registered customers actively using its email service had passed the 425 million mark (cf. D'Orazio 2012). Statements from the company also suggest that several million business customers have migrated part of their IT support to Google, including household names such as Capgemini, General Electric, Roche and Genentech. The dynamic growth shown by Amazon and

[5] 1 exabyte = 1,000 petabytes = 1,000,000 terabytes.

Google is impressive, and casts the achievability of economies of scale and efficiency in a new light.

These two companies serve as excellent examples of the predominant market dynamics in IT, and the requirements that these entail. In certain areas such as infrastructure or the kinds of business process-neutral IT services offered by Google, CIOs and companies are demanding that services provided meet new standards in scalability and efficiency.

2.2.3 The Customer Factor

The following quote from a DAX 30 CIO, from an interview held in summer 2012, illustrates the growing importance of customer expectations: "*... this attitude has been drastically changed by Amazon, Google and eBay. When you go to Amazon today, then Amazon just knows the last thing I bought there. Customers have no problem with this and in fact see it as a plus. And our customers are now starting to lose patience with us if we don't know which product it was they bought. The customers project these experiences onto us.* [...] *Customers expect this to be a standard, but in some areas we're nowhere near that right now.*"[6] Customers want to exert more influence on the design of information systems. Their experiences as consumers—and in particular through the use of platforms such as Facebook, Blogger, Instagram and a range of applications on Apple's iPhone/iPad—are having a major impact on their expectations for application systems and the design of user interfaces. Compared to usability, requirements for data protection and data security appear increasingly to be of lesser concern, especially among the younger generation. For CIOs, the consequence is a new set of demands for the development and operation of these systems. Priority is given to agility and customer involvement, even at an early stage of development. At the same time, new skills are in demand from development unit staff in order to implement the requirements in software.

Hand in hand with customer influence goes the trend towards consumerization, i.e. the reversal of the traditional flow of IT innovation from large organizations in the direction of the end consumer. This means that software and IT innovations are increasingly being created at the point of use or specifically for consumers, before then going on to influence corporate software design (cf. Escherich 2011). Customers and employees are increasingly "emancipated" in how they use and select software and hardware. IT services can be sourced from the cloud—e.g. as "Software as a Service" (SaaS)—for almost any department in a company, such as for sales support, enterprise resource planning (ERP) systems, video conferencing systems, etc. The cloud software provider Salesforce.com has become well-known in this context.

[6] Interview with a DAX 30 CIO from summer 2012.

Interest is similarly strong in corporate "bring your own device" (BYOD) strategies. Here, companies encourage employees to bring IT equipment of their choice to work and use it in the office. Apple devices are particularly popular in this context. Consumerization thus offers IT organizations and CIOs new opportunities to participate in innovation processes and allow for change processes within the company. Such chances are also associated with new challenges, however, such as the management of "shadow IT", i.e. workplace-deployed software and hardware that by definition lies outside the CIO's knowledge domain and sphere of influence (cf. Brenner et al. 2011).

2.2.4 Technologies

Moore's Law[7] has proven true for decades—and no end is yet in sight. The transition with regard to information and telecommunication technology is in full swing, and influences both people's daily lives and the ways in which companies do business.

Smartphones Smartphones are currently the strongest driver of technological change. Devices such as Apple's iPhone or the Samsung Galaxy are not so much telecommunication devices but fully-fledged computers. Equipped with high-powered processors, sensors and cameras, GPS, accelerometers and high-resolution displays, these devices now take center-stage in terms of people's communication with their surroundings. If we assume that Moore's Law will continue to apply, future versions of these devices will exhibit enormous processing power and deliver high-precision sensor data, which could lead to new applications such as virtual reality. In addition, the use of the phone's screen as the sole means of presentation is no longer essential. Data can now be displayed in real-time on glasses, headsets or on external displays.

Collaboration/Broadband and Wireless Networks In the digital era, the provisioning of global networking and network bandwidth for data communication that is accessible, of high quality and available worldwide will be one of the most important factors for success. 3G and 4G networks are already rising to the challenge of meeting growing demands. Driven by colossal growth in the field of collaboration and communication, demand will continue to increase in the future. To match it, network structures will need to offer substantially better agility and flexibility. The ability to bring employees together at the right time, despite their spatial and hierarchical disparities within the company, will remain one of the core challenges in the future. Existing solution strategies include unified communication and collaboration (UCC) systems, video conferencing and chat rooms.

---

[7] Moore's Law states that the number of transistors on a computer chip doubles over the same area within a period of 12 months.

Cloud Computing In the future, large volumes of data will need to be available anywhere and at all times for both companies and individuals. The underlying technology is known as "cloud computing": Professionally managed data centers use distributed (usually worldwide) data storage to make data permanently available to its users. The market offers only a few successful providers. In the private consumer segment, one can point to services such as Apple's iCloud (iTunes Match) or GoogleDocs. In the commercial client segment, Salesforce.com is one of the leading cloud providers. This technology can be leveraged to design integration scenarios between individuals and organizations involving entirely novel approaches to architecture. Case studies from Europe's German-speaking regions reveal that, in a professional capacity, CIOs primarily rely on private cloud products from IT service organizations. In the Infrastructure as a Service (IaaS) and Platform as a Service (PaaS) segment in particular, CIOs have a large portfolio of services to choose from.

Big Data A direct corollary of the many sensors in use at home and in the office—combined with the growth in machine-to-machine communication (M2M communication[8] as well as smartphones as "social sensors")—is the rapidly increasing volume of data now available to companies. "Big data" is used as an umbrella term for technologies that enable the storage and processing of these vast quantities of data. One example is Apache Hadoop, a distributed storage and processing framework for very large quantities of data that relies on highly-standardized—and thus low-cost—computing and network infrastructure. Other technologies will follow in the years to come, primarily based on non-SQL databases.

2.3 The Evolution of IT

Which process led to the developments described in the last section? And what informs the prevailing patterns of strategy and action for contemporary company CIOs? Part of the answer can be found by considering IT development from a historical perspective (cf. Brenner and Witte 2007).

The Age of Production The 1960s and 1970s were a time when companies began their foray into IT in the form of electronic data processing. Company accounting was one of the first areas to benefit from IT: this was a highly repetitive task featuring mature processes and structures. Initially, the majority of such work involved the automation of bulk data processing by using "batch runs". Later, the systems were also deployed to support and optimize production workflows. Networking as we understand the term today was unknown at this stage, and was

[8] M2M = machine-to-machine communication, refers to the concept of the growth of networking between machines for the mutual exchange of transactional information.

limited to no more than the interconnection of the various information systems within the company. The only workplace computers visible were terminal devices, and they were few and far between. The job of IT management at this point in time was limited to simply keeping the IT up and running. There was no real sense of connectivity between the business units and IT. On the contrary: the IT unit in fact wielded considerable power, since expertise for its complex machinery was fairly limited within the company, although its use was already regarded as business-critical.

The Age of Supply Chains and Major Projects The second era was characterized by large-scale projects and collaboration across corporate boundaries. Until this time, data repositories had generally been maintained and stored individually per application system, and integration between discrete application systems was uncommon. It was only the process of advancing industrialization in the IT sector that created a need to integrate application systems along the supply chain, so as to facilitate the exchange of data beyond the confines of a single company. For CIOs, work at this time focused on large-scale projects and transfer programs. Their core competency was no longer "merely" managing data center operations, but involved guiding major projects in line with traditional parameters such as time, budget and quality. This produced the first significant change in the CIO role: The earlier, technology-focused image of the IT unit faded away as business units came to associate the CIO with application system development. Senior IT management nonetheless continued to maintain a certain distance from the business units.

The Age of Information and Communication From 1990 onwards, the utilization of information technology to support the communication, aggregation and processing of information and data began to gather momentum. One factor in this development was the runaway success of the personal computer (PC). System architecture became distributed and the reach of technology extended far beyond the walls of the data center to the employee or user's desk. Unfamiliar issues about centralized and decentralized information technology were suddenly part of the agenda. Many CIOs saw the introduction of the PC as a threat rather than an opportunity. Yet the deployment of these PCs marked the start of a new era. The first knowledge processing systems were created—the era of "knowledge management" projects had arrived. This was also the time when the business departments first exhibited an interest in getting to grips with application systems. Intelligent telecommunications systems—the precursors to today's UCC technology—started to be introduced, and the take-up of email spread like wildfire. At the same time, use of integrated software packages—such as those offered by SAP—also became more widespread. CIOs were tasked with helping to revise existing processes and organizational structures to work with these software systems.

The Age of the Customer We describe the contemporary era as the "age of the customer". As shown in the previous section, customers are no longer merely consumers, but have expectations and ideas about requirements that, with the aid of IT, fundamentally impact the corporate development and production process. As one example, the Adidas product configurator used in the "mi adidas" range (cf. Adidas 2012) presupposes not only a highly efficient and effective IT backend but also a radically customer-focused company. The service lets fitness enthusiasts configure an individual sports shoe perfectly tailored to their requirements and then have it manufactured as a custom item. Starbucks involves customers in the development and continuous improvement of new or existing products via its "My Starbucks Idea" (MyStarbucks 2012) web portal. Customers can provide feedback and offer ideas that can then be taken further by the responsible development team at Starbucks. The French ski manufacturer Rossignol serves as another example. The "Ski Pursuit" application (Rossignol 2012) gives the company real-time field data from both potential and existing customers. Such data can then be utilized by product development. The list can be continued ad infinitum. One thing is clear, however: The distance between companies and customers has shrunk significantly in the last few years. Information technology has extended its reach far beyond the data center and the workplace. Sensors in smartphones, machine-to-machine communication (M2M), mobile wireless networks, modern production procedures, etc. have all led to a situation where IT is present in almost every product and has matured into a distinguishing factor within many industries. CIOs need to adapt to this change. Supplementing technological expertise for the implementation and operation of mobile applications, CIOs must improve the skills of their own workforce to meet the demands of the digital natives.

2.4 Rethinking the Role of the CIO

How do these changes impact the work of CIOs, both today and in the future? This was summarized as follows by the CIO of a prestigious insurance company: "*As modern CIOs, our responsibility is threefold: costs, security and innovation*".[9] The last sections clearly show that IT will take on an expanding sphere of responsibility. The approach taken by CIOs to leverage and personalize this functional remit will vary from individual to individual. While CIOs must ensure tasks remain manageable, this also requires harmonizing a range of aspects. This challenge is also reflected in the new understanding of the CIO's role.

2.4.1 Balancing the Needs of Optimization and Innovation

The CIO's sphere of responsibility continues to expand in the direction of business and the customer. This goes hand-in-hand with a shift in the duties required of the

[9] Quote from an interview held in March 2012.

CIO by the CEO (cf. CIO Executive Council 2010). CEOs increasingly expect company IT units to be a partner of other business units, so as to promote a high level of integration, business focus and customer orientation. This is driven by the realization that IT is not merely a commodity, i.e. a standard product (cf. Carr 2003), but has a crucial role to play in deciding the success of products, services and business models in the future. In this future, IT will make up a considerable proportion of most products in the market, from the family car to the washing machine. One CIO described the situation as follows: "*The large monitors used by IT staff display not only system availability, but also the latest e-commerce figures.*"[10] The example reveals an ever-growing degree of integration between IT units, the company and its business. Indeed, this practice is taken so far that the same key performance indicators are used to measure both business success and the CIO's performance.

In practical terms, we observe increasing involvement of the CIO throughout the company's planning process for new products and services. From brainstorming to product development, production and marketing, CIOs now have a key role to play. As a result, CIOs are fostering business expertise in their units. In return, the business side is granting deeper insights into the mechanisms and procedures behind production and service provision. This process of expansion is still very much underway and is by no means complete. Corporate development teams no longer work exclusively "transactionally", i.e. guided by formal processes, sequentially organized and rarely engaging in interdepartmental work: instead, they operate in a collaborative, team-oriented fashion. Diversity within these groups is no longer seen as a disadvantage but as a benefit. Knowledge from production and product development is supplemented with technological expertise from IT. In this context, the IT unit is not only tasked with defining and implementing standards for infrastructure and technologies: instead, its work increasingly involves the joint development and provisioning of platforms to be used as springboards for future innovations.

As a corollary of the greater integration of CIOs into the company's core business, they are expected to do more than direct the standardized and planned rollout of systems and components. Especially in the early phases of brainstorming and development, a world undergoing such rapid change requires methods and processes with the agility and flexibility shown by "rapid prototyping" or "need finding"[11] (cf. Vetterli et al. 2011). Often, situations arise in which there is a lack of knowledge about the requirements for new software systems, infrastructure or business models. Conventional IT methods for development and planning are overburdened by this task. Successful projects at the University of St. Gallen's Institute of Information Management with companies such as SAP, Audi, FIFA, Swisscom and Clariant have shown how new methodological approaches such as

---

[10] Leading retail multinational. The interview was conducted in summer 2012.

[11] Need finding is a method for analyzing customer requirements and its development has been pursued primarily at the University of Stanford.

"design thinking" can help IT and business departments gain customer proximity while becoming more flexible and more agile.[12] Deutsche Bank has even gone a step further: design thinking has been an integral and successful part of the company since 2009[13] (cf. Vetterli et al. 2012). Design thinking and similar methods are also associated with a change in the approach taken to decision-making. The familiar "top-down" style of decision-making in companies is replaced by a customer-focused decision-making process. New solutions and products are presented in short, iterative cycles to customers, whose feedback is used as the criterion for deciding whether to proceed with the solution. Simultaneously, however, this kind of approach ushers in momentous cultural change for both management staff and employees. Permission to fail must be granted in line with the principle of "fail often and early in order to succeed sooner", so as to free up the idea process, offer room to innovate and engage in the occasional wild goose chase. In the final analysis, implementation of these paradigms leads to an organization driven by need and effectiveness, whose overarching goal is customer utility. Boundaries between IT and core business grow diffuse or disappear entirely.

The CIO's conflict results from the combination of his or her existing and future tasks, as one set of duties focuses on safeguarding IT operations in all of its manifold forms, such as costs, avoidance of downtime (quality), optimized business processes, security and global aspects, while the other works to ensure integration into the company-wide process of innovation and development for new products, services and business models.

According to the latest IT trend report from Capgemini, the trend is clear (cf. Capgemini 2012): CIOs see their future role more as the business partner and technical innovator. The existing image of the service provider and business processes optimizer seems to have had its day. "*I'm stepping on the gas over there* [*in innovation work*], *without slowing down over here* [*in IT operations*]", was one CIO's take on the situation.

2.4.1.1 Challenges in IT Operations

Cost Optimization and Standardization There has been no let-up in the need for continuous optimization of cost structures within IT over the last few years. In fact, the opposite is true: the growing uncertainty within global markets is exerting greater pressure on IT to reduce the costs of operating the company's IT systems (cf. Capgemini 2012). One viable instrument here is to standardize the core processes within IT and the technologies used by business. This was summarized by the CIO of a car maker as follows: "*Everyone has to follow set processes, methods and standards*."

In addition, continuous optimization is also viewed as a "cleanup process". While routine activities such as the consolidation of application environments are

[12] See http://www.dthsg.com

[13] Design Thinking —The Value to the Company; see Deutsche Bank Group YouTube channel http://www.youtube.com/watch?v=ZIKMZ7c5L0I

well underway, these are nowhere near complete and require a major commitment of resources. "We *currently run 4,600 applications and we want to further reduce this volume*", was the recent comment of a CIO from a leading chemicals company. This not only enables IT units to reduce their costs, but to establish a clear starting point for agility and flexibility, and thus the integration of new (mobile) applications into the existing IT environment. Opposing these efforts are company acquisitions or the implementation of applications with the help of new technologies, which act to reduce the degree of standardization.

Quality and Security Ensuring quality and security are two core competencies now expected to be demonstrated by a good CIO. "*If you're not performing your core duties, you're not doing a good job*", reports a CIO working in the automotive sector. These include both the stability of IT operations as well as the development of high-quality application systems in accordance with customer requirements. Requirements stemming from new and more stringent legal frameworks—such as in banking—must be implemented with particular speed and precision, and are currently generating new challenges for IT organizations.

Global and International Aspects At the operational level, a further challenge has arisen in recent years, namely the IT unit's ability to ensure worldwide delivery (cf. Zelt et al. 2013). Due to the dismantling of legal and economic barriers, company production and development sites are now distributed all over the planet. This development has been promoted by the IT industry itself. IT services must be provided worldwide to the business departments in a standardized, cost-effective way. In the process, a trade-off must be made between global standardization and local flexibility in the respective markets (cf. Zelt et al. 2013). The contours of this boundary between flexibility and a global standard will differ for each industry. Then again, globalization within the IT industry means that the selection and management of service providers must also be conducted internationally. Ultimately, this means establishing and operating processes capable of facilitating worldwide procurement.

Sourcing Outsourcing information technology to IT service organizations or IT service providers has a long tradition and has attained an advanced stage of development, at least in terms of core infrastructure services (cf. Brenner et al. 2012). Various models, such as the buy-in of individual personnel resources (especially in development) through to the tendering of complete projects or the purchasing of infrastructure according to units of consumption can be found within the market. The dominant trend in the market is in the direction of performance contracting, i.e. procurement no longer focuses on individual resources—such as servers or licenses—but on the output of these resources. For CIOs, the key challenge is to ensure a flexible and dynamic approach to managing the remaining in-house activity of their IT units. This management is necessary, since, depending on the company's current situation, a relatively low or high share of sourcing is advisable. Companies with a lower degree of sourcing typically attempt to modify their IT more rapidly to new circumstances, while, in contrast, companies with a higher degree of sourcing aim to ensure the greatest freedom of movement for innovation projects by the delegation of routine activities. We observe that CIOs' expectations regarding external service providers are also increasing in terms of their abilities to contribute to the innovation process. One insurance CIO describes the following core challenge in sourcing: "How *can we guarantee the pursuit of innovation in our outsourced units*?"

2.4.1.2 Challenges for Innovation

Agility and Speed One CIO described the phenomena mentioned with the phrase "IT of two speeds". This refers to the fact that CIOs are increasingly being asked to produce (and then operate) ready-to-run software capable of implementing business requirements in just a few weeks. Conventional methods for software development—and for operations alike—appear unsuited to these requirements. One topic repeated in many of our interviews was that traditional bureaucratic processes are well-suited to standard requirements, but are a poor match for a fast-moving, agile world. That applies both to software development and to IT operations, which in many of its task areas often requires more than 20 working days to provision the requested infrastructure. Above and beyond this, the software frameworks themselves must also be able to connect to new software products via standardized and modular interfaces.

Products, Services and Business Models "*Innovation is a sensitive plant.*" This description of the status quo by an insurance CIO applies to many IT organizations. The transition from a data center operator and service provider to a business partner engaged at the level of corporate management for product, service and business model innovation is a long and stony path. Often, CIOs lack the authority to originate innovation, even as it gradually dawns on the business world that IT is a critical element for success in almost all industries—a fact not merely important today but likely to be even more so in the future (cf. Brenner and Witte 2007). Accordingly, the key challenge faced by CIOs pursuing change will be to obtain the legitimation that permits them to make a valuable contribution to core business.

2.4.2 The CIO's Scope of Duties

As the previous sections have shown, the successful CIO of the future will be expected to master and cross-connect a wide range of competencies. Then again, the complexity of the CIO's job profile—at the nexus of innovation and IT operations—necessarily means that most CIOs will find the simultaneous fulfillment of all duties impossible, due to conflicts of interest. To be effective, managers must be able to "change their hats" depending on the specific situation prevailing at the company and flexibly refocus their activities. Both internal and external factors are responsible for this positioning. By 2007, it had already been clearly shown that the role of the CIO would be split into two "camps" (cf. Brenner and Witte 2007). First, the "Designers", who primarily seek a way into business and actively engage in innovations related to the portfolio and the company's business model. Second, the "Chief Technology Officers", who concentrate on the efficient and effective operation of production resources. One should emphasize that a drawing-down of the scope of duties is not to be equated with a curtailment in the sphere of responsibilities.

Responsibility for IT Operations *"In an IT unit operating worldwide, tasks need to be completed rapidly, at high quality and at low cost."*[14] Reliability and a high level of quality continue to be of paramount importance in IT operations, a situation justified not least by the critical dependence of the business on IT. Responsibility for this area encompasses not only the safeguarding of stability and security, but also the ability to scale IT operations to match the growing needs of the business and the demands of its customers. This also includes the management of subcontractors supplying IT services, as well as process services (business process outsourcing) and back office processes. Beyond this, new significance has been given to the management of IT employee training profiles within IT operations. Emerging technologies require proactive re-skilling and continuous professional development.

Managing IT at a qualitatively optimum level requires standardization, formalization and an optimized division of work in the unit's strongly repetitive areas. Supplementing the well-established ITIL framework (IT Infrastructure Library), guidance can be found in the form of popular standards such as COBIT (Control Objectives for Information and Related Technology) or the eTOM framework (Enhanced Telecom Operations Map) originating from the telecommunications industry.

Interviewed in 2006, Rainer Janßen, CIO at Munich Re, stated: *"First and foremost, the basic expectation* [*on the part of business*] *is that things run smoothly*." That is, responsibility for IT operations cannot be delegated, while actual execution can. Accordingly, the same standards also apply to external IT service organizations. Comparable to Maslow's hierarchy of needs, the "hygienic factors" relating to basic, existential and security needs on the part of both the business and its customers must be supplied by IT. Only the satisfactory completion of these tasks establishes a position from which the CIO can actively engage with responsibilities and tasks as a technology adviser or innovator.

Responsibility as Technology Adviser As a technology adviser, the CIO has a high level of technological expertise in all matters relating to IT. Aided by highly persuasive communications skills, s/he is capable of maintaining networks both within his or her own company and externally to suppliers—to technology suppliers in particular. Empowered by his or her personal technological know-how, this role

[14] Statement made during a 2012 interview with an insurance CIO.

enables the CIO to help incorporate market developments and trends into IT and business strategies at an early stage.

Responsibility as Process Specialist The CIO is generally accorded the process specialist title per se, due to the historical development of the role. Many corporate processes are now digitalized and mapped out within application systems. The transformation of these processes into the world of IT—not forgetting process operations themselves—normally means the CIO is the person responsible for process operation and design. This task is associated with a profound knowledge of the company's various business units, i.e. "vertical knowledge", and the markets it targets—knowledge that may first need to be acquired, depending on the CIO's skill profile. This acquisition requires the CIO to be fully integrated into the company, both organizationally and in terms of personal networks. Closely associated with process operation and transformation is the capability to change these same processes. This not only assigns the process specialist the responsibility for mapping out processes and managing their operations, but also for process optimization, in the form of business process re-engineering.

Responsibility as Innovator The search for new—for "real"—innovations, is something that does not come naturally to the majority of CIOs, at least if the series of personal interviews we conducted with managers can be taken as representative. On the contrary: the path from simply feeling like an innovator to actually achieving innovation is a long one for most people and companies alike. From the authors' point of view, the commonest fallacy among CIOs is to equate—and thereby confuse—the identification of new technologies in the market with innovation itself. The identification and systematic exploration of technologies ("trend and technology monitoring") naturally forms part of innovation. But it is indeed only a part of the process. In addition, the CIO as innovator must create the right working atmosphere for employees. Alongside a suitable working environment, such as facilities, equipment, etc., this also includes an optimum workplace culture and agreed working conditions that stimulate employees' creative and conceptual freedom. One management paradigm we might mention would be "fail often and early", which means promoting a culture of tolerating error in the workforce, so as to identify and embark on new approaches in development and research processes as early as possible. Beyond this, the CIO also bears responsibility for establishing agile and iterative working processes informed by prototypes. Only the direct contact with customers and team-based collaboration with employees from the business units can guarantee the necessary diversity of novel perceptions required to develop new IT-driven products, service portfolios and business models. One characteristic typical of this breed of CIO is the capacity to consciously view unexpected interim project results not as destructive or a hazard in the sense of a project risk, but instead as an opportunity to discover or create something new.

To summarize, we may state that the scope of duties and sphere of responsibilities assigned to the CIO have both seen considerable expansion and are now oriented more towards customers and the business. Alongside purely operational responsibilities, CIOs are expected to contribute actively to change in core business. The authors firmly believe that only a small proportion of management staff will be capable of leveraging their existing teams to fulfill this weighty portfolio of duties (IT operations, technology adviser, process specialist and innovator) at the level of quality both necessary and expected to satisfy the discussed challenges. Accordingly, this situation generates major potential for providers of IT services to extend the value chain as guarantors of effective and efficient task completion.

2.5 Positioning IT Service Organizations

How can IT service organizations and IT service providers position themselves effectively in the IT sector's dynamic market environment—with its complex requirements for operations and application system development? What are the critical factors for success that result from the company's strategy in each case? Our reply to these two questions will certainly not involve locating a universal answer, and will need to be contextualized in terms of the organization in question. That said, it is possible to derive two generic and textbook strategy models for IT service organizations from the contemporary and future positioning of IT organizations and CIOs. The basis is formed by the numerous interviews conducted with CIOs in recent months. The CIO support service model certainly appears to offer providers tremendous scope, with professionalism, quality and subject expertise all being in great demand.

2.5.1 Strategies for IT Service Providers

2.5.1.1 Strategy A: Business Partner

The "Business Partner" strategy positions the IT service provider as a partner for the CIO in all of the latter's task areas, and encompasses not only IT operations but also the fields of development and innovation. This strategy is based on a definition of the value contribution that goes beyond traditional parameters for IT service providers. That is: negotiations with the customer are not oriented exclusively on costs, production quality and security, but also incorporate qualitative aspects and expertise relevant to the industry in question.

If we look at the IT market of recent years, we see a vacuum developing between IT organizations and providers of infrastructure-like IT services. Infrastructure providers are engaged in the large-scale standardization of servers, networks, databases, and so on. The goal is to maximize economies of scale while achieving cost optimization to a degree that cannot be accomplished at the orders of magnitude found in conventional IT organizations. This objective consciously dispenses with the establishment of industry-specific expertise, however, and offers no direct knowledge of specific markets, such as the insurance sector. The strategy adopted by Amazon, Salesforce.com, etc. consciously attempts to minimize relevance for any one industry, so as to ensure portfolio complexity remains manageable, and thus sustain their hard-won responsiveness, agility and cost leadership.

On the other hand, both IT organizations and the role of the CIO are currently in transition, as has been touched on in previous sections. Both business and customers are demanding new (mobile) application systems, including rapid turnaround and integration into existing infrastructure. This is accompanied by the need to establish IT platforms able to handle entire value chains—such as the energy or automotive sectors (see car sharing)—so as to offer customers new services based on integrated data repositories.

This is the environment in which the authors see major potential for IT service organizations to position themselves in the vacuum between these two poles. These organizations would have an opportunity to partner with CIOs in a particular value chain in the shared design, setup and operation of new platforms offering integration and market potential. In terms of perspective, IT service organizations would no longer focus exclusively on the technological aspects of networks and servers, but on the core business of the customer organization. IT service organizations could offer their expertise to each and every member in the value chain, thus facilitating new platforms for the energy industry or in car sharing for the automotive sector, for example. In the final analysis, however, this does mean that IT service providers need to engage with the customer's market, business processes and technologies at a fundamental level: only in this way can they even begin to support CIOs with innovative proposals of their own. Acceptance into the CIO peer group is not achieved merely by the simple operation of high-quality cloud services.

This positioning strategy will first require sweeping changes to be made at some IT service providers, however—not only in terms of providing basic and further training for the company's own workforce (e.g. to develop specific industry expertise) but as regards implementing structures and processes of far greater agility and innovative focus. Performance parameters traditional to the IT service provider sector (i.e. costs, security and quality) naturally retain their validity for IT organizations—although their relative importance in evaluating IT service providers decreases.

The authors firmly believe that the companies who navigate this transition will be offered opportunities to work in partnership with CIOs in the future and to support them in many different ways. Inevitably, this would be linked to a shift in the business model to one that is no longer focused exclusively on cost/price reduction and standardization, but which looks beyond this to place industry know-how and market expertise center-stage.

2.5.1.2 Strategy B: IT Operations/Development Partner

The "IT Operations/Development Partner" strategy is based on the establishment of cost efficiency, economies of scale, standardization, global availability/delivery capability and production quality. From the perspective of tomorrow's CIOs, IT service providers adopting this strategy acknowledge they will be benchmarked directly against current industry titans like Amazon, Google or IBM. Achieving vast economies of scale is the primary objective here, as mentioned in the introductory sections.

Once achieved, these economies of scale automatically amplify the degree of IT production automation and industrialization in several dimensions. As early as 2007–2008, joint research work carried out between the University of St. Gallen's Institute of Information Management and T-Systems International had already demonstrated that ERP-like systems are capable of end-to-end automation of IT service production (cf. Ebert et al. 2008): from the initial design of the IT service portfolio to IT service consumption with the aid of self-service portals and the delivery and operation of the IT service for the customer, including the provision of continuous monitoring and quality assurance services. At the time, it was possible to reduce the window required for provisioning IT services and bringing them online from several days to just a few hours. One key insight here was that core business was now focused on the configuration of standard services instead of the customization of IT services: accordingly, standardization needed to be increased across the board (cf. Brocke et al. 2011; Dudek et al. 2011). In action behind the scenes is the principle we espoused as early as 2004, namely end-to-end process optimization and industrialized information management, combined with a systematic focus on customer needs. The starting-point for this work comprised parallels drawn with traditional industry. In the current analysis, the textbook example of this strategy is Amazon's S3 service. Within just a few minutes, highly-redundant storage space is both configured and available. This has been facilitated by the setup of highly-available "IT factories", i.e. IT production facilities featuring almost 100 % standardization.

Comparable requirements are being demanded of software development teams in terms of their division of labor and internationality. IT service providers operating internationally maintain development centers worldwide: this permits them to leverage local cost benefits while also exploiting regional differences—in Asia or South America, for example—in adapting the design of application systems.

For most IT service providers, the only viable option now available is the "me too" strategy—i.e. copycat models that mimic the activities of the undisputed market leaders. Efforts to innovate at such companies often have a strong technological bias: the aim is rapid service provision at the best possible price point and for a wide range of application scenarios, while also generating a high degree of scalability in their infrastructure. Work focuses on unrelenting optimization of cost structures by adopting a dual strategy of radical growth of the customer base combined with the continuous improvement and automation of internal processes.

Companies adopting this strategy handle the completion of core tasks for IT organizations and CIOs in terms of IT operations and development work. The generalized nature of the services provided does lead to a certain "interchangeability" among providers, however. In addition, IT service providers in this market are being confronted with increasingly tough competition on a global scale: ultimately, the size of the company will be decisive in determining the victors.

2.5.2 Critical Success Factors for IT Service Organizations

The most important factors for success in the case of the two strategies described—in their idealized, textbook forms—are derived from the discussions in this section and are summarized definitively in Table 2.1.

The Ability to Innovate The ability to deliver a continuous stream of innovations for the CIO is central to both model strategies. There are practical differences, however. While technological innovations will suffice in meeting the expectations of the CIO in Strategy B, companies following Strategy A will also be expected to make contributions to innovations affecting the business model, products and services—both in terms of core company business and the respective value chain. Companies in the Strategy A group must therefore seek to prepare and train their employees for the forthcoming transition as early as possible while also establishing business competency. Meeting the challenges of the ability to innovate will require changes to the style and structure of management, and to its methodological toolbox. The guiding principle for these companies is simple: "Innovation is not a game!"

Customer- and Market-specific Business Know-how In many cases, the CIO will accept or reject IT service organizations based on their knowledge of business-relevant topics. Strategy A requires a high degree of engagement with market circumstances and mechanisms of action along the entire value chain. For the CIO, the service organization's contributions must be specialized to have any value. For Strategy B companies, this kind of specific expertise is not required. Such IT service providers only need to provide sufficient know-how for preparing the company's business portfolio to handle future change.

Customer Focus For Strategy B, customer focus involves aligning the IT service portfolio and IT production in general as closely as possible with the needs of the customer. End-to-end orientation of organizational processes on the customer also applies in the case of both model strategies.

Global Delivery Capability IT service providers of the future must be capable of offering IT service provision worldwide at the same high level of service quality. This factor for success applies equally to both model strategies. Practical implementation is likely to differ in each case, however. Group A companies can leverage partner models (for example) to supplement their own, globally-distributed infrastructure.

Product and Service Quality As is the case today, the assurance of product and service quality will continue to be a fundamental entry barrier to the provision of IT services. Regardless of the strategy model they adopt, companies who struggle to orchestrate their processes and procedures or are unable to supply quality to the required standard will face difficulties in gaining market acceptance.

Table 2.1 Critical success factors for IT service organizations

Success factors	Strategy A: business partner	Strategy B: IT operations/ development partner
Ability to innovate	CIOs expect technological innovation to be matched by the achievement of innovations in business, products and services	Focus on the generation of technological innovations and their optimum deployment
Business know-how specific to the customer and market	Mandatory, to enable participation on innovative brainstorming within the CIO peer group	Important, to be able to define market-specific offers and architecture based on standard services
Customer focus	Customer focus means having an empathic understanding of the challenges facing the customer organization in its markets, and responding with both standard and tailor-made services	Aligning standardized IT services with the needs of the customer
Global delivery capability	Global delivery capability is a key requirement for working with major clients	
Product and service quality	Maximum compliance with security and availability requirements in the relevant IT service categories	
Cost leadership	Transparent price/cost structures	The objective is to achieve cost leadership

Cost Leadership The success factor of cost leadership is primarily a factor for companies following the Strategy B model. Due to increasing cost pressures in the market and the fact that IT service quality has now been harmonized at the highest possible level among the market's biggest players, cost leadership will constitute a key criterion for customer organizations in the IT service organization selection process. IT service organizations must respond by achieving major economies of scale and widespread automation.

2.6 Summary

In authoring this chapter, our aim was to isolate and discuss the success factors applicable to IT service organizations. At the outset, we considered the general market situation in the IT sector and a number of trends, such as greater customer proximity and advances in technological developments. Working from this analysis, and incorporating a total of 50 interviews with CIOs and senior management, we then sketched out the implications for a new CIO role in IT organizations. The result is a palpable expansion of both the CIO's responsibilities and duties in terms of business and the customer. Our discussion has also shown the great potential offered to IT service organizations by the market of the future. Section 2.5 of this article then sketched out two generic model strategies: (1) Strategy A, the "Business Partner" and (2) Strategy B, the "IT Operations/Development Partner". Strategy A empowers companies to engage in fields of business that are new to IT service providers. This option requires an immense commitment of resources, however, to acquire the necessary business expertise and establish the "authority to innovate" vis-à-vis CIOs. Due to a simple lack of resources, many companies are likely to focus on specific industries. IT service organizations that pursue Strategy B are entering a global competition that will be decided by sheer size and cost efficiency. The standard for success here is the ultra-integrated value chain as established by industry titans like IBM, HP, and others. The outcome of this competition will affect both traditional IT service provision and new services provided from the cloud computing sector. We also described six critical factors for success that support these two strategies and are decisive for business success: the ability to innovate, customer- and market-specific business know-how, customer focus, global delivery capability, product and service quality, and cost leadership.

References

Adidas. (2012). Retrieved December 20, 2012, from http://www.adidas.de/mi%C2%A0Predator%C2%A0Lethal-Zones/15001945_M,de_DE,pd.html?cgid=customise-Shoes&config=true#is_configurator

Airbnb. (2012). Retrieved January 2, 2013, from https://www.airbnb.com/home/press

Bravo-Sànchez, C., Uebernickel, F., & Zarnekow, R. (2005). Lean IT – Die Industrialisierung des Informationsmanagements. *Is.Report – Magazin für betriebliche Informationssysteme, 9*(10), 12–17.

Brenner, W., & Witte, C. (2007). *Erfolgsrezepte für CIOs – Was gute Informationsmanager ausmacht.* Munich: Hanser.

Brenner, W., Györy, A., Pirouz, M., & Uebernickel, F. (2011). *Bewusster Einsatz von Schatten-IT: Sicherheit und Innovationsförderung.* St. Gallen: Universität St. Gallen. Retrieved January 14, 2011, from http://www.salesforce.com/de/form/pdf/brenner.jsp?d=70130000000s91I

Brenner, W., Uebernickel, F., Wulf, J., Zelt, S., Györy, A., Heym, M., et al. (2012). *Strategies for application management services.* St. Gallen: University of St. Gallen.

Brocke, H. F., Uebernickel, F., & Brenner, W. (2011). Balancing customer requirements and IT service standardization – a procedural reference model for individualized IT service agreement configurations. *Enterprise Modelling and Information Systems Architectures, 6*(2), 4–20.

Capgemini. (2012). *Studie IT-Trends 2012 – Business-IT-Alignment sichert die Zukunft.* Capgemini.

Carr, N. G. (2003). IT doesn't matter. *Harvard Business Review, 81*, 5–12.

CIO Executive Council. (2010). *How are CIOs meeting evolving CEO expectations?* Retrieved December 28, 2012, from http://www.cio.com/article/594396/How_are_CIOs_Meeting_Evolving_CEO_Expectations_?page=2&taxonomyId=3174

D'Orazio, D. (2012). *Gmail now has 425 million active users.* The Verge. Retrieved December 28, 2012, from http://www.theverge.com/2012/6/28/3123643/gmail-425-million-total-users

Dudek, S., Ubernickel, F., & Brenner, W. (2011). Variant configuration for IT-services and its impact on the service request fulfillment process. Research in Progress – 18th Americas Conference on Information Systems, Detroit.

Ebert, N., Vogedes, A., Uebernickel, F., & Brenner, W. (2008). Production planning for IT-service providers: An ERP-based concept. Proceedings of the Nineteenth Australasian Conference on Information Systems (ACIS 2008): University of Canterbury, 2008, 19th Australasian Conference on Information Systems (ACIS), Keystone, CO.

Escherich, M. (2011). *Search analytics trends: The inevitable consumerization of corporate IT*. Gartner Analytics. Retrieved December 28, 2012, from http://my.gartner.com/portal/server.pt?open=512&objID=260&mode=2&PageID=3460702&id=1591515&ref=

Gartner. (2012). *Gartner says worldwide IT outsourcing market grew 7.8 percent in 2011*. Press Release. Retrieved December 28, 2012, from http://www.gartner.com/it/page.jsp?id=2021215

MyStarbucks. (2012). *My starbucks plattform*. Retrieved December 28, 2012, from http://mystarbucksidea.force.com/

Rodriguez, A. (2011). *Too big to backup*. Nasuni. Retrieved December 28, 2012, from http://www.nasuni.com/blog/22-too_big_to_backup

Rossignol. (2012). *Ski pursuit*. Retrieved December 28, 2012, from http://www.rossignol.com/US/US/skipursuit.html

Schaffry, A. (2012). *Top 10 CIO-Prioritäten 2012*. CIO-Magazine. Retrieved December 28, 2012, from http://www.cio.de/strategien/2299663/

Vetterli, C., Brenner, W., Uebernickel, F., & Berger, K. (2011). Die Innovationsmethode design thinking. In M. Lang & M. Amberg (Eds.), *Dynamisches IT-management. So steigern Sie die Agilität, Flexibilität und Innovationskraft Ihrer IT*. Düsseldorf: Symposion.

Vetterli, C., Uebernickel, F., & Brenner, W. (2012). Initialzündung durch Embedded Design Thinking — Ein Fallbeispiel aus der Finanzindustrie. *Zeitschrift für Organisationsentwicklung, 2*, 22–31.

Zarnekow, R., Brenner, W., & Pilgram, U. (2005). *Integriertes Informationsmanagement*. Berlin: Springer.

Zelt, S., Uebernickel, F., & Brenner, W. (2013). Managing global IT delivery networks: A literature review from the supplier's perspective. Proceedings of the 46th Hawaii International Conference on System Sciences: IEEE Computer Society, 2013, Hawaii International Conference on System Sciences (HICSS), Maui, Hawaii.

Part II

Industrial Reformation

Transformation in the IT Industry 3

Katharina Grimme and Peter Kreutter

3.1 Industry Lifecycles and Competitive Dynamics

Using a selection of headlines from business papers as an indicator for the competitive dynamics in the IT industry, the signs of the times are clear for IT outsourcing: Consolidation. Smaller providers are not the only ones fighting for survival; the trend has not stopped at the doors of the well-known names in the global business. The one-time pioneer of the IT services revolution, EDS, was taken over by HP as early as 2008. Since 2006, only five big names, IBM, Oracle, Microsoft, Hewlett-Packard, and SAP, have conducted more than 70 take-overs and are continuing to push for more consolidation. Other providers, such as Atos or Dell have also discovered acquisitions as a tool for gaining new market share by way of inorganic growth. These are just selected examples from a list that could be expanded at libitum.

From a scientific standpoint, this is not a chance accident, but rather the expression of a trend that the U.S. economist Steven Klepper (1997) introduced to academic discourse under the term of "industry lifecycles". Studies following Klepper are considering how "young" industries are changing over time and how the changing rules of the game are affecting the companies operating within them.

K. Grimme (✉)
Pierre Audoin Consultants (PAC) GmbH, Holzstraße 26, 80469 Munich, Germany
e-mail: K.Grimme@pac-online.com

P. Kreutter
WHU – Otto Beisheim School of Management, Campus Düsseldorf, Erkrather Str. 224A, 40233 Düsseldorf, Germany
e-mail: Peter.Kreutter@whu.edu

F. Abolhassan (ed.), *The Road to a Modern IT Factory*, Management for Professionals,
DOI 10.1007/978-3-642-40219-7_3,

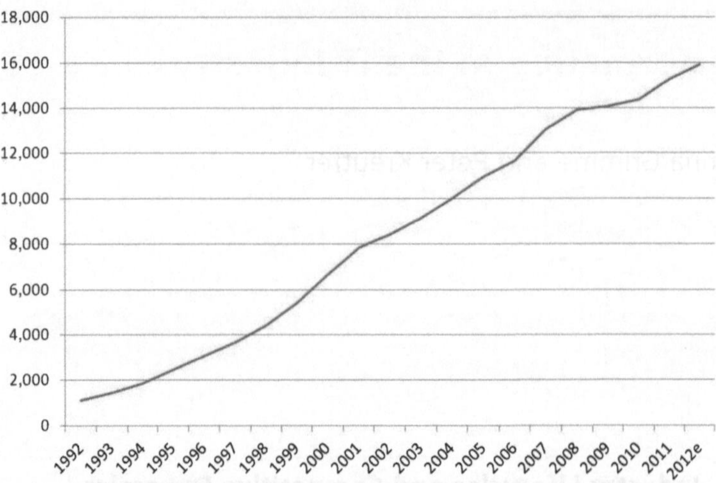

Fig. 3.1 Volume of the German IT outsourcing market (*Source*: PAC 2012)

Apart from the extensive structural changes that often taken the form of consolidation among providers (e.g. Günther 2009), a characteristic feature is that these mechanisms take hold in growing markets. The volume of the German IT outsourcing market has also seen unabated growth since the early 1990s, as the chart above shows (PAC 2012) (Fig. 3.1).

From the point of view of competition strategies, the decisive factor is that a maturing market will see decreasing relative growth rates and, in the long run, a decrease in the overall market size. In this specific case, it is evident that the relative growth of the IT outsourcing market has indeed slowed down, with the extreme growth of the 1990s having become a thing of the past. Over time, relative growth rates have been declining, and the market is only seeing single-digit growth in Germany, as it is elsewhere in the world (PAC 2012).

This development in the market volume, and the relative growth that can be achieved, clearly seems to follow the expected pattern for the industry lifecycle, which means that fundamental structural changes are to be expected. As in many other industries (see the overview in Peltoniemi 2011), more mature markets mean substantial changes to the "dominant design" (Suarez and Utterback 1995) of business models.

Traditional models saw services produced and sold in close regional proximity to each other. This has changed under a new paradigm, where the separation of production and sales has become the norm, not the exception (Fig. 3.2). We can see four interdependent factors that are the drivers and, at the same time, also the results of this trend. On the sales side, the trend towards consolidation means—in academic terms—more differentiation, leading to new sub-industries and specialist niches. On the production side, the global nature of value creation has become an established fact, whereas automation and industrialization of service processes are still in their infancy. These four aspects will be reviewed in more detail in the following section.

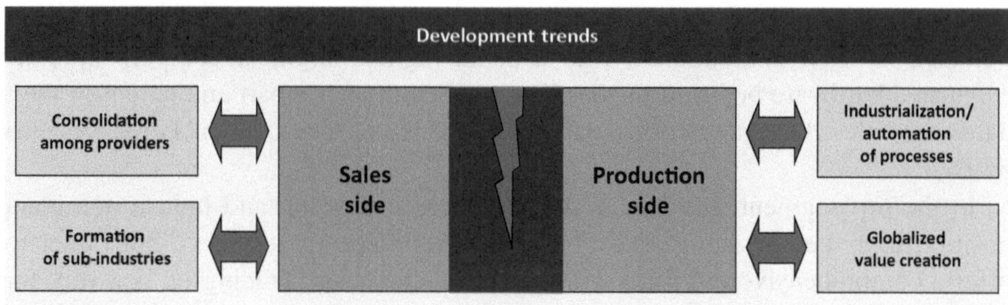

Fig. 3.2 Systematic representation of the forces in the IT service industry (illustration by the authors, 2012)

3.2 Consolidation

The forces of consolidation on the IT provider side have already been mentioned. Their effect is becoming visible e.g. in the on-going take-overs of companies in the market, leading to ever greater concentration. Fewer providers are holding relatively greater and more dominant market shares—"relative" being the operative word. We are not witnessing traditional oligopolies or the beginnings of such a market. Rather, the IT service market continues to be highly fragmented, which can, for instance, be seen in the fact that the top ten IT outsourcing providers taken together were only holding a mere half of the German market in 2011 (PAC 2012).

Competition has heated up for a variety of causes, including excess capacities that are the result of the systematic overestimation of future growth rates (cf. on a theoretical level: Hopenhayn 1993). At the same time, the pressure on prices has increased from the customer side: Customers are expecting real cost savings from new outsourcing contracts, which is a form of passing on the commercial pressures they themselves are facing. This is made worse by the generally smaller size of the contracts compared to a few years ago. Megadeals worth nine-figure sums are now definitely an exception to the rule. At the same time, smaller-scale contracts give providers fewer opportunities to offer a cost advantage. One essential problem here is the absence of economies of scale due to costly technology investments on behalf of the customer.

In the outsourcing business in particular, many providers are facing the challenge of having to offer significant price reductions to customers even when "simply" renewing existing contracts. More likely than not, this means eating into the profit margin. Customers have learned to make the most of their bargaining position, especially in high-volume areas like IT infrastructure. It has generally been noted that the prices—and the margins—for IT services are now, in the global financial crisis, nowhere near as high as they were at and before the turn of the millennium (cf. PAC/Berlecon 2012).

This trend is made worse by the arrival of an increasing number of new players from the margins of the market, i.e. from neighboring industries. This not only includes hardware or software makers or resellers trying to compensate for the dwindling margins in their core business by adding IT services to their portfolio. For such providers, the rationale is to seize the higher margins in comparison to the exhausted hardware business or to sell service contracts as part and parcel of their hardware sales. One noteworthy example here is the take-over of Perot Systems by Dell.

In the top segment, the aim is not as much to develop and hold a dominant position in a specific sub-market (hardware, software, or services), but rather to offer a comprehensive portfolio with a holistic character. Trading up is a way for actors who used to be confined to the low-end commodity area to develop their stakes in the high-end IT service and outsourcing business.

New international actors—in particular Indian service providers like TCS, Infosys, Wipro, or MahindraSatyam—are pushing into the market. Since their high growth of the past is nearing its logical limits in the domestic and the Anglo-American markets, these companies are increasingly looking to continental Europe, Germany in particular, as the new engine for growth and target market. With the IT outsourcing business being worth €230 billion worldwide, and Germany's €16 billion constituting a 7 % share, the size of the pie is considerable, even if most of its slices are already taken and nobody expects more than moderate growth (PAC 2012). Good growth rates are thus only to be had by conquering parts of the market from competitors or, simply, by taking them over.

For such regional expansion coupled with systematic trading-up, companies need more local resources, both in quantitative and qualitative terms. With its acquisition of the Swiss consultancy house Lodestone, Infosys has paved the way. Cognizant has followed suit by taking over parts of Germany's C1 Group. We can expect more such take-overs to follow soon (cf. Bäumer et al. 2010).

3.3 Sub-industries

While the sweep of consolidation is thinning out the top spots, the markets are continuing to differentiate by size and maturity. Niche and new sub-markets or sub-industries are forming (cf. Buenstorf 2007) which give smaller specialists an opportunity to establish themselves and challenge the larger generalists by banking on greater specialization and more flexibility. Software testing and high-end recovery services can be named as two examples. Amadeus IT has become one of the leading IT service providers for the travel industry. In a similar vein, Wincor Nixdorf is known as a specialist for retail banks and the retail industry.

The increasing number of sub-markets is making decisions more complex for larger players. Given that all resources are finite, not all niches can be covered. A product mix has to be found that matches the available competencies, but also offers sufficient uniqueness to stand out from the competition. Another option is to make use of different competitive strategies or supply partnerships with other companies.

Accordingly, success depends not only on simple quantitative growth, but also on the effectiveness of specific, very differentiated strategies governing the company's service portfolio, skills profile, and position in a consolidating global IT industry. This is just as relevant from the point of view of the sales markets as it is for the company's own relative costs.

The cost landscape of a company is determined above all by its value creation architecture. Seen in more procedural terms, it is the internal architecture that needs to be seen in terms of its strategic value contribution. Apart from understanding how individual activities contribute to differentiation in the company's core business, companies need to ask themselves to what extent sourcing these activities from external suppliers presents a cheaper alternative. Particular attention should be paid to the wage gap between different regions in the world.

3.4 Globalized Value Chains

Other industries can look back on decades or even centuries of globalization in their value chains, whereas IT only caught on to the issue in the wake of the Y2K problem. The need to have substantial and, above all, cheap programming and development resources available at a moment's notice has shifted attention to countries like India or regions like Central and Eastern Europe. By providing cost-efficient services in near- or offshoring hubs, these offer a low-cost alternative to the local providers, still entrenched in their high-wage environments. This move is supported by the rise of more and more standardized products and improved technological flexibility, especially in terms of the global availability of broadband networks.

The formerly predominant prejudice against "cheap" and "low-end" offshoring has been shown to be baseless. It is hard to deny that playing the salary card was one of the drivers for the rise of the Indian IT industry in particular. Low wages allowed custom solutions to be produced at much lower costs than in Western nations. However, the limitations of the Indian "mega-factory" are beginning to show. The strong rupee is eating into the cost savings. Increasing salaries and a slimmer talent pool of experienced and qualified Indian IT specialists are further factors. In the end, the considerable costs of coordination and language barriers must not be underestimated. For certain activities, near-shoring to e.g. Eastern Europe is much more attractive, even if full-cost or salary-cost analyses would mean that a few jobs are indeed returned back on-shore. In this sense, we can already speak of a truly global delivery model that works with production capacities across the world to produce cost-efficient, but high-quality services.

3.5 Industrialization

Another source for sustainable competitiveness is industrialization. For IT service providers, remaining agile under the increasing cost pressure while still producing an acceptable level of profit requires a fundamental review of how they deliver their services and a commitment to industrialization. Compared to other sectors of the economy, such as the automotive or industrial engineering industries—IT service providers, as is true of their peers in the service industry at large, have significant potential for optimization.

Three aspects deserve particular attention: The standardization of service portfolios, the modularization of solutions, and the automation of service delivery. All of these measures are aimed at making the service offerings more scaleable and reducing the costly complexity of selling and delivering services.

This resembles an important evolutionary step that manufacturing took about 120 years ago in its own era of industrialization, namely the replacement of manual labor with technological means. European entrepreneurs in particular, who had exhausted their ability to compete on labor costs alone, could gain a massive competitive advantage as a result. Automating and codifying services in software solutions allows a similar evolutionary leap. For IT specialists in particular, increasing numbers of formerly manual service processes have recently been automated. Software and software updates are no longer delivered in physical disc or CD format and installed manually, but distributed from a central and automated source. Intelligent applications that support the IT infrastructure with monitoring and admin processes also need far fewer personnel resources than only a few years ago.

Technologies like voice recognition, data analysis tools, or software for service or business process management are continuing to push this "productification" of services, to the extent that one could speak of a trend towards "Service as a Software". Replicable, prefabricated results built on best practices determine whether something is the right, suitable choice. Creative thinking in this vein allows many other services to be "productified". BPO providers are leading the way: With highly automated processes, e.g. for accounts payable, invoice processing or expense management, the need for manual intervention has been minimized.

Summary and Outlook

As our inquiry has shown, the IT sector is in the grip of massive structural change. Consolidation and the formation of specialist sub-sectors on the supply side, and globalized value creation and industrialization on the production side are challenging its established paradigms. All actors in the industry are forced to review their current position and the competencies they possess to develop a future-proof business model for themselves.

These rebuilding efforts must not be limited to some cosmetic retouching or new marketing approaches alone. What is needed is a true reformation in every respect. Critics might argue that such strategies are always a risky choice, fraught with uncertainties. However, much of that uncertainty is, in the end, only due to the simultaneous changes that are under way on the demand side, in the demand patterns and structures at the client. This calls for entrepreneurship, just as the famous quote by Nicholas Negroponte (1985) encouraged long ago: *"It is far easier to predict the future when you are helping make and distribute it."*

References

Bäumer, U., Kreutter, P., Rothauge F. (2010). Higher Hanging Fruits – Zielsegmente und Strategien indischer IT- und Technologieunternehmen in der DACH-Region. M&A Review, Dezember, pp. 590–596.

Buenstorf, G. (2007). Evolution on the shoulders of giants: Entrepreneurship and firm survival in the German laser industry. *Review of Industrial Organization, 30*, 179–202.

Günther, C. (2009). *Pioneer burnout: Radical product innovation and firm capabilities.* The Papers on Economics and Evolution (# 0922).

Hopenhayn, H. A. (1993). *The shakeout.* Barcelona: Universitat Pompeu Fabra

Klepper, S. (1997). Industry life cycles. *Industrial and Corporate Change, 6*(1), 145–182.

Murmann, J. P., & Homburg, E. (2001). Comparing evolutionary dynamics across different national settings: The case of the synthetic dye industry, 1857–1914. *Journal of Evolutionary Economics, 11*(2), pp. 177–205.

Negroponte, N. (1985). Heise. Retrieved January 12, 2013, from http://www.heise.de/tp/artikel/2/2035/3.html

PAC. (2012). *Outsourcing Research Program 2012.* Munich: Pierre Audoin Consultants.

PAC/Berlecon. (2012). *IT services Preisdatenbank.* Munich: Pierre Audoin Consultants.

Peltoniemi, M. (2011). Reviewing industry life-cycle theory: Avenues for future research. *International Journal of Management Reviews, 13*(4), 349–375.

Suarez, F. F., & Utterback, J. M. (1995). Dominant designs and the survival of firms. *Strategic Management Journal, 16*(6), 415–430.

4 From Project to Product Orientation

Markus Löffler and Felix Reinshagen

Reducing the costs of IT services has been the ambition of many companies over the last few years. Substantial savings have indeed been achieved by consolidating hardware assets, standardizing technologies, and streamlining processes. Nonetheless, even the most effective cost-reduction drive will hit a barrier at some point: namely, the inherent complexity of infrastructure and applications. Moving from a project-oriented to a product-oriented approach can reduce that complexity and push back this barrier. This approach will be reviewed by taking a closer look at IT infrastructure as discussed by Kaplan et al. (2004) and Chubak et al. (2011). Similar approaches can also be pursued for the application side of the equation.

4.1 New Opportunities for Standardization

The reason for this new complexity lies in the project-oriented, built-to-order concept that most IT organizations espouse. However futuristic the typical infrastructure might seem, it essentially resembles an old-fashioned motor vehicle: Hand-built by experts and designed to the specifications of a single customer. The current situation has application developers choosing the specific server configuration for each application and the infrastructure team following their orders. The consequence: Thousands of disconnected application silos, each using bespoke hardware and suffering from a mess of incompatible equipment and devices. In the end, this is a severe burden on the flexibility and market responsiveness of businesses.

Since every server is configured to match the peak demand for every application—a peak that is hardly ever reached in real-life practice—a substantial part of these expensive capacities are left unused, and the close connection between

M. Löffler (✉) • F. Reinshagen
McKinsey & Company, Birkenwaldstraße 149, 70191 Stuttgart, Germany
e-mail: Markus_Loeffler@mckinsey.com

F. Abolhassan (ed.), *The Road to a Modern IT Factory*, Management for Professionals,
DOI 10.1007/978-3-642-40219-7_4, © Springer-Verlag Berlin Heidelberg 2014

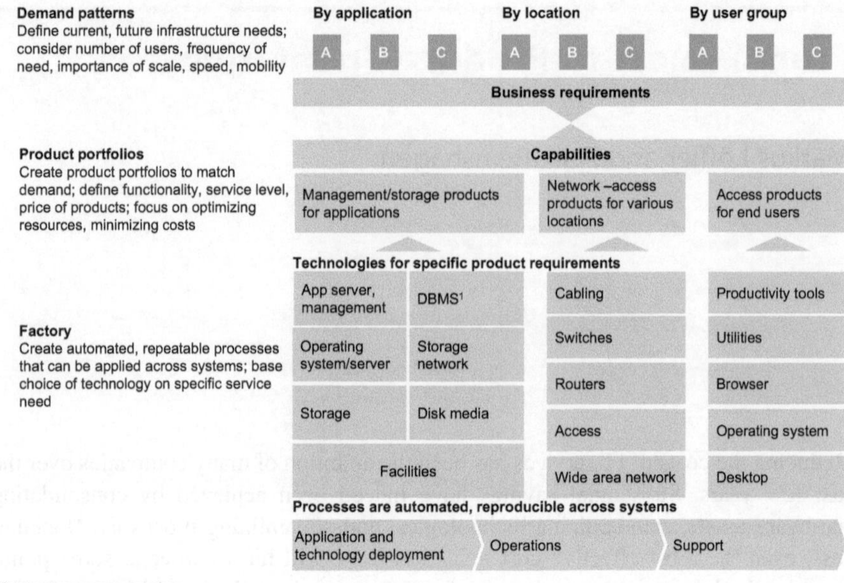

Fig. 4.1 The product-oriented model in IT infrastructure (*Source*: McKinsey 2004)

applications and their server and storage hardware prevents unused capacities from being available for use elsewhere.

Companies have begun to move beyond this build-to-order approach by using technical innovations—in combination with new capabilities and leadership practices. A decade after introducing distributed data processing, client–server or web-based architectures have become the norm. Businesses are introducing standardized application platforms and programming languages. Thanks to modern processors, storage units, and networks, individual infrastructure elements now need little manual adjustment to fulfill the needs of their users.

In response to these changes, leading actors in the industry have begun to introduce new concepts for managing and standardizing their infrastructure (cf. Fig. 4.1). Instead of defining the hardware and configuration required for a business application ("I need this brand, this model, and that configuration for networked servers. . ."), they define the service requirements ("I need storage that can be scaled up immediately. . ."). Rather than tailoring bespoke systems, their infrastructure teams are producing a selection of standardized, but versatile services.

In the product-oriented model, the specification of IT requirements can be compared to buying from a catalog. A developer looking for a storage product would thus choose one of multiple options with different service levels (e.g. in terms of their speed, capacity, and reliability). The final price will depend on the services actually bought. With this level of transparency, business clients know exactly how their demand will affect costs and resources.

4.2 Segmenting User Requirements

Any product-oriented model is built—as its name implies—around defined products or standard services. The product catalogue is aligned with the needs of the user: these needs should be explored and segmented accurately.

Large IT organizations can support thousands of applications, hundreds of sites, and tens of thousands of end users. All of these have their unique requirements concerning the infrastructure: Applications need service and storage capacity, physical locations need connectivity, users want desktops, laptops, PDAs etc. Standardizing all of these elements means that IT organizations first need to understand the current demand for infrastructure and predict how it will develop. The requirements should then be clustered in individual segments of relevance for the end user (e.g. operating times, throughput, or scalability).

Most applications can be allocated to a quite small number of clusters. For pharmaceutical companies, for instance, there could be two prominent clusters: Sales applications that need 24/7 support and should be available offline, and business applications that can be scaled to thousands of users and have to cope efficiently with batch transactions.

By contrast, the application portfolio of a bank for commercial clients will cover a much broader spectrum of requirements. Some applications—such as the tools for managing financial instruments, pricing, or risks—need enormous processing power to handle calculations in minutes, not hours. Applications for simple account transactions need to guarantee minimum downtimes. Finally, applications for program trading need to handle transactions in the blink of an eye.

Even if the requirements of physical locations or user groups are relatively simple, they can be clustered in a similar way, e.g. clustering the network architecture by size (organizations with over 1,000 users, with 250–1,000 users, or remote offices with fewer than 250 people). For a cable company, the user groups can, similarly, be clustered by executives with comprehensive support needs, specialists, call center personnel, and field technicians.

In most cases, the definition of the specific infrastructure needs for applications, locations, and users is the hardest challenge when segmenting requirements. The greatest difficulties can be the frequency and timing of demand, the number of users, the acceptable level of downtime, and the importance of speed, scalability, and mobility.

4.3 Product Standardization

When the current and the future needs have been assessed, work can begin on developing "productified", replicable services. On the level of the portfolio, the decision has to determine the scope, depth, and range of the products on offer, always keeping an eye on the optimum use of resources and lowest possible costs. Any exceptions should be clarified beforehand. For instance, the team can decide against offering products for applications with strict requirements, such as those that have extremely short latency. In other cases, no changes should be made, for example to established products that work well and are harder to transition to new hardware. The decision should also consider how new technologies will be introduced and how established applications will be migrated over.

On the level of products, the team needs to determine the required functions, service levels, and prices. Application support products need to have a defined programming language, an acceptable level of downtime, and a certain price for using the infrastructure. That price depends on transparent costs for data processing, storage, processing, and network usage, which makes it easier for the end customer to understand and work with. The pricing model can offer discounts when the demand is predicted exactly, so as to reduce overhang capacities and to use strategic pricing to coax the user in the direction of standardized products.

Producing a catalogue of products with a high degree of standardization enables the people in charge of infrastructure functions to pick which software, hardware, and processes to use. Once this has been achieved, they can set to work on optimizing their delivery model and developing integrated regional strategies to reduce the number of data centers needed for the business. In this way, more functions can operate off-site—at low-wage or even off-shore locations.

A careful selection of products and product portfolios is essential for successful infrastructure functions. Developers and users will not put up with portfolios that limit their choice—whereas a portfolio offering too many options does not offer scalability and reusability. As is the case for any maker of consumer goods, understanding the customer's needs is a sine qua non.

4.4 Organizational Changes

Focusing consistently on the product will have major implications for the roles, responsibilities, and governance in the infrastructure organization (cf. Chap. 9).

The most important new roles are the role of the product manager, who defines the product and product portfolios and oversees their lifecycle, and the role of the "factory architect", who designs the shared processes for enabling, operating, and supporting the business (cf. Fig. 4.2). Product managers need to concentrate on the service portfolio and are responsible for achieving certain productivity targets. They also need to maintain excellent relations with end users and application developers to understand and cluster their requirements, define the right product portfolio, and convince developers and end users alike of the worth of their product portfolios.

Factory architects make sure that the product promise can actually be fulfilled. They select the technologies and tools required for the purpose, put processes into place, and plan process automation.

For the new infrastructure to work efficiently and produce a lasting boost to performance, IT executives should concentrate on five key areas:

1. **Demand forecasting and capacity planning**. Getting supply and demand in a perfect balance means no resources go to waste. To be able to achieve this, the IT

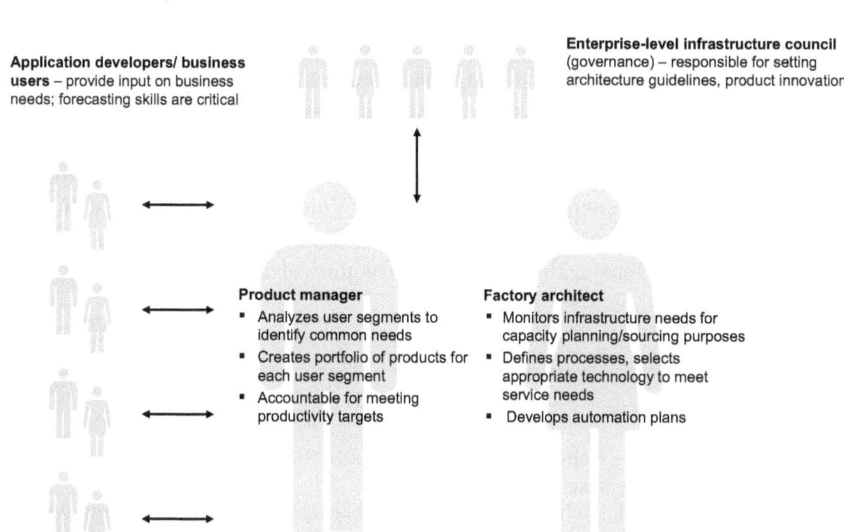
New roles in IT production
Application developers/ business users – provide input on business needs; forecasting skills are critical
Enterprise-level infrastructure council (governance) – responsible for setting architecture guidelines, product innovation
Product manager
Analyzes user segments to identify common needs
Creates portfolio of products for each user segment
Accountable for meeting productivity targets
Factory architect
Monitors infrastructure needs for capacity planning/sourcing purposes
Defines processes, selects appropriate technology to meet service needs
Develops automation plans

Fig. 4.2 Organizing IT production with a product focus (*Source*: McKinsey 2004)

team needs to work closely with the line organization to predict actual demand and plan capacities more accurately.

2. **Financing and budgeting**. Product demand determines the budget. Since the new model predicts the actual demand, budgeting becomes easier, and price transparency also ensures clarity. The business divisions now know what their IT decisions will cost; their infrastructure teams understand how user requirements affect the budget and can produce more detailed financing plans.
3. **Product portfolio management**. Developing new product portfolios should be expected to take 6 months at least. Infrastructure managers should check these portfolios two to three times in the first year to establish whether they match the expected workload and new requirements of the end users. After this first hurdle has been passed, the cycle can be brought down to one review per year. The teams should, however, monitor all phases of the product's lifecycle, from planning and the procurement of new products to end-of-life for old service offerings and the reallocation of freed-up resources.
4. **Release management**. In order to guarantee the effective integration of new technologies or upgrades and to prevent downtime or loss of productivity as a result of changes, leading companies make sure that release processes run in parallel for infrastructure products and applications. Planning ahead means keeping application developers informed about any changes in the infrastructure portfolio.
5. **Procurement and supplier management**. It is up to IT executives to make sure that sufficient data resources are available for the various service levels in the

product portfolio. Infrastructure managers should therefore check their procurement strategy on an annual basis and keep looking for ways to reduce costs and improve productivity.

Alongside establishing and staffing the roles described here, the success of any business concept depends on a strong governance model that allows a meaningful balance of risks and costs, while allocating responsibilities for taking action and producing results. For greater transparency, the roles and responsibilities should be defined for the development and enforcement of guidelines, as well as methods for monitoring and reporting. The organization could, in this sense, produce an inventory of all applications and related infrastructure elements to enable effective productivity checks.

References

Chubak, D., Kaplan, J. M., Kelly, C. (2011). A business-back approach to technology consumption. McKinsey on Payments.

Kaplan, J. M., Löffler, M., Roberts R. P. (2004). Managing next generation IT infrastructure. McKinsey on IT.

5 The IT Product Factory

Markus Löffler and Felix Reinshagen

Turning IT products into cost-efficient industrial goods means rethinking their production in terms of modern management principles. The following chapter will consider three core aspects on the path towards efficient IT production "factories": The application of lean principles in IT, the optimization of data center operations, and the globalization of the value chain. The aspects and suggestions in this chapter owe a debt to the contributions of Chatrin et al. (2007), Chatrin (2011), Kaplan et al. (2009), and Forrest et al. (2008).

5.1 The Arrival of Lean in IT

Toyota invented lean management to minimize waste in its manufacturing processes and establish a culture of continuous improvement. For a process to become lean, it was first scrutinized to see which parts of the manufacturing system were redundant and could be removed. At the same time, Toyota developed new organizational principles and performance management systems designed to instil a long-term commitment to these changes in the company.

The past few years have seen the application of these lean principles not only in the manufacturing industry, but also in the service sector. Among the pioneers in this area were banks and insurers, who began to revise their back-office processes accordingly and later applied their findings to the customer-facing side of their business. Popular opinion holds that cost reductions always imply a reduction in service quality. This has been disproven by the experience of the industry, which showed that increased productivity not only brought costs down, but that it improved quality whilst simultaneously accelerating business (just as Toyota had

M. Löffler (✉) • F. Reinshagen
McKinsey & Company, Birkenwaldstraße 149, 70191 Stuttgart, Germany
e-mail: Markus_Loeffler@mckinsey.com

F. Abolhassan (ed.), *The Road to a Modern IT Factory*, Management for Professionals, DOI 10.1007/978-3-642-40219-7_5, © Springer-Verlag Berlin Heidelberg 2014

managed in the automotive industry). Frequently, there are far more "redundant" IT processes than people would assume (including activities that actually produce additional costs rather than benefits for providers and their clients alike).

We can distinguish between eight forms of redundancy, explained for our purposes with examples drawn from real-life client projects:

Redundant work (Not produced to match demand): Server management produced monthly 20-page reports on server operating times that users almost never consulted. None of the reports ever touched on the users' main worry, the slow server response times, and the problem was never resolved.

Inventory (Too much on hold): A helpdesk manager lacked the means to allocate jobs to his team. His people simply picked jobs at random, with no regard for completion times or the complexity of the task. This led to imbalances in their workloads, more inventory on hold, and to the constant reprioritization of jobs.

Waiting periods (Idle time that interrupts workflows): A helpdesk call center had timed its break periods to coincide with the greatest number of calls during the day. This led to unnecessarily long waits for the user and complex callback routines.

Logistics (Longer routes than necessary or interim storage/hold required): The storage of hardware equipment was not designed for optimum efficiency: A previous consolidation drive meant that all server parts were kept in a single location, but this was far from the actual servers and caused unnecessary to-ing and fro-ing with individual components.

Movement (Unnecessary manual intervention, poor workplace ergonomics): Bottlenecks in the IT system meant that helpdesk personnel could only complete their work by manually changing the job ticket title.

Excess production (Producing too much for current demand): The capacity of the new servers was based on the peak demand expected in 2 years' time. Despite this, all new servers were brought on line immediately.

Reworking (Producing flawed products that need to be reworked): Software had been installed with different settings and at different times in the various units. A new software package was then only offered for a single configuration. Test cycles and emergency processes were not aligned and required several reworkings before functioning.

Intellect (mismatch between competencies and tasks): Internal support employees were overqualified and far too experienced, leading to a lack of motivation and/or to over-engineered solutions.

Identifying redundant activities and optimizing processes makes up only one of the four pillars of lasting change. Equally important pillars are the introduction of improved performance management, a change in the attitudes and behavior of employees, and a revision to the organization's make-up (cf. Fig. 5.1). To make sure that continuous improvements continue to be seen after the first 6 months, lean programs introduce work concepts that allow employees and executives to continue to define and implement ways of improving performance.

Experience with lean programs has revealed three important success factors: (1) The involvement of executive management and their support from the start of the project, with particular focus on aspects of change management; (2) The

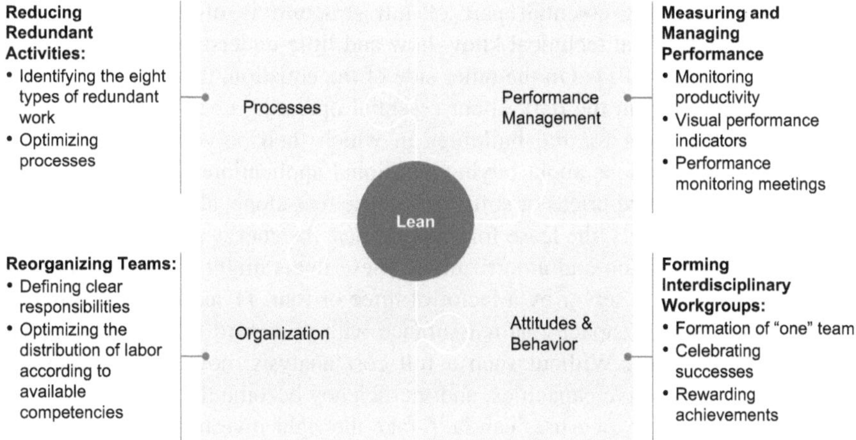
Lean Transformation
Reducing Redundant Activities:
• Identifying the eight types of redundant work
• Optimizing processes
Processes
Performance Management
Measuring and Managing Performance
• Monitoring productivity
• Visual performance indicators
• Performance monitoring meetings
Lean
Reorganizing Teams:
• Defining clear responsibilities
• Optimizing the distribution of labor according to available competencies
Organization
Attitudes & Behavior
Forming Interdisciplinary Workgroups:
• Formation of "one" team
• Celebrating successes
• Rewarding achievements

Fig. 5.1 The four pillars of a lean program (*Source*: McKinsey 2004)

selection of the pilots to showcase the importance of the program, and (3) The selection of lean experts to apply the methods.

Executive managers must take a leading role in giving the work the right presence and stopping the program from degenerating into a pure cost-savings exercise. It is also important that the top managers support the middle managers below them during the implementation period and consider all aspects of the target vision when taking their decisions.

Second, the right pilots need to be picked to demonstrate the importance of the program and to make sure that the business at large accepts its responsibilities.

Third, people need to make sure that the project is not limited to the fine-tuning of processes alone. For sustainable, continuous improvement, mindsets and patterns of behavior need to change. In practice, this means the careful selection of lean experts as change managers, the early involvement of line managers ("it is their project"), and the assurance of constant and undivided attention for the entire course of the project.

5.2 Optimizing Data Centers

Data centers are the factory floors of IT production. This where the IT sector encounters traditional concerns of industry: Infrastructure investments, capacity planning, facility maintenance, and energy consumption. The high costs of hardware and long-term commitment to the chosen location make careful planning essential. Only too often, poor planning and weak utilization make data center operations unnecessarily expensive (cf. Chap. 15).

Considering the costs for data centers, the responsibility for their financial performance is often astonishingly poorly defined. Financial and commercial responsibility for this essential part of infrastructure is often left to facility managers with minimal technical know-how and little understanding of the commercial significance of IT. On the other side of the equation, the people operating the servers are often in the dark about essential operating costs like energy consumption or the costs for the buildings in which their servers are housed. IT managers make decisions about buying additional applications or new servers by looking at the hardware prices or software license fees alone, although they should consider operating costs, the lease for the facilities, the energy prices, support, and the costs of depreciation and amortization. These items might exceed the upfront purchasing price for a server by a factor of three or four. IT managers also like to buy additional server capacity as reassurance with no regard for the costs or the actual business needs. Without such a full cost analysis, however, unnecessary building work, excessive capacities, and inefficiency become the rule.

The following four measures can help take the right investment decisions and keep data centers efficient.

Proactive IT facility management: A disciplined approach should be taken to the use of existing servers and facilities. The spots occupied by retired servers can be used by new ones before more physical data center space needs to be added. Older servers can be upgraded or taken off-line if they are not used. Virtualization can help reduce the need for active services. By these means, a sample data center managed to increase its average utilization rate from 5.6 % to 9.1 %. A new data center that had already been approved by the company's management and would have eaten up the lion's share of that year's investment budget was no longer needed.

Companies can also save costs by ensuring tighter control of increases in their data needs. Business units should check how much data actually needs to be stored and whether some labor-intensive data analyses might not be drawn down. By removing some processing activities, peak demand can be brought down, and not all of the business's data needs the same recovery capacities in the form of comprehensive backup systems.

Better supply of information: Good forecasts and good planning are the foundations for greater efficiency in data centers. Companies should track any deviation between the expected and actual capacity needs and give their line units incentives for better forecasts. The managers of data centers should build their models with a comprehensive sense for future trends, such as growth or business cycles. With this strategy, a global communications company managed to introduce a planning process with data growth scenarios for each of its business units that allowed it to shelve 35 % of the originally planned investments.

Calculating the actual costs: Most companies do not treat their data centers as a scarce and expensive resource, but as containers waiting to be filled to capacity. To counter this, companies should take decisions about new servers, additional applications, or more data on the basis of an understanding of the actual operating costs (Total Cost of Ownership—TCO). Achieving transparency and avoiding excess capacities requires the early definition of all costs over the entire lifecycle of the system.

The business departments and the IT unit both to understand which investments into software actually produce adequate results. This is essential for the discipline needed to take the right decisions—decisions that affect the costs of data processing.

Centralized responsibilities: In large companies, it can be hard to push through these changes. Oftentimes, people do not realize what the provision of data costs, although many parts of the business need data center services. Sharing the responsibility across multiple IT units (including application development), capacity management, shared service groups, or facility management only worsens transparency. This problem can be countered by introducing clear and—if necessary—centralized responsibilities.

5.3 International Value Chains

As in manufacturing, industrialization in IT will give a new significance to international value chains. Considering the minimal "transport costs" in the industry and its high organizational complexity, the offshoring models used elsewhere cannot simply be copied over (cf. Chap. 18 on sourcing strategies and Chap. 19 on make-or-buy decisions). Here, we will look at the most important aspects in IT offshoring.

With more trust being placed in remote management, the ready availability of cheap bandwidth, and the spread of fast networks, offshoring has seen a growth spurt in India, other parts of Asia, and Europe since the turn of the millennium. It has led to amazing achievements. A global financial services company, for instance, managed to reduce its labor costs by more than 20 % as early as the half-way point of a 36-month program.

Such successes should not tempt companies to rashly introduce a completely new procurement model. The long-term strategy should also not be forgotten in all the focus on short-term necessities. Short-term action on overcoming bottlenecks or responding to diverse challenges, e.g. in user support or network management, often leads to patchwork offshoring, which can make the process much more complicated and limit potential savings. Finding the right procurement model needs time and care. First, companies need to consider their commercial goals in deciding between an internal model—in which they own the offshore provider—and an external model. Experience shows that most companies benefit from an external solution that relies on multiple providers. Indeed, many companies have come to sell off their own offshore operators to dedicated outsourcing providers looking to grow their business. Irrespective of how this decision pans out, companies then have two options: They either keep all project management in their control and only try to cover shortfalls in their labor capacities, or they enter contracts with defined service level agreements. This option would generally offset the performance risks, as the provider would have to reach the defined milestones or face contractual penalties. Using offshore capacities in response to personnel bottlenecks is the simpler option, but experience shows that guaranteed service levels tend to lead to greater satisfaction and additional savings in the medium or long run. They also create a natural incentive for more efficiency.

Despite the increasing reliance on offshoring, most companies still look predominantly to the traditional industry players, and India in particular. This can be problematic: the volatile world economy of the recent past has shown how drastic currency and wage fluctuations can undermine even the best-laid business plans. There are many highly promising alternative destinations for offshoring. Pan-European companies who, for instance, need French- or German-speaking support staff, could look to Africa or Eastern Europe. For truly global organizations with 24/7 operations, on the other hand, the "follow the sun" model tracks time zones to cover all shifts. The advantages are evident: Immediate response, lower costs, and continuous availability. However, only few companies have the size or budget for such a comprehensive solution. For many, centers of competence with pools of talented people concentrated on the key hubs will be the better solution. These offer the advantages of global reach and pooled expertise with better utilization of human capital. One European banking house with multiple infrastructure sites decided to pool these processes in one hub in India, which meant that it could supply the same number of customers with fewer resources and at much lower costs.

When picking the right provider, companies need to pay attention to aligning the available capacities with their actual needs. Since many IT applications can be considered business-critical, the services of the chosen provider need to live up to exacting standards. A well-established application development provider might also not be the perfect choice for infrastructure support, as some companies have had to learn to their cost. Providers need to show that they have the required recruiting, training, and staff retention capabilities to ensure the supply of appropriate human resources. To avoid the loss of key personnel, many companies have begun to support their offshoring providers in their efforts to retain staff and are offering top performers interesting and exciting jobs.

Even if the provider has sufficient and sufficiently qualified people at hand, not all functions or roles are indeed suitable for offshoring. Certain activities need to stay in close physical proximity to the end user. In other cases, keeping certain expertise in-house can guarantee a competitive advantage that should not be watered down through offshoring. Despite this, a considerable part of the labor required for developing and maintaining IT infrastructure and applications can be outsourced. Large companies do so by identifying activities that are difficult or impossible to off-shore for regulatory, technical, or security reasons, and clearly demarcating these within their organizational structure from activities that can be off-shored. The top technical support level, a level 3 team, might be very hard to offshore, because its technicians need access to confidential information and might be subject to special regulatory requirements. A financial services provider would therefore split the L3 team into two groups: One team to support the customer on site, and one team for purely technical activities that can be located elsewhere.

How fast an offshoring solution is actually implemented depends on how urgent it is for the company to reduce costs and on how ready it is for risks. Rapid decision-making is called for, since the head of steam the company has built up can soon be spent in a long search for the perfect solution. Two factors should never be forgotten, as they are absolutely essential. First, the responsibilities for all actors need to be clear and unambiguous. If multiple suppliers team up to provide a service, their client needs one defined interface to work with. Whoever acts as this interface will, for instance, take charge of coordinating the response to downtime or escalate problems that cannot be passed on directly to one of the involved functions. Second, there needs to be clarity about the expected service, not least in terms of how it is monitored and the response to take if it does not live up to expectations.

The most successful companies follow a specific approach to offshoring: They begin by defining a comprehensive corporate strategy and combine top-down decisions with bottom-up experiences and insights. By clarifying the most important cost factors, their performance, and the characteristics of the locations in question at the very beginning, they mitigate potential risks in offshoring and establish a basis for better sourcing decisions. Saving time means investing enough time into planning and preparation. Companies that have learned to follow this maxim are in the best place to gain most from their offshoring investments.

References

Chatrin, C. (2011). *Bringing lean to a highly skilled workforce: An interview with Thierry Pecoud of BNP Paribas*. Lean Management: New frontiers for financial institutions.

Chatrin, C., Kaplan, J., et al. (2007). *Making IT infrastructure operations lean*. McKinsey White Paper.

Forrest, W., Kaplan, J., et al. (2008). *Data centers: How to cut carbon emissions and costs*. McKinsey on Business Technology

Kaplan, J., Libarikian, A., et al. (2009). *Getting infrastructure offshoring right*. McKinsey on Business Technology

Industrialization in IT and Traditional Industries: Similarities and Differences

6

Katharina Grimme and Peter Kreutter

6.1 Industrialization: A Short Historical Detour

In recent years, increasing pressure on cost-cutting and performance has brought one issue onto the agendas of executives at IT service providers and in company's internal IT units: the industrialization of IT. According to Brenner et al. (2010, p. 132), industrialization in IT can be described as the "*application of successful management concepts and methods from industrial production to IT production*". While this call to copy successful principles from industry—and the automotive industry in particular—may seem natural, the gamut of concepts proposed as guidance is confusing to say the least: from Kaizen to TQM, from modularization to assembly line production, or from automation to rapid prototyping.

This chapter will try to outline the many similarities between today's IT sector and the automotive industry of yesteryear. There can be no doubt about the great potential of fundamental industrial concepts for the IT business. Implementation, however, requires at the very least, a basic sense of why a particular concept was introduced in other industries at a given point in time.

The early twentieth century was the time of Taylorism and Ford's principles. Compared to earlier manual cottage industries, these models of industrialization meant a radical boost to efficiency. The Toyota production system that the wider public first learned about in the MIT study "The machine that changed the world" (Womack et al. 1990), represented a similarly fundamental leap. Western

K. Grimme (✉)
Pierre Audoin Consultants (PAC) GmbH, Holzstraße 26, 80469 Munich, Germany
e-mail: K.Grimme@pac-online.com

P. Kreutter
WHU – Otto Beisheim School of Management, Campus Düsseldorf, Erkrather Str. 224A, 40233 Düsseldorf, Germany
e-mail: Peter.Kreutter@whu.edu

F. Abolhassan (ed.), *The Road to a Modern IT Factory*, Management for Professionals,
DOI 10.1007/978-3-642-40219-7_6, © Springer-Verlag Berlin Heidelberg 2014

companies like Porsche copied this production system relatively quickly and achieved a level of costs and quality that had been unthinkable for mass production only years earlier. What the concepts of Frederic Winslow Taylor, Henry Ford, and Taiichi Ohno (Ohno 2005) have in common is that they present basically identical paradigms: They are the optimum answer to the unique political, social, economic, and technical circumstances of their times and can be boiled down to a set of fundamental, universally applicable principles of effective and efficient network optimization (Pfeiffer and Weiß 1992). We should not ask about "whether", but about "how" these principles can be applied to IT. At the same time, we need to raise our awareness of the unique environment in which these principles are to be used.

6.2 Customers' Expectations in Modern Industrialized Markets: Tailor-Made Mass Production

Applying the textbook distinction between sellers' and buyers' markets, there can be no doubt that IT has become a stereotypical buyers' market. Customer focus, in the sense of providing highly customized solutions, means enormous complexity for IT production. Henry Ford's legendary saying "You can have any color as long as it's black" reflected a car market where the seller was in the driving seat and the buyer had to be happy to get a cheap, quality product in the first place. Special equipment, like custom colors or additional extras, was not an option. The users of the first generation of PCs were similarly undemanding. Many of them built their own hardware and wrote their own software (Campbell-Kelly 2004).

For the automotive industry and the computer industry, these times are now long past. In both cases, it was the move into mass markets that created the pressure to reduce costs while adding more and more differentiation to cover different customers' needs. Joseph A. Schumpeter (1950, p. 82) described this very vividly: *"[...] the capitalist achievement does not typically consist in providing more silk stockings for queens, but in bringing them within the reach of factory girls in return for steadily decreasing amounts of effort!"*

The following illustration shows how the methods of production in the automotive industry have evolved in close interaction with the scope and complexity of demand (Fig. 6.1).

The same is happening on the customer side of the IT industry. Success in customers' core business demands highly customized and highly-available IT systems. These systems differ not only from industry to industry, but also within individual industries or even single companies. One need only think of the different requirements for trading systems in asset management and for point-of-sale terminals in retail banking (PAC 2012). This means exceptional flexibility in the

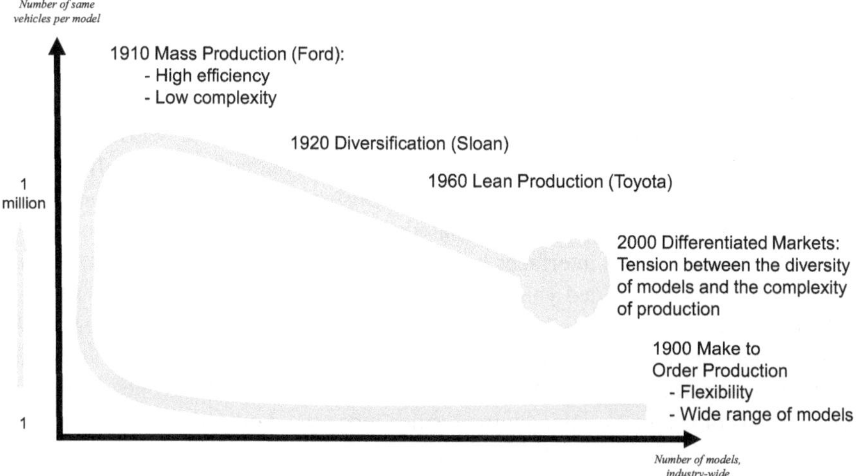

Fig. 6.1 Diagram showing the positioning of various industrialization concepts in the context of market conditions. (Source: illustration by the authors, 2012)

production paradigm and in the means of IT industrialization. Brenner et al. (2010, pp. 129 ff.) name four pillars of industrialization:

- Standardization and automation
- Modularization
- Continuous improvement
- Concentration on core competencies

In a similar vein, Pfeiffer and Weiß (1992) have proposed a set of principles as the fundamental factors in the transformation of the entire value creation network of industrial businesses as a form of systemic innovation. Although there is an overlap in the basic principles and in the extent of the changes, we should not underestimate the many differences between the products of traditional industry and IT service production. The aspects introduced below in section 6.3 have been chosen as particularly illustrative of the key point to bear in mind here: the transformation must be introduced in an intelligent and problem-oriented fashion, with due consideration for the unique nature of service business models and the technical value creation infrastructure.

6.3 Challenges in the Industrialization of IT Services

6.3.1 Basic Considerations

The essential difference between an industrial product, like a car, and a service lies in the fact that services can usually only be produced with the involvement of the client and that services are intangible in nature. This intangible nature also makes it harder to define a set of specifications for the service. Even simple services, like a haircut, can soon lead to unhappiness about the quality of the service when poor communication or unclear expectations come into play.

In the case of outsourced IT services, which are usually delivered over longer periods of time, the situation becomes even more complex as the services need to follow changing expectations. Again, the burden is on clients to get involved: they need to work with the service provider to ensure meaningful and continuous demand management. Properly coordinated governance models can be the answer by regulating the various interfaces between clients and service provider(s). Industrialization offers real added value, as it is a consistent attempt at "productifying" services that can be described and measured in clear and non-complex terms. As Chap. 3 has shown, the automation and codification of services in software solutions is the way forward. For service providers, the challenge lies in getting the client to come along on this journey, since more standardized services will need a rethinking and adjustment of the client's systems and process world.

6.3.2 The Tension Between Objective and Subjective Quality

The potential tension between objective quality problems and subjective quality defects has already been mentioned in passing. The special nature and complexity of services means that service quality is often not immediately measurable or that it is measured with indicators (e.g. SLAs concerning downtime) that do not relate immediate to the actual business activities of the client.

More commercially aware service and quality definitions—breaking with the technological fixation—can be the solution. These would provide a manageable set of indicators to counter the (often subjective) dissatisfaction of clients. IT service providers have already begun to extend their feelers in this direction.

This environment offers exciting, innovative forms of cooperation between clients and providers: These concepts are used to develop new shared business models for both parties. One example of this is the joint venture between the Indian mobile phone company Bharti Airtel and Infosys. The two partners set up a payment network that uses the mobile phone system and works independently of the banking system, giving many Indian consumers their first opportunity to make electronic transactions. This virtually invented a new line of business from which both partners can benefit. A characteristic trait of such partnerships is their thorough focus on commercial (and commercially measurable) services and their sharing of risks and rewards alike.

In order to use all of these opportunities, both clients and providers need to open up to one another. Clients need to let go of their vision of exclusive ownership of technologies or processes in all their details. Providers have to shape the design of the architecture and the services they deliver, and the delivery of these services needs to become transparent in the form of commercial performance indicators. Providers need to convince the client of this close, mutually interdependent cooperation—and they need to accept that they will share both the risks and the rewards with their clients.

6.3.3 No IT Service Contract Is Ever Fully Watertight

Viewed from the perspective of economic theory, all contracts are notoriously incomplete. This stems from the fact that contract drafters are unable to predict all eventualities that might affect the execution of the contract. Not all contractual claims can be enforced with third-party support, i.e. there is always a certain degree of uncertainty that no legal interpretation or review could remove. Highly service- and/or technology-oriented projects are a prime example for this natural incompleteness of contracts. How "incomplete" a contract is depends on a variety of factors. First, innovative concepts, such as cloud solutions, require innovative technologies by definition. However, such new technologies have a naturally higher degree of uncertainty, since they are in an early phase of their lifecycle. At the time of the contract, it might be hard to predict how cost and performance parameters will develop over time. The sometimes massive under- or overestimating of these factors is a common problem described in the literature on strategic technology management. Incomplete contracts are particularly likely when they concern complex system innovation, which represents the coming-together of many (partial) technologies, each with a unique level of maturity, that need to be embedded in existing technological and human-organizational environments and the service networks that complement them.

Such loopholes offer the stronger party a foothold for opportunism, e.g. for making additional, supplementary, or later demands, especially in circumstances where long-term contractual relationships are encumbered with switching barriers.

This makes it important for both sides in the IT outsourcing partnership to stay aware of the potential problems when negotiating their contracts. Necessary changes—be it in response to changing customer requirements or to technical innovation—can be covered by innovative contractual mechanisms or regular amendments. An important criterion for success is regular, open communication and a real partnership between client and provider.

For service providers, the particular challenge lies in not letting tough negotiators detract them from their established long-term purpose. They need to avoid any systematic overbidding, which often becomes a cause for later contractual problems. In low-growth, high-competition markets in particular, clients also need to understand that they should not overshoot their target in supplier negotiations, as the eventual choice of provider might try to recuperate a lost profit margin in some other form. Contracts that do not close every possible bolt hole always give providers some opportunities to do so.

Summary and Outlook

Chapter 3 took a brief look at the many changes affecting the IT industry which call for a stronger focus on core competencies and a new strategic stance in an industry that is changing at its core. This means rethinking old partnerships and the ecosystem of more or less strategic alliances. New forms of partnership are being created in the sense of mutual value creation networks. These networks rely on hierarchical, but also flexible structures and try to satisfy specific needs of clients, which are often of an only temporary nature. In this respect, the IT industry will have to follow the automotive industry's 20-year lead in taking a completely new path and daring to introduce sweeping reforms in such value-creation networks. What this requires is decisions about activities and partnerships that try to expand the reach of their know-how value chains. Partnerships aimed at purely regional expansion are a second type, whereas technology partnerships constitute another, third form. Most exciting, however, are those new and innovative forms of cooperation that bring clients themselves on board and try to develop entirely new, cooperative business models. The trend is clear: Away from traditional supplier-client relations to multi-faceted partnerships in open eco-systems whose purpose is to work on common (exclusive and unique) solutions, sharing all risks and profits together along the way. For these to flourish, systematic industrialization is a fundamental and ever-present requirement.

References

Brenner, W., Resch, A., Schulz, V. (2010). *Die Zukunft der IT in Unternehmen*. Frankfurt am Main: Frankfurter Allgemeine Buch.

Campbell-Kelly, M. (2004). *From airline reservations to Sonic the Hedgehog: A history of the software industry*. Cambridge, MA: MIT Press.

Ohno, T. (2005). *Das Toyota-Produktionssystem*. Frankfurt am Main: Campus.

PAC. (2012). *Status quo and trends in Germany's banking market*. Munich: Pierre Audoin Consultants.

Pfeiffer, W., Weiß, E. Lean management. Berlin: Erich Schmidt.

Schumpeter, J.A. (1950). *Capitalism, socialism and democracy* (3rd ed.). New York: Harper.

Womack, J. P., et al. (1990). *The machine that changed the world*. New York: Rawson.

Part III

Tools for Short-Term Optimization and Greater Efficiency

7 Short-Term Quality Improvements

Stephan Kasulke

From the point of view of many clients, IT has become a key piece of basic infrastructure—like water and electricity, it should simply be there without any effort on the part of the consumer. IT is changing into a commodity business where very few features distinguish one provider from the next. For providers, this means having to rise above their competitors by offering premium quality at ever-lower prices. Since many of their clients will be operating business ventures in many countries, they will also have to be able to act as one-stop, full-service providers with global availability.

IT service organizations need to win the trust of their clients by guaranteeing reliability. For the client, reliability—meaning service quality—mostly refers to three key aspects, guaranteed over a suitably long period of time:

- No downtime affecting critical systems
- Fast and transparent responses to disruptions of service
- Continuous compliance with delivery deadlines.

At the same time, clients expect the quality of the service to increase measurably and production costs to decrease over time.

For IT service providers, this means providing both fully scaleable and customized solutions for the client's specific needs, as well as models for optimum data security and service reliability. The real expectations of clients often go far beyond the actual service level agreed in their contracts. Tolerance of system outages is diminishing, especially after longer periods of stable and reliable operations. Clients are building their business processes on the assumption that the underlying IT infrastructure is permanently available. IT applications that might

S. Kasulke (✉)
T-Systems Austria, Rennweg 97-99, 1030 Vienna, Austria
e-mail: Stephan.Kasulke@t-systems.com

F. Abolhassan (ed.), *The Road to a Modern IT Factory*, Management for Professionals,
DOI 10.1007/978-3-642-40219-7_7,

initially have been non-critical for the business are often expanded or used in such a way that their absence would mean a major disruption to business processes. One typical example would be the rapid rise of email for business communication: this trend has turned potential disruption to mail exchange servers into a serious problem.

"Zero Outage" is the goal. People are right to fear outages in their IT infrastructure: Every stoppage of critical processes costs money. European companies with more than 50 people lose over 37 million hours of labor every year due to IT downtime and the time needed to recover data. If such disruptons are prolonged, they can threaten the very existence of the business. One example: In 2008, a German subsidiary of a US-based bank, experienced several hours of downtime affecting its online banking services. Only shortly before, the bank had received hundreds of millions of euros in private investment for a new, online-only savings product. An Icelandic bank had recently shut down its online services to stop people withdrawing their savings in the financial crisis. Faced with the outage of its online banking system, the German bank almost faced a bank run, which could have had a critical impact on its short-term liquidity.

All parts of a quality drive in IT service organizations need to be focused on the "greater whole": Promoting global standardization, integrating the perspectives of the overseas branches and the business units, and ensuring a holistic sense of customer awareness.

How can one best pursue short-term improvements in quality? The first phase of any quality campaign, the "quick-fix phase", relies on immediate actions to reduce the number of incidents and escalation of client issues. The second phase, the "fix phase", turns its attention to longer-term activities for structural optimization. In the final stabilization phase, the measures adopted are anchored in the organization. The achievements are used as a stepping stone—what works well is maintained, while other aspects are developed further to achieve a lasting improvement in quality.

In all of this, it is essential to include all relevant actors—from employees to top managers and from suppliers to sales people—in the pursuit of a shared global quality standard. Perfection should be the be-all and end-all of the entire value chain and every individual's contributions. This is how security and high availability can be guaranteed for the client.

7.1 Quality Management

Weekly reviews of the essential quality indicators (key performance indicators, KPIs) by top management can help achieve a lasting increase in quality. In this way, top management is not only notified about critical incidents or projects, but also about specific improvement activities that are ongoing to resolve quality issues for good.

7.1.1 KPIs in Operations

For monitoring quality, indicators can be defined for the core processes of incident, problem, and change management:

(A) Incident Management

Incident management usually employs two specific indicators to measure operational stability. The most prominent KPI is the number of major incidents (MIs). A major incident is any disruption of an IT system that affects an important business process of the client so that the latter incurs severe financial losses or a loss of reputation.

The correct classification of incidents requires documentation of the client's "critical landscape", i.e. the business-critical IT systems, which should be aligned with contractual agreements. Should a disruption occur, the provider also needs to work with the client to establish the extent to which the IT service is actually affected.

Achieving an improvement in the number of major incidents means first understanding the most common causes of disruptions and the various responsibilities involved. This should distinguish between disruptions of critical IT services that lead to a total outage (MIs) and partial losses that create a risk of a later complete outage ("High Incidents", "HIs").

The analysis should also distinguish between the three main causes of major incidents:

- Client error: The client or the client's supplier has caused the disruption or is responsible for the affected IT system.
- Error by IT service organization subcontractor: Disruptions caused on this side can be kept to a minimum by introducing shared quality initiatives or faster escalation procedures.
- Error of the IT service organization itself: Disruptions in this category can be influenced directly by the provider's quality initiatives.

It is important to remember that IT service providers need to get to work on all three factors if they want to achieve high quality over the long term—even those factors that are outside their immediate control.

For short-term improvements, the most obvious step would be to explore the factors that lie within the organization's immediate area of control. Here, there are four common causes of problems: Flawed or poorly defined processes, technological problems (hardware, network, low-level software), application problems (application software), and human error.

Stabilizing the major incident situation can rely on change freezes, i.e. completely prohibiting all changes to critical systems, e.g. while annual statements are being prepared.

The second KPI in incident management is the "Mean Time To Repair" (MTTR). This indicator defines how long it takes on average for an IT service to be brought back on line. The MTTR is a good measure of incident management quality and reveals, among other factors, whether the notification chain has worked well or how quickly the people with the right qualifications were on site to resolve the incident. Regular tests ("fire drills") and a sound organization can have an immediate positive impact on the Mean Time To Repair by simulating outages in cooperation with the suppliers or members of staff that are involved and providing training for the necessary steps to recover from the incident.

In special circumstances, the time might be right to establish a war room with a permanent complement of personnel. The war room staff coordinate the monitoring of critical systems and can notify all relevant people whenever an incident needs a response. The war room should have board-level legitimation for taking every action necessary to ensure stable operations.

(B) Problem Management

Problem management is an add-on to incident management, whose job it is to analyze the causes of problems in detail and find ways to prevent or remove them for good. A common indicator in this area, the "Root Cause Rate in Time", defines whether the cause for an incident has been identified in the exploration period agreed with the client (for instance, 3 days).

Another related indicator is the "Problem Management Solution Rate in Time". It determines the percentage of countermeasures that were executed successfully in the defined response period.

Problem management is an indispensable part of short-term quality improvements, since many disruptions have similar causes. This enables problem management to reduce the number of major incidents effectively by tackling these repeat causes.

(C) Change Management

The change management process concerns the active management of IT infrastructure elements—their addition, adaptation, or removal—by means of standardized methods and procedures. Monitoring the quality of changes can again be performed with specifically chosen indicators.

The number of major incidents caused by changes shows how many outages occurred despite dedicated change management. To learn from failed changes, this topic should be explored in close cooperation with problem management.

Other indicators for measuring how well change is prepared and introduced is the "Ratio of Successful Changes" and the "Ratio of Changes in Time".

The successful and disruption-free introduction of changes is not enough. Planned downtime should be complied with and generally kept to the bare minimum. A fourth common indicator is therefore the "Ratio of Changes in Time": this indicator shows the degree of change introduced in the planned period (change window).

7.1.2 KPIs in Project Work

In project work, the key indicator is "Time, Budget, Quality" (TBQ). Tracking this indicator shows whether the provider complied with the project milestones, budget limits, and quality standards agreed with clients.

As in the case of problem management in regular operations, any short-term quality improvement in projects depends on qualified, results-oriented project reporting. All such reporting should be based on sound facts, and it should show the progress towards the planned results with details about risks encountered and support needed along the way. The most effective measure in the case of projects that deviate from their planned corridor is to introduce fact-based, daily reporting.

7.2 A 360° Perspective for Top Clients

If top clients have experienced quality issues and a visible improvement needs to be achieved as soon as possible, a 360° response over 3 months has proven to be a viable tool for quality improvements.

Temporary intensive support is given to the client in the form of a team of experts, seconded to the client to work on the major problems, working outside the scope of normal departmental activities.

Intensive support begins with a brief risk assessment: Comparable to a roadworthiness check, this assessment looks at the typical fault lines in processes, technologies, or human resources. Discussions about quality definitions and key issues are then held with the client. In the next step, concrete activities are defined on a weekly basis for all three categories, which can include training people, optimizing core processes—particularly incident and change management—and remedying technical risks, such as obsolete hardware. The success of these activities is verified by means of regular customer surveys.

To safeguard the long-term quality of operations for important clients, 360° reports should be produced to cover all relevant aspects of the relationship: The quality of basic operations, the quality of projects (KPI: Time, Budget, Quality), the quality of service in order management and customer support, and the profitability and quality of the IT service organization as perceived by the client.

Top management should again use these reports actively, and it should be seen to do so among the wider workforce to encourage people to actively include quality factors in their daily work.

7.3 Central Change Advisory Board

Thorough change management prevents disruptions. The Central Change Advisory Board (CCAB) acts as part of global de-escalation management by tracking all important and critical changes to the IT landscape and supervising their introduction at every stage along the way.

In specific terms, this means planning any change, such as migrations, updates, etc. with care and a commitment to quality, to keep planned downtime as short as possible, and to generally cause as few outages as possible.

The CCAB should have global authority and make sure that all change processes follow the same binding standards wherever they occur.

For the change management process to function smoothly, it needs accurate risk assessments from two angles: What are the possible implications of a planned change, and which risks might come about when it is not introduced?

In the case of internationally active IT service providers, global change advisory boards are an important addition to the work of local change advisory boards. Their central counterpart comes into action when complex, far-reaching, or particularly risky changes are proposed and makes sure that these changes are planned and executed in line with the given quality standards. By contrast, the local change advisory boards oversee all minor changes according to the same quality criteria.

The scope of a change is determined by its possible effect on the client, the so-called "Customer Business Impact" (CBI).

Every IT service organization lives off the qualifications of its people and invests regularly in their training. However, even highly trained people make mistakes. To avoid human error in the introduction of changes, major or significant changes should never be introduced by a single actor without peer review and counter-checks.

7.4 Global 24/7 Incident and Problem Management

Effective de-escalation needs a central change advisory board, global incident management, and centralized problem management. The mission of the incident management process is to recover normal operations as quickly as possible, whereas problem management processes serve to uncover the causes for disruptions and help prevent their reoccurrence by introducing a defined set of solutions.

The general processes for incident, problem, and change management are built around IT Infrastructure Library (ITIL) processes. ITIL generally refers to a collection of best practices for IT processes, published initially in 1989 by the Office of Government Commerce (OGC) and developed since that date. The current version of ITIL, version 3, has been integrated with other important standards like ISO20000, Six Sigma, COBIT, and Prince 2.

For better incident response quality and a reduction of the MTTR, major incidents should be handled from one central point: A single team can develop a certain routine for handling extremely critical problems, actively take on outside supplier management during incidents, and work on replicable solutions for recurrent problems. It is aligned with the client's critical business processes, to which it gives absolute priority.

Professional incident handling needs a full set of information about the client. It needs to understand how a major incident could impact the client's business processes. For this purpose, "critical landscapes" are drawn up to outline the service chain that is at stake.

To enable global incident management to truly fulfill its mission, it needs to be involved from the very first warning sign of a possible critical incident—even if the incident's final classification (critical, high etc.) is not yet known. The earlier incident managers get involved, the sooner work can start on remedying or preventing the disruption.

The most important factor for successful global incident management is a culture of urgency, which encourages every actor to do his or her best to recover full service at every point during an incident. Incident managers need exceptional stress management abilities, and they need to be able to establish a dependable structure immediately, even in complex circumstances, and to lead teams that might be spread out across many different locations.

Central problem management would then supervise the production of a root cause analysis after every major incident and the introduction of remedial measures in the case of disruptions. It is there to make sure that problems at a client or in a country organization will lead to a set of preventative measures for other clients of the service organization. In this sense, the scope guaranteed by the size of the provider can become an inherent quality advantage for the client.

8 Optimizing Costs and Efficiency

Stefan Bucher and Carsten Glohr

In today's globalized, supercharged, and supercompetitive economy, companies increasingly encounter situations that call for immediate and tangible relief of the cost burden without compromising the quality of their products or services. Such situations affect companies of all sizes and in all industries, and offer only two options: Reducing costs or improving efficiency—immediately, if possible. IT production is no exception. The following chapter will take a look at possible first-response measures for the immediate improvement of efficiency and costs.

8.1 Definitions: Efficiency and Costs

This chapter will define efficiency as the output volume that is possible with a given input. Following the principle of maximum returns, the following considerations will view efficiency improvements as the increase of output with stable input or means of production. Increasing the output by increasing the input is not true efficiency, as it does not improve the productivity of the means of production. In other words: Activities that cost additional money upfront should be treated very carefully—or preferably, not even considered—in the first, acute phase of a crisis intervention.

A distinction must be made between the increase in production output and sales volumes. Neither can be fully separated from the other, but the sales volume falls within the remit of sales, whereas efficiency is a matter for production managers. Where efficiency improvements are concerned, the feasible sales volume is one factor to consider, but not the actual target.

S. Bucher (✉)
T-Systems International GmbH, Dachauer Str. 651, 80995 Munich, Germany
e-mail: Stefan.Bucher@t-systems.com

C. Glohr
Detecon International GmbH, Sternengasse 14–16, 50676 Köln, Deutschland
e-mail: Carsten.Glohr@detecon.com

F. Abolhassan (ed.), *The Road to a Modern IT Factory*, Management for Professionals,
DOI 10.1007/978-3-642-40219-7_8, © Springer-Verlag Berlin Heidelberg 2014

Reducing costs means producing the same output with less input. Reducing the input by reducing the output is usually not the aim, even though there can be instances when it makes sense to put the brakes on production output to keep costs in line. At this point, we are, however, concerned with a clear definition of the term 'cost reductions'.

Immediate efficiency and cost optimization basically means: "Do more with less as quickly as possible!"

8.2 Efficiencies and Cost Reductions: The Principles

8.2.1 Predicting Possible Efficiencies

The first step has to be to predict how much more output could be achieved with the same amount of input. Not being honest with oneself in this forecast will lead to major problems with reaching targets, as they will be based on incorrect assumptions. Ideally, the forecast should consider data from a reliable production planning and scheduling system. For the purposes of this chapter, we assume the presence of such a system and a perception of IT as a commercially understood production unit that produces and sells fully costed and sensibly priced products.

Considerations like the sales potential of individual products should always be included when determining the target output volume. The most important factor in this respect is assured sales volume from established contracts. Other sources for the forecast can be market data or analysts' assessments. It makes most sense to dig for immediate efficiencies where the market is growing and where a growth in sales volumes can be expected. Increasing the production efficiency—and thus the output—of a product that has a shrinking market needs strong arguments, like an innovative or unique feature that justifies this approach in a time of crisis.

The areas that should be prioritized are defined in the following matrix (Table 8.1).

8.2.2 Defining the Viable Cost Reductions

The most important yardstick for prioritizing objects and means of cost reduction is their immediate impact in a time of crisis. This often limits the available measures, as many activities take a while to have an effect or at least have no immediate impact (cf. Chap. 8.3). If an activity promises great potential, but needs time to take effect, the intended savings might arrive too late. Table 8.2 illustrates this balance and shows the areas that should have precedence.

Table 8.1 Prioritized efficiencies. Preference should be given to activities in the top-right quadrant, to account for their major impact, followed by the top-left, bottom-right, and bottom-left quadrants

Potential Efficiencies	Volume	
	High-volume, limited efficiencies **Example:** Consulting Services	High-volume, substantial efficiencies **Example:** IaaS customers
	Low-volume, limited efficiencies **Example:** License contracts	Low-volume, substantial efficiencies **Example:** Usage of legacy platforms such as BS2000

8.2.3 The Perfect Balance Between Efficiency and Savings

A restructuring process benefits from having a percentage target for the improvement of the company's production performance within one year. This overall target is made up of the effects of increased efficiency and reduced costs:

$$Improvement_{\text{total}} \text{ in } \% = Increase_{\text{Eff}} \text{ in } \% + Reduction_{\text{costs}} \text{ in } \%$$

For individual products, the improvement can be calculated by comparing the produced units and the production costs over time:

$$\left(\frac{units_{year+1}}{units_{year}} - 1\right) \cdot 100 + \left(1 - \frac{costs_{year+1}}{costs_{year}}\right) \cdot 100 = \text{overall improvement in } \%$$

The degree to which efficiencies and costs contribute to the overall aim can differ from case to case. The right balance needs experience, profound knowledge of the company and the industry it is operating in, and a certain measure of simple instinct. After all, efficiency can only be improved when the production volume itself also increases.

Table 8.2 Priorities in cost reduction potential: the activities in the top-right quadrant have preference, followed by the top-left quadrant and finally the bottom-right and bottom-left quadrants

Effectiveness	Potential for Cost Reduction	
	Quick effect, low potential **Example:** Reducing catering costs	Quick effect, great potential **Example:** **Fewer outside providers**
	Slow effect, low potential **Example:** Standardizing employee cell phone contracts	Slow effect, great potential **Example:** Data center consolidation

The restructuring process should always follow a distinct cascade, breaking down the overall goal into targets for the lower organizations units. It helps to determine which part of the overall goal each organizational unit has to contribute with efficiencies or with savings.

The company also needs to be ready to change its weighting of the components if the intended balance turns out to be unrealistic, if the circumstances change, or if the chosen assumptions were not precise enough. This happens often in dynamic markets—nothing is as permanent as change!

Finding the right balance between efficiencies and costs needs to consider the unique circumstances at the company. Companies offering consultancy services have little opportunity for greater efficiency by simply ramping up utilization—after all, a given consultant cannot simply multiply his or her capabilities. The focus should lie on costs. The case is different when the company offers IaaS (Infrastructure as a Service) on the basis of an established infrastructure. Companies can usually get more out of their resources without additional investments, e.g. by making more use of the floor space in their data centers and avoiding idle costs.

In the case of in-house service providers, greater volumes might not be the best option, since the higher revenue could affect the crisis-stricken company itself. Usually, any activities here should focus on the cost side of the equation.

8.3 Possible Interventions

8.3.1 Improving Efficiency

Which efficiency measures will have an immediate effect depends strongly on the actual company in question. The first and foremost measure is to ramp up the utilization rate of the available infrastructure and labor resources, and thus generate more output with identical resources. This can mean speeding up throughput, clocking up operating cycles, or offering unused collocation space for lease.

When consolidating work, one should move beyond a simple fixation with time and move to a focus on actual activities. This helps pinpoint the teams with excessive workloads, setting them apart from the teams that have free capacities going to waste. People can be reallocated to such high-workload teams or the responsibilities can be rearranged to ensure better sharing of the workload and avoid delays in processes caused by resource bottlenecks.

Immediate efficiencies can also be gained by providing all of the IT unit's staff with the automation tools that are commonly used in their sector.

All core processes should be subjected to a critical review. There is often lots of redundancy or repetitive busywork hidden in them. One typical candidate is the order-to-deploy process, that is, the activities that take place between the intake of an order and the delivery of the service. Accelerating throughput in this sense not only lessens the workload on employees, but also frees up resources for truly value adding work. It also boosts customer satisfaction and could have an immediate effect on sales, as more orders can be completed in the same time.

8.3.2 Reducing Costs

For most IT organizations, the prime foothold for immediate savings is the reduction of outside labor costs, as IT organizations often employ substantial numbers of external personnel. By contrast, measures targeting internal labor costs or infrastructure factors often need considerably longer before real savings can be made. In a crisis, all agreements with consultants, freelance programmers, administrators, or other service providers should be rechecked. The tasks covered by them could be handed back to internal employees, even if this leads to greater workloads for them. The best approach is to make a list of external resources and the areas they cover, which are then ranked according to their criticality. Client projects that need expertise not normally available within the company naturally need to be treated as a special case: here, the necessary external resources should only be released in absolute emergencies.

In times of crisis, recruitment often needs to be frozen and/or may need special clearance from executive managers. Jobs that become vacant by natural fluctuation may not be filled immediately. This can have a relatively rapid impact on labor costs that are otherwise only susceptible to slow-working, long-term interventions.

Bringing down the company's labor costs immediately means slimming down areas with staffing overhangs by voluntary means. This can avoid the lengthy and often very expensive severance schemes needed for other forms of headcount reductions. Common approaches include:

- Partial retirement.
- Termination agreements.
- Internal reappointment to understaffed areas.

Seemingly run-of-the-mill maintenance and support commissions also offer lots of potential savings. These can be found in a variety of ways, including:

- Shortened service windows (e.g. 18/7, instead of 24/7)
- Slower response times
- Consolidation of multiple OEM support/maintenance contracts into single third-party contracts to realize economies of scale and make for easier contract management.

When urgent IT or software purchases are required, extending the write-off period beyond the usual 3- to 4-year window is also possible, as it will have an immediate impact on financial calculations. Laptops, desktop PCs, displays, switches, or storage systems can certainly be used for 5 years or longer, and it is even true of operating systems or office and ERP applications made by professional vendors. Support contracts with the right extended duration are available. However, any decision in this respect should consider the implications and restrictions on the side of balance accounting or general business economics.

A fast, but often minor effect can be had from saving on popular, but often unnecessary spending habits, like conference catering, travel, partner invitations, or complimentary gifts. Such cutbacks can have a certain psychological effect. They say: We have nothing to waste—often an important signal for getting a company's people to fall in line. Even if they offer only little in the way of savings, these decisions should be taken to achieve this psychological side-effect.

9 Governance Models

Carsten Glohr

The term "IT governance" refers to the system for managing and regulating the structures of an IT organization (its procedural and organizational make-up). Its job is to make sure that IT management and its organizational structures and processes are arranged in such a way that they support the wider strategy of the business in the most effective and cost-efficient way possible.

IT organizations have to cope with enormous cost pressures. They are forced to fulfill critical business requirements with increasingly limited resources. Modern IT governance models help balance these tensions with professional customer-supplier relationships.

In response to the above-mentioned cost pressures, the supply side is witnessing an increasing trend towards industrialization and standardization. On the demand side, IT needs to keep adjusting to the business and its requirements. The result is a degree of complexity and diversity required by the business that cannot be reduced or consolidated down beyond a certain minimum without a negative effect on the business's responsiveness. The resulting pressure is particularly strong in more mature sectors of industry that have to cope with higher cost burdens, where IT often becomes an integral part of the product (e.g. in telecommunications or modern retail banking) or of the business model itself. The internet age means that most industries are already conducting a significant part of their business via "Business-over-IT" platforms. Virtually every aspect of their business processes is supported by IT systems and would now be unthinkable without IT. Reduced time-to-market, leaner, automated business processes, and improved business intelligence mean that IT has had to become more dynamic and agile than ever before.

C. Glohr (✉)
Detecon International GmbH, Sternengasse 14–16, 50676 Köln, Deutschland
e-mail: Carsten.Glohr@detecon.com

F. Abolhassan (ed.), *The Road to a Modern IT Factory*, Management for Professionals,
DOI 10.1007/978-3-642-40219-7_9,

What this has created is an inherent target conflict, as the other side of the equation is the increasing cost burden for the IT supply side, which has responded with more and more industrialization. The standardization and reduction of diversity in IT operations has had a positive impact on many cost drivers.

Increasingly standardized IT services are thus becoming cheap "commodities", IT components with less variety and diversity between them. This has made them less distinctive and more easily replaceable, which allows companies to procure them from other providers in the market and simply assemble them into the final IT service packages that they sell as custom solutions for their clients. As in many manufacturing businesses, this move towards less variety has led to faster learning curves and greater productivity. Using standard software or technologies like SOA, object orientation, or virtualization boosts this process of industrialization even further. However, the basic business still defines certain limits to the extent of standardization and complexity alike.

We have to distinguish between two types of complexity. First, there is the complexity that is imposed by the business model (e.g. the need to add more process variants) and that cannot be reduced further. Second, there is the redundant, unnecessary complexity that is often a legacy of the past (e.g. mixed-bag IT landscapes in different country organizations that actually have similar business models). It is this second type of complexity that offers potential for standardization and consolidation. At the same time, the complexity and variety enforced by the demand side of the business makes this pursuit of standardization more difficult and creates major tensions in IT organizations.

These tensions mean that most IT organizations and governance models in the industry can be allocated to one of three basic functions (cf. Fig. 9.1): The demand function (1—Demand Organization), the supply function (2—Supply Organization), and the heavily industrialized delivery function with its economies of scale (3—IT Factories). With less and less vertical integration in modern IT organizations, the definition of a professional supply–demand interface has become essential.

A similar picture can be found in IT units kept in-house. Most in-house shared service centers are, in this sense, using professional supply–demand interfaces between service management functions in the business departments and standardized IT service accounting.

As shown in Fig. 9.1, this triple split allows each organizational function to concentrate on its core competency and balances the tensions between the business departments and IT.

IT factories possess cost management as their core competency and are dedicated to bringing the unit costs down. They are the ones that produce the actual IT performance on an operational level. Usually, these IT factories would specialize specifically on operational IT services, in which they can achieve economies of scale (size or learning curve effects). The end product is an independently organized delivery unit that can concentrate on a specific set of competencies, e.g. for:

- Data center operations (computing services)
- Desktop services and service desks

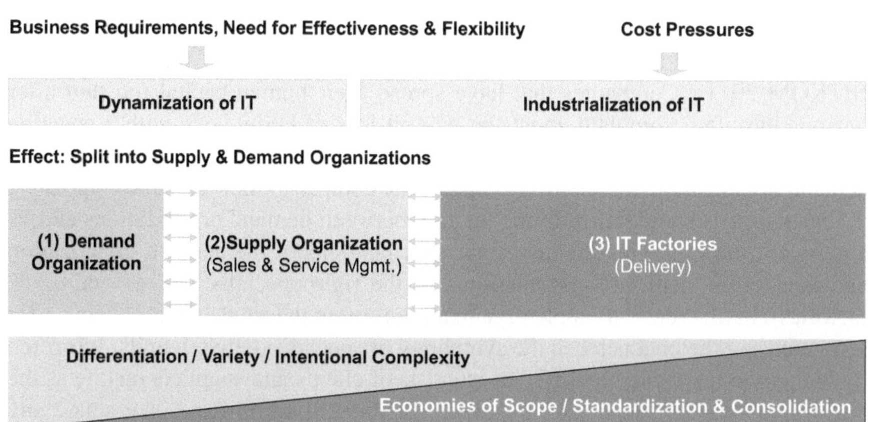

Fig. 9.1 Almost all IT organizations in the market can be represented as supply and demand organizations (cf. Detecon 2010)

- Network services (WAN, LAN, RAS ...)
- Application operations
- Application development (project services and system integration, often split further into functional application or standard software packages, such as SAP, CRM, billing, logistics)

Packaged like this, many services are sourced from outside providers. In such cases, the commissioned provider takes over the function of the IT factory and the supply organization. Most of the personnel in the IT factory will have a technical, operational background. The strong commoditization and easy replaceability of their services has put their wages under increasing pressure, made worse by the cut-throat competition with offshore or nearshore providers.

The **demand organization** represents the interests of the client and is typically an integrated part of the various business departments/divisions (client organization), albeit with more and more decentralization. This trend has led to many people speaking of the end of the line for CIOs, since the splitting and decentralization of demand organizations on the one side and the outsourcing of IT budgets on the other leaves little justification for the CIOs' presence in top management. However, there are still many centralized models, often federally organized. Many demand organizations operate their own competency centers with people who possess unique expertise about certain business processes and are in charge of e.g. defining functional specifications. This keeps core competencies (often a detailed insight into essential business processes) in the right place. Many demand organizations are also organized as service management functions that take over procurement functions or, at least, work hand in hand with procurement departments. The close proximity to the client means that demand organizations ensure the required customer focus, while maintaining the agility and responsiveness of IT. A Detecon study conducted in cooperation with BITKOM surveyed 1,000 executives in

Germany, Austria, and Switzerland and revealed that IT organizations without dedicated demand functions are usually regarded as failures (cf. Detecon and BITKOM 2011). Companies that have spread their human capital too thin after outsourcing often complain about the painful loss of know-how, with a negative impact on IT's ability to innovate, optimize, or evolve further. For a well-structured demand organization, the motto is "Change the company", not "Run the company".

The **supply organization** forms the link between demand organizations and IT factories. It takes the requirements and specifications of the demand organization and transforms them into commissions for the right specialist delivery units (IT factories). In this sense, a supply organization is often the single point of contact for its clients and the conductor in the symphony of specialist delivery units. It is often up to them to reconcile the different interests of clients and suppliers (acting as the client's advocate in dealings with the IT factory) or to mitigate or escalate any problems with integrating the specialist IT factories. The governance model must be designed to support this balancing of interests. At the same time, the supply organization has a certain sales function and manages existing commissions or accounts with external IT service providers. A similar (even if less formal) sales function can also be found in in-house shared service centers. There need not be an explicit distinction between IT factory and supply organization, but a poorly-defined distinction can mean that the operational costs and pressures that the IT factory labors under can lead it to forget the necessary customer focus: the pressure stops the supply function from focusing, as it should, on acquiring and developing new client business.

The customer-specific definition and the 'final assembly' of the standard IT services produced in the IT factories is also often the job of the supply organization. This makes it another link in the value chain, as it now handles operational functions like application management services, with highly standardized infrastructure services being procured from IT factories. Competency center functions (storing the know-how about business processes or functional specifications) are also better placed in the supply than the demand organization if the standardization of processes makes the bundling of these functions necessary. In most cases, the organization is then arranged by industry or process clusters (e.g. logistics processes, finance and management accounting, CRM, product lifecycle management, etc.) that are handled across business units or customer groups. In many other cases, the supply organization is, however, focused on service management and sales functions alone.

9.1 How Tripartite Governance Models Function in Practice

Modern governance models are tasked with getting these three basic functions to work together effectively. Apart from the structural arrangement, a governance model has to include the following components:

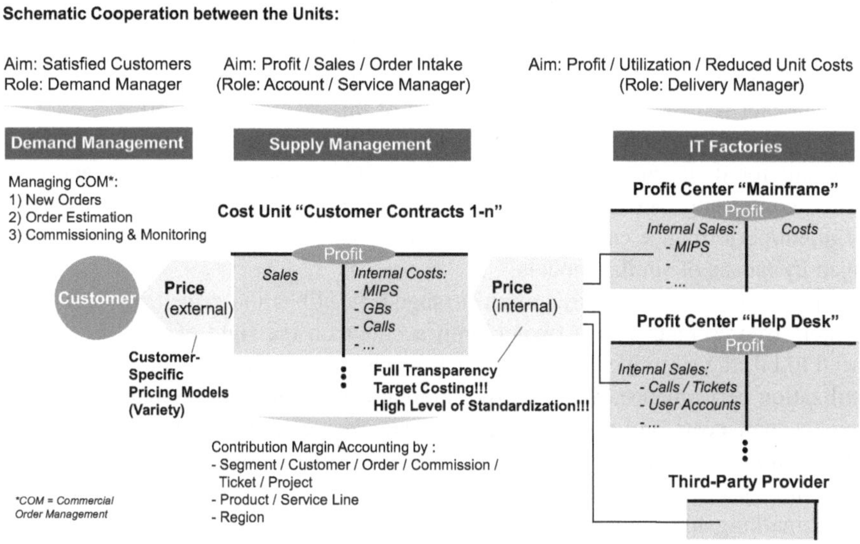

Fig. 9.2 Cooperation in a tripartite supply and demand organization (cf. Detecon 2010)

(A) An appropriate controlling and management model to provide suitable indicators, pricing models, and controlling data.
(B) Clear roles and responsibilities with a targets system to set the right incentives for employees.
(C) Clearly structured administrative processes with suitable support from tools and applications.

If outsourcing is chosen, the responsibility is limited to demand management on the client side. Supply management and the IT factory are then turned over to external providers. When internal shared service centers are used, all three basic functions fall within the responsibility of the company (Fig. 9.2).

The interplay between the three basic functions can be explained with the process applicable when IT has to respond to new business requirements.

(1) Our example begins with the specification of the new client requirements by demand management.
(2) The requirements are reviewed in cooperation with supply management and an offer is estimated and prepared. This cost estimate provides a basis for managing the commercial profitability of the commission and contract.
(3) To monitor and manage the profitability of the order (project or contract), a separate cost unit can be introduced (here represented as a simple two-column account). On the earnings side, the pricing model arranged with the client and the order estimate are recorded. Usually, an additional internal pricing model would exist for the internal handling of the processes between supply organization and IT factory. In contrast to the unique, specially negotiated pricing model for the client, this is highly standardized and not open for negotiation, as it serves only internal controlling purposes. The end result is the planned cost side of the estimate. The profitability of the cost unit (be it a single order,

project, or contract, managed by an account or service manager) is determined by comparing planned earnings and planned costs. As part of the ongoing controlling process, the supply organization's performance is measured by whether it meets, exceeds, or falls short of this planned profitability.

Supply organizations are usually given revenue targets that are particularly relevant for their sales personnel. By consolidating the customer contracts/cost units, controlling can also cover contribution margins by customers and market segment/performance calculations. Internal shared service centers are often managed by means of similar models.

IT factories are nowadays often arranged as utilization-driven profit or cost centers (represented by the two-column account on the right of Fig. 9.2). They need to bill their services via the internal service accounting system to show their utilization performance. Standardized internal service accounting makes calculating the unit costs and target costing for each center possible, and even allows benchmarking with multiple delivery units spread out around the world. Both the customer-specific and the internal, standardized pricing model are suitable for benchmarking and can thus be revised to match current market prices. The utilization of IT factory resources is kept transparent by their being managed as profit centers, and by volume and cost unit planning. To optimize utilization, incentives can be set by means of marginal cost or fixed cost calculations. To increase standardization, companies often rely on policy-driven pricing to make standard services cheaper and custom, non-standard services more expensive.

IT pricing is therefore one of the main levers in the working of any IT governance model. There is much room for creativity, especially when working with customer-specific pricing models. At the one end of the spectrum (cf. Fig. 9.3), there are business-oriented volume/pricing models, just as the prices in the automotive industry go by car sold or by seat taken in the airline industry. The drawback of such business-oriented models is that they might be too far removed from the actual IT costs. For instance, the earnings of the IT service organization of an airline would simply collapse if fewer tickets are sold after a terrorist incident, irrespective of how unrelated its operations are to actual bums on seats. From the customers' point of view, however, these pricing models offer appealing simplicity, since customers are more familiar with simple order volumes than with the technical details behind them, such as gigabytes or data center floor space.

Business-oriented models allow risk management to be handled using established commercial indicators. IT costs are adjusted flexibly when business volumes stagnate or contract. IT providers know the risks and operate with higher risk premiums. In the high-risk environment of our airline example, this can result in margins of 30–40 % or more, which might not be overly advantageous for the client.

The other end of the spectrum uses technical pricing models. These are often closely related to actual costs and can be calculated with minimal risk. However, their technical nature means that not all clients can relate to them immediately. The demand organization therefore needs a lot of technical expertise to be able to influence this situation, which is often not actually wanted in the business.

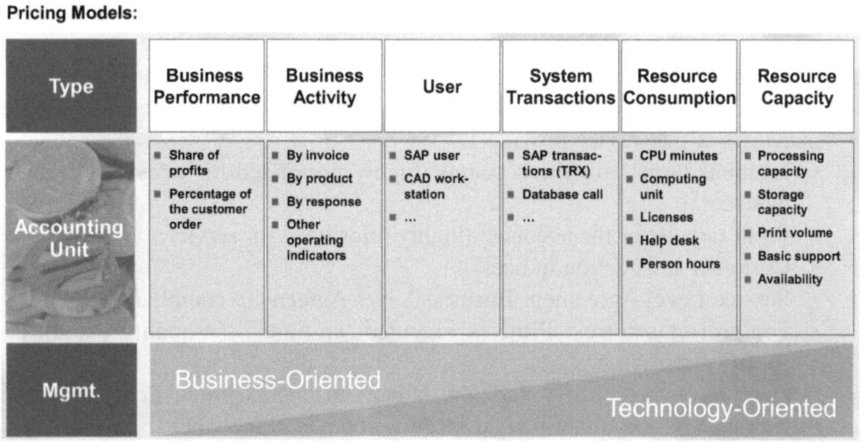

Pricing Models:

Type	Business Performance	Business Activity	User	System Transactions	Resource Consumption	Resource Capacity
Accounting Unit	▪ Share of profits ▪ Percentage of the customer order	▪ By invoice ▪ By product ▪ By response ▪ Other operating indicators	▪ SAP user ▪ CAD work-station ▪ …	▪ SAP transac-tions (TRX) ▪ Database call ▪ …	▪ CPU minutes ▪ Computing unit ▪ Licenses ▪ Help desk ▪ Person hours	▪ Processing capacity ▪ Storage capacity ▪ Print volume ▪ Basic support ▪ Availability
Mgmt.	Business-Oriented					Technology-Oriented

Fig. 9.3 Range of IT pricing models from business-oriented to technology-oriented (cf. Detecon and T-Systems 2006)

To make the right choice of pricing model, one should therefore always take into account the competencies in the organizational units: this is one of the reasons for the mass of different pricing models in today's markets.

Customer-specific pricing models often use the entire range of possible approaches and aim for maximum flexibility. Providers are trying to secure top profitability for their accounts with clever financial engineering in their pricing models. Customers would, if they had a choice, prefer an easily manageable and transparent price.

Both sides would do well to structure their pricing models in such a way that they allow optimum management. Possible optimization is particularly important in this respect. It can, for instance, make less sense to arrange prices on the basis of physical server resources when planning to consolidate the server landscape, since it would take away the actual incentive for such consolidation (as it would cannibalize the basis of its earnings). Pricing models should be arranged to produce a win-win situation for both the supply and the demand side, and to promote and allow potential optimizations on both sides.

9.2 Performance Targets and Variable Remuneration

Another important component of the governance model is the right performance target system for the organization's personnel. In an ideal scenario, it would be coupled with a variable wage component and cover important indicators/targets like:

(a) Demand manager (demand side)—Targets for:
- Delivery capability, i.e. the execution of projects "in-time", "in-quality", and "in-specification"
- Quantified cost savings/budget compliance

- Customer satisfaction indices (with structured questionnaires in the business units, e.g. the TriM index method)
- Service Level Agreement/Business Level Agreement compliance

(b) Supply manager (delivery side e.g. sales and account managers, service managers at the service provider):
- Earnings targets for the accounts (highly prioritized for sales and account managers)
- Profit targets for the accounts (highly prioritized for service managers)
- Customer satisfaction indices
- Service Level Agreement/Business Level Agreement compliance
- For project services: Projects executed "in-time", "in-quality", and "in-specification"

(c) IT factories on the delivery side (e.g. delivery managers, production managers):
- Unit cost targets/quantified cost savings/budget compliance
- Profitability/resource utilization
- Service Level Agreement/Operational Level Agreement compliance
- Customer satisfaction indices

9.3 The Need for a Central Program

The model outlined here has its limitations and is rather focused on operational management. One such limitation concerns wider optimizations or circumstances when continuous improvement to the operational management models is no longer sufficient and an immediate, sweeping intervention is required (e.g. in the case of external crises/shocks). It can make sense to add a central, comprehensive optimization program with board-level support. This could allow the company to introduce unpleasant economy measures (e.g. recruitment freezes, redundancies, or the wholesale removal of external personnel/service providers). More far-reaching interventions, such as the consolidation of applications, are also only possible with such a program in place. Such interventions need shared contributions and a united front of demand management, supply management, and IT factories. Industries working with a constant pressure to improve and optimize would do well to establish such central optimization programs as regular and permanent parts of the business.

References

Detecon. (2010). Service Offering Präsentation "Optimierung von IT Governance".

Detecon, & BITKOM. (2011). *IT-organisation 2015 – Fit für die Zukunft. Facelift oder Modellwechsel?* http://www.detecon.com/de/studies

Detecon, & T-Systems. (2006). Standardpräsentation Complex Deal Management – Preismodellgestaltung.

Performance Management and Reporting 10

Jörn Kellermann, Tom In der Rieden, and Gregor Altmann

10.1 Cascading Targets: Cascading Reporting

As discussed in Chap. 8, the managers of a company would commence a restructuring/optimization process by defining improvement targets, usually in the form of percentage improvements, that are then cascaded down and detailed further in targets for the company's various units, all the way to the level of individual departments and teams. Department managers often define their departments' targets by stipulating how much each unit has to contribute, as they do so, they make sure that all individual targets are in line with the overall purpose. Each unit and sub-unit would therefore have unique targets, made up of efficiency improvement and cost reduction elements that come together to form a joint goal. Depending on the given instructions and the unique nature of each unit—e.g. considering whether it operates in a growth segment—the right balance between efficiency and cost reduction needs to be found.

Every measure needs to be defined and quantified in detail: Everybody needs to be clear about what the measure covers and what its aims are. In order to do so, the target needs to be quantified, cost reductions need to be defined precisely in terms of the relevant cost type and cost unit, and the deadlines and responsibilities need to be known. Taking all of these individual efficiency or cost reduction measures

J. Kellermann
T-Systems International GmbH, Heinrich-Hertz-Str. 1, 64295 Darmstadt, Germany
e-mail: Joern.Kellermann@t-systems.com

T. In der Rieden (✉)
T-Systems International GmbH, Mecklenburgring 25, 66121 Saarbrücken, Germany
e-mail: Thomas.In-der-Rieden@t-systems.com

G. Altmann
T-Systems International GmbH, Johannisberger Straße 74, 14197 Berlin, Germany
e-mail: Gregor.Altmann@t-systems.com

F. Abolhassan (ed.), *The Road to a Modern IT Factory*, Management for Professionals, DOI 10.1007/978-3-642-40219-7_10, © Springer-Verlag Berlin Heidelberg 2014

Intervention	Area	Person in Charge	Category	Affects Cost Types	Affects Cost Units	Deadline	Planned Savings 2012	Actual Savings 2012	Performance 2012
Improving processes for higher utilization of IT capacities	IT Produ ction	Joe Miller	Efficiency impro- vement	HR Hardware Software	10XXXX 31XXXX	30 Sept 2012	$4.5 million	$4.3 million	96%
Reducing the number of active software tools	IT Produ ction	Marie Maher	Cost reduction	Software licenses Software mainte- nance	10XXXX 25XXXX 47XXXX	31 Dec 2012	$2.8 million	$3.2 million	114%

Fig. 10.1 Layout of an action plan for a "Network" unit

together, the activities need to add up to match the overall target of the unit as a whole. On the practical side, this is done effectively by recording all measures, targets, and additional information of note in a dedicated chart (Fig. 10.1).

Progress on all of these measures is monitored by people assigned for the purpose and financial controlling, using a peer-review principle in this tandem approach between the people on the ground and controlling. A longer cycle allows too much leeway for deviation, whereas shorter cycles make for reporting that is too labor-intensive and complex. It can, however, make sense to send weekly abstracts about current progress to the management board or the supervisor in charge.

Controlling consolidates the data into a 360° view that gives executive managers and the line managers on all levels an up-to-date overview of current activities and enables them to intervene if the need arises.

When it becomes clear that certain measures are not getting anywhere at the level they are intended to work on, they need to be replaced with other means that can contribute better to the intended outcome (compensation principle). The failure of a specific measure should never be cause for criticism, since nobody can predict their effectiveness with any certainty beforehand, especially in the case of efficiency measures that are built on certain assumptions about volume growth. Interventions or penalties should only be introduced when the general target for the unit in question itself is in danger of being missed (cf. Chap. 10.4).

10.2 Integration in Finance and Reporting Systems

On a basic level, targets, measures, and the reports used when pursuing them should be designed in such a way as to allow all relevant reporting data to be sourced from the established enterprise resource planning (ERP) system. In turn, the reports should be ready for easy and straightforward integration into established financial reporting, i.e. they need to match the structure and contents of standard reporting used in management accounting, e.g. in terms of defined cost types. This keeps additional effort for management accounting personnel to a minimum, which helps them include all such planned measures in their normal planning tools—and annual planning in particular.

This does not mean that the sub-units in question have to input their data into the ERP system. Rather, lower-level units in particular are encouraged to use more straightforward tools like Excel spreadsheets to plan their activities. A very helpful tool is a company-wide tracking system to record all activities and the progress they are making. Yet restructuring or optimization activities should be monitored in any case, even if such a tool is not available or not commercially viable. In that case, the process needs to rely on what it is there in the toolbox. Anything else would put the company's general goals at risk.

More important than practical tools for planning cost reduction measures is the right definition of the relevant cost types and cost units in compliance with the system used by the company's accounting personnel. For measures relating to business transactions, e.g. when redesigning the order-to-deploy process, the right timeframe is similarly important, because many procedural efficiencies can only come into effect when the relevant processes have been revised in full.

10.3 Monitoring Methods and the Management of Change

Reporting needs to be clear and well-ordered. This means that the indicators in question should be tracked with monitoring methods that are established and accepted at the company as a whole. This is best left to management accounting staff, working with executive managers and the business departments in question.

Cost data can be monitored relatively easily: One simply adds up the spending of the relevant cost units. When trying to reduce labor costs, the plans are calculated on the basis of the average headcount and average labor costs over a given period of time. The eventual savings are then reported on a monthly basis with the actual figures achieved as a result.

As a criterion for improved efficiency, the growth of business volumes should be tracked on a monthly basis. However, the make-up of companies often changes intrinsically as a result of restructuring or optimization campaigns. Their headcount can change when major outsourcing contracts are introduced and new employees are recruited. In such cases, the basis for comparing efficiency has changed.

To compare such growth between different time periods, one would define a sample "basket" containing as many of the company's products as possible, allocate fixed prices for these products—discounting for inflation—multiplied with the planned and actual volumes, and total the weighted prices for the products to reach a sum that can be compared for different points in time. The calculation should ignore any industry- or market-specific discounts. It allows the company to track the development of production volumes over several years and makes efficiency transparent, even if it has to account for very mixed sets of products. In the case of global processes, these "baskets" need to be defined on a country-by-country basis, since the programs and products of different country organizations often differ considerably from each other.

Despite the principle of utmost precision, efficiency measures often leave no option but to use fictional indicators, like annual average production volumes.

When higher production volumes come at higher costs, these need to be offset with the growth in production to understand the actual gains in efficiency. After all, efficiency is only that part of additional production that was achieved without additional costs (cf. Chap. 8.1).

It helps to design reporting processes in such a way that the data for certain product groups or cost units can be sourced without major effort. This can help benchmarking cost or activity groups with similar companies, e.g. the costs for operating mainframes, for training measures, travel expenses, or simple floor space. Such benchmarks can provide important insights about how well the company is doing in certain areas and which aspects should be pulled into focus for further restructuring or optimization activities.

10.4 Escalation Management

As in normal business, restructuring or optimization processes can always encounter difficulties or crises that call for a corrective intervention. Usually, there are three occasions that demand a response from higher up in the hierarchy:

- Regular reporting shows that the planned targets are not being reached at some stage in the chain.
- Milestones, i.e. deadlines, are not being complied with.
- The people in charge of the measures or their supervisors responsible for actioning them are asking for support, because targets are in danger of being missed.

In all three cases, it is important for the next-higher level to try to understand where the stumbling blocks are as soon as possible. If this reveals that the people actioning the measures do not have the means or the authority to remove the obstacles, the issue should be escalated upward. This escalation should not stop until the problem has been removed or a level has been reached that has the authority to act on the problematic process component. If need be, escalation proceeds to the top-level process governance committee or board-level management.

No report should try to obfuscate or whitewash the presence of difficulties or delays in a restructuring or optimization process, be it for the team or for higher management audiences. This can endanger the continued well-being of the company as a whole, which is another reason for the mentioned peer-review principle. In extreme cases, such strategies can call for immediate disciplinary actions. A problem-solving process should only be considered finished when the critical issue has returned to a "green light" state or when the process has been fully redesigned, for instance if the original target turned out to be unrealistic or not achievable with the planned measures. All reporting formats should be designed to allow the report recipient to dig deeper (drill down) to the reports covering lower levels of the corporate hierarchy.

Part IV

Structural Changes

Elements of Structural Change and the Management of Transformation

11

Henryk Biesiada

Successful industrial transformations mean moving beyond insular one-off solutions to standardized product and platform environments. As discussed in Chap. 2, industrialization in the form of standardization in the automotive industry has produced unified workflows and platforms, substantially streamlined processes, and achieved major improvements in quality, effectiveness, and efficiency. The first milestone on that journey was the switch from manual production ("cottage industry" manufacturing) to assembly line scenarios. This tectonic shift was followed by an era of standardization, prefabrication, and modularization. Modern developments include a turn towards more consolidation, less vertical integration, and the global sourcing of supplier services and components. All of these measures are designed to counter the impact of tougher competition, the rising burden of costs, and the deteriorating margins in the industry. IT service organizations, which are facing challenges not dissimilar to those faced by carmakers, can learn a lot from this pioneering role-model. For a lasting boost to efficiency, they would do well to scout other industries for industrialization models that could reasonably be applied to their own processes.

Experience tells us that such transformation processes proceed in two successive steps[1] (cf. Fig. 11.1).

The first step has already been explained in more detail in Chap. 3. Its purpose is to achieve immediate improvements in terms of quality and costs in the IT service organization, relying on levers that act quickly and directly. Concerning quality, this can mean the almost complete removal of all potential disruptions and errors or

[1] These can be further subdivided into four phases: Step 1 = Correct (1) and Fix (2), while Step 2 = Stabilize (3) and Transform (4).

H. Biesiada (✉)
T-Systems International GmbH, Mecklenburgring 25, 66121 Saarbrücken, Germany
e-mail: Henryk.Biesiada@t-systems.com

F. Abolhassan (ed.), *The Road to a Modern IT Factory*, Management for Professionals, DOI 10.1007/978-3-642-40219-7_11, © Springer-Verlag Berlin Heidelberg 2014

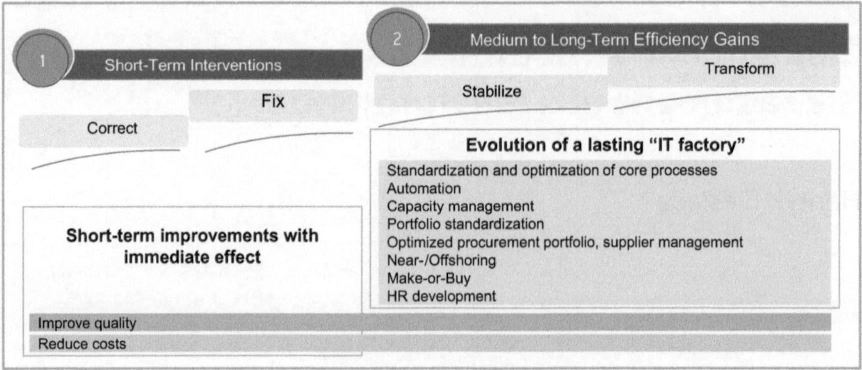

Fig. 11.1 Steps in the transformation process (*Source*: T-Systems)

the acceleration of repairs (commonly called a Zero Outage culture in the IT industry). Concerning costs, one common aim is a quick reduction in all operating expenses. Comparatively fast-acting interventions are possible for a variety of cost factors. The effect is a tangible improvement in the organization's competitiveness and more satisfied customers who enjoy greater quality for less money: two signs of a more viable and profitable IT service organization.

Such interventions can be introduced at virtually every company, but only up to a certain point. After that threshold has been reached, no more savings can reasonably be expected from working on cost drivers. Usually, this first phase takes from 1 to 2 years to reach that point.

11.1 En Route for Industrial IT Production

This chapter will take a closer look at the purpose of the second step: the medium- to long-term, sustainable improvement of the efficiency of IT service organizations, which includes the consolidation of the progress made in step 1.

The activities in step 2 are governed by the vision of an industrialized "IT factory", that is, the evolution of the IT service organization into an efficient and effective structure, with an organization, processes, and tools befitting its purpose as well as a standardized product portfolio. The essential means for achieving the necessary changes include learning from other industries, innovation, and continuous improvement, with the focused development of skills in the workforce playing a major part.

High-quality solutions and services or cost advantages built on economies of scale are made possible only by the determined transition of the organization and its production methods into structures that are coherently and holistically standardized and automated. However, this calls for a steady hand on the right tiller: Levers need to be chosen that will have a longer-lasting and more extensive impact on efficiency than the on-the-spot interventions of step 1. For instance, any attempt at consolidating the quick-win quality improvements from step 1 also means standardizing, optimizing, and automating the core production processes on a global scale. The aim should be service of the same, high quality anywhere in the world.

One essential element of the vision of standardization and automation is increasing the role of the cloud in IT production. This can be done by tackling multiple aspects in sequence, including overcoming or reducing the barriers to entry into the cloud in terms of the difficult migration from the traditional ICT world, providing the right infrastructure automatically, and virtualizing the necessary resources.

Efficiency can be improved with two other levers, namely the best-possible utilization of computing capacity in large-scale server pools and the standardization of the portfolio. Establishing energy-efficient data processing centers has a twofold impact: It reduces costs considerably and it can boost the organization's reputation for quality among increasingly eco-aware clients.

Companies that want to succeed competitively need to focus on their core competencies. In this sense, it makes sense to review the portfolio regularly and to decide whether all of its elements should continue to be produced and, if so, how. Make-or-buy analyses (i.e. relying on in-house production or external service providers) can optimize the value chain and give rise to tangible cost advantages. Strategic partnerships with other companies are also a common source for synergies to add to the portfolio, to improve quality even further, or to open up new markets.

A final, essential driver of lasting efficiency improvements is the optimization of the procurement portfolio and supplier management and, not least, the development of the workforce and their abilities. Another strategic question that should be asked is to what extent efficiencies can be gained by outsourcing certain parts of production to near- or offshore partners. A reasonable benchmark for the ICT industry would seem to be 50 % near- or offshoring of services.

Completing the activities in step 2 can be expected to last between 2 and 3 years. A complete transformation—both steps 1 and 2—therefore needs around 4 or 5 years of change.

11.2 A Central Body for Change Management

The levers of step 2 have a generally indirect effect and cannot be expected to be switched on or off at a moment's notice. Their use involves considerable challenges that demand professional change management. The evolution from a provider of "hand-made" custom solutions into an automated, standardized IT factory needs a central body in place to manage and oversee the necessary activities. This body should also act as the engine powering the cycle of continuous improvement and rejuvenation in the production processes.

For executives, the special challenge lies in engaging meaningfully with employees in these transformation processes and allaying their fears of change. People will only bring to life the changes and get passionate about them when they understand the benefits and opportunities they can bring for the company. Since they are the point where company and clients meet, staff also become the public face of the advantages of industrialization. They should have the conviction that their clients will benefit considerably and sustainably from industrial IT production and "*IT on tap*" when costs, quality, and future prospects are concerned—with, for instance, both the company and its clients saving costs or developing and introducing pioneering solutions at a constant and reliable level of product quality.

12 Improving Quality over the Medium and Long Term

Stephan Kasulke

Winning a client's trust means delivering top quality. The benchmark should be: little to no downtime, fast responses to critical incidents, giving clients comprehensive and high-quality support, and improving core processes systematically.

How can these exacting standards be maintained over the long term? Diversity is the enemy of profit—making standardization a must-have. Anybody in charge of supporting clients in an IT landscape will usually be faced with a legacy of complex systems with many sub-systems added on: this often stands in the way of the quick and straightforward identification and removal of faults or errors. This calls for a migration to standardized, tried and tested platforms and modules. The degree of standardization is the root and measure of success.

12.1 Standardizing Technology

Standardizing technology means reducing its complexity: complexity is the primary cause of disruptions and reducing it is the best foothold for a quick response if a crisis occurs. Standardized technology means fewer parts and less specialist expertise or procedures are required, and fewer unexpected side-effects to consider when introducing changes.

12.2 Standardizing Key Processes

Standardizing key processes produces a replicable, globally uniform level of quality, creates simpler means of controlling and management, and avoids fluctuations in service quality. A learning organization will apply the same standard to all core processes, wherever they might take place.

S. Kasulke (✉)
T-Systems Austria, Rennweg 97-99, 1030 Vienna, Austria
e-mail: Stephan.Kasulke@t-systems.com

F. Abolhassan (ed.), *The Road to a Modern IT Factory*, Management for Professionals, DOI 10.1007/978-3-642-40219-7_12, © Springer-Verlag Berlin Heidelberg 2014

Standardized global incident management will respond to and resolve sudden incidents as quickly as possible by aiming for the highest possible degree of professionalism in the form of replicable solutions. It feeds into problem management, where the lessons learned are identified and future prevention strategies are developed to avoid a repeat incident somewhere else on the global stage. This helps remove many typical sources for error in standardized change management. Every critical change is checked and scrutinized according to a structured, uniform process and has to live up to exacting quality standards checked and approved by the Central Change Advisory Board (CCAB).

The foundations for standardized processes are provided by configuration management (CFM). Its job is to provide up-to-date and consistent information on the current configuration of the IT infrastructure. It does so to allow all higher processes (such as incident, problem, change, or license management) to take decisions on a sound basis of concrete and reliable information.

Configuration management makes sure that all configuration items (CIs)—that is, all elements of the IT infrastructure that are subject to configuration management—are known, monitored, and recorded and that the data is always kept up to date.

The Configuration Management Database (CMDB) stores all of the information about IT components and their relationships and interdependencies. It is the heart of all IT processes and all processes relate to it.

Changes to IT components have to be recorded in the configuration management database by change management—ideally in an automated process. No configuration item should be added, modified, replaced, or removed without it being documented in the change management process.

In complex IT landscapes, it can be difficult to cover the configuration items from all IT areas in a single data model or physical configuration management database. Usually, there are multiple dedicated configuration management databases to track the configuration item data. A master configuration management system (CMS) allows logical access to all configuration management databases and the information stored in them. With this in place, entire service chains can be represented.

Configuration management has to maintain high quality in the sense of its information being complete and correct, and the status of every configuration item being transparent at all times. High-quality data is essential for all subsequent processes that have to work with the data in the configuration management system.

A well-maintained configuration management system acts as a form of procedural catalyst, unifying the heterogeneous landscape and handling important processes, such as global patches or release management. All of this helps prevent disruptive incidents.

12.3 Standardizing Suppliers

Suppliers can be standardized in two distinct ways: first, by focusing on selected, high-quality suppliers; second, by setting out clear rules for suppliers.

As a precondition, the IT service organization must have clearly defined quality standards that it can then apply to its suppliers. This can mean using only material or software that is known to be flawless or auditing the service processes of suppliers regularly according to defined internal norms. The people in charge and the response chains need to be clearly defined on the supplier side to achieve full availability in the case of any critical incident. Essential services and service chains should be designed with redundant safeguards.

12.4 Standardizing HR Training

The long-term improvement of quality is heavily dependent on the human factor. People need to be qualified to be able to comply with processes and deliver the expected quality.

Important processes and behavioral norms should be established in a well-structured and well-designed global training program that is anchored in the organization. Its purpose is to help people use core processes in a globally standardized manner, especially in the areas of change management and incident management. The training can rely on blended e-learning and video training, and progress can be monitored with regular tests.

A company's workforce can be reached most efficiently with a train-the-trainer concept: Selected members of staff are invited to learn about changes or innovations in special training events, and are then asked to take their new know-how into their units or global organizations. Be it web training or full-scale roadshow—they are free to choose the method for disseminating their knowledge.

Certification should not be too easy for members of staff, as they should be encouraged to deal actively with the concrete procedural and quality standards of the company. If it costs nothing, it is worth nothing—this principle also applies to quality certification. Quality training is one of the levers for improving quality, and it is the key to the effective management of core processes.

12.5 Enforcing the Zero Outage Doctrine

Long-lasting quality depends essentially on reliable project execution and the holistic awareness of all risks affecting operations. This makes a systematic processing plan a helpful tool, as it surveys all risks that have led to or might lead to critical incidents.

The next step is to record which risks already have suitable countermeasures in place and which IT services are still subject to risks without adequate responses. Depending on current investment constraints and on urgency, a regular review can decide which other risk mitigation measures are introduced. It also establishes transparency about the dangers to be expected.

When priorities change, a defined part of the processing plan can immediately spring into action. For instance, the risk of industrial action might have long been considered marginal and acceptable, but it can gain much more topical relevance when political changes suddenly occur.

The second essential part of embedding the principle of quality in the organization lies in the systematic evolution of the corporate culture. It is being formed, slowly and steadily, by quality awareness on the part of the organization's people and managers. Quality should already play a defined part in human resource management, beginning with recruitment and continuing in other elements, such as salary development, the selection of executives, or the annual appraisal process.

The values and norms of the workforce can also be shaped and influenced with meaningful and patient communication efforts.

12.6 Play

A well-known yardstick for these considerations is "play". Originally an engineering term for the gap between two components, such as a door and its frame, it has become a hallmark of quality. In the car industry, a tight fit—minimal play—is a sign of high quality, as it allows only minor deviations from the standards. For IT, play is defined by management as a visible measure of compliance with quality standards.

To measure this "play", one can introduce a set of questions that reveal the degree to which defined processes are actually followed in everyday work. Other instances in project work include "quality gates", in which certain parts of a project, such as the specifications or project plan, are subject to regular quality checks.

Minimal play is essential for keeping an eye on progress towards better quality. Its standards should be raised year on year to match increasing expectations.

The IT Factory: A Vision of Standardization and Automation 13

Carsten Glohr, Jörn Kellermann, and Holger Dörnemann

The similarities between manufacturing and IT are striking. IT services can be split down into their constituent parts like the parts of a machine. An order processing solution would, for instance, be made up of a software application, database capacities, middleware components, servers with their operating systems, hardware, storage facilities, network capacities, and monitoring tools.

By reducing component variety and increasing its standardization, manufacturing gained enormous economies of scale. Standardization is similarly reducing variety in the IT sector. As in traditional industries like car making, where vertical integration is on the way out and car brands are buying entire assembly units from suppliers, IT organizations have also begun to outsource major parts of their value chains and are now buying standard services from outside providers. Their unique addition consists of integrating these standard services into bespoke packages for the client.

Standards are not only developing for IT services themselves. The various layers that form these services are becoming increasingly decoupled and interoperable by relying on standard interfaces (examples: XML, databases, virtual OS).

C. Glohr (✉)
Detecon International GmbH, Sternengasse 14–16, 50676 Cologne, Germany
e-mail: Carsten.Glohr@detecon.com

J. Kellermann
T-Systems International GmbH, Heinrich-Hertz-Str. 1, 64295 Darmstadt, Germany
e-mail: Joern.Kellermann@t-systems.com

H. Dörnemann
VMware Global, Inc., German Office, Freisinger Str. 3, 85716 Unterschleißheim, Germany
e-mail: HDoernemann@vmware.com

F. Abolhassan (ed.), *The Road to a Modern IT Factory*, Management for Professionals,
DOI 10.1007/978-3-642-40219-7_13,

Processes and tools are also experiencing standardization. Standards like ITIL are playing their part in this evolution. At the same time, the vendors of standard software are enabling ever higher degrees of automation by producing more tightly integrated software packages to cover the required IT processes (e.g. service desks, provision and monitoring tools, etc.).

13.1 Cloud-Based Automation and Standardization

One important driver behind this trend towards standardization and automation is the rise of cloud technology. The new technical capabilities of virtualization are creating entirely new opportunities for running a business. Modern delivery models are already matching cloud computing criteria, such as the following:

- Self-provisioning (capacity provisioning requested directly by the user)
- Very fast delivery (on-demand or highly responsive delivery systems guaranteed by OLAs and SLAs)
- Substantial reduction in manual installation requirements (zero touch)
- Scalability, rapid elasticity
- Fully monitored services/pay-per-use
- Multi-tenancy, broad network access
- Resource pooling

This can be explained by looking at the on-demand provision of an SAP sandbox system as is often used by developers (cf. Fig. 13.1): Immediately after the user has sent the request by picking the right SLA class, a "machine" installs a complete SAP system on virtual hardware. This includes an operating system (LPAR), a database, and an SAP instance. The system is ready for immediate use. Where traditional procurement processes often took months, not least because of lengthy hardware orders, the cloud allows the system to be provided in seconds. Virtualization, above all, cuts out the slow hardware provisioning process. The installation also takes place automatically, which removes the need for complicated manual installation, testing, and release of software components. The system behind this operates like a script that installs the three components—operating system, database, and SAP—automatically and flawlessly. Recording a standard installation process in the form of a script that can be repeated ad libitum represents not only a great reduction in manual labor, but also a boost to standardization and thus less susceptibility to human error.

For this to function, the service offerings need to be similarly standardized. The client needs to enter all of the relevant information, e.g. SLA classes, performance classes, etc., when making the service request. With this in place, the process continues automatically. The machine produces an ITIL-compliant service request, a change, updates the CIs in the CMDB, and informs the billing engine of the requested volume for later invoicing. Manual work and unnecessary provisioning costs are removed from the process. By tailoring processes and products to the

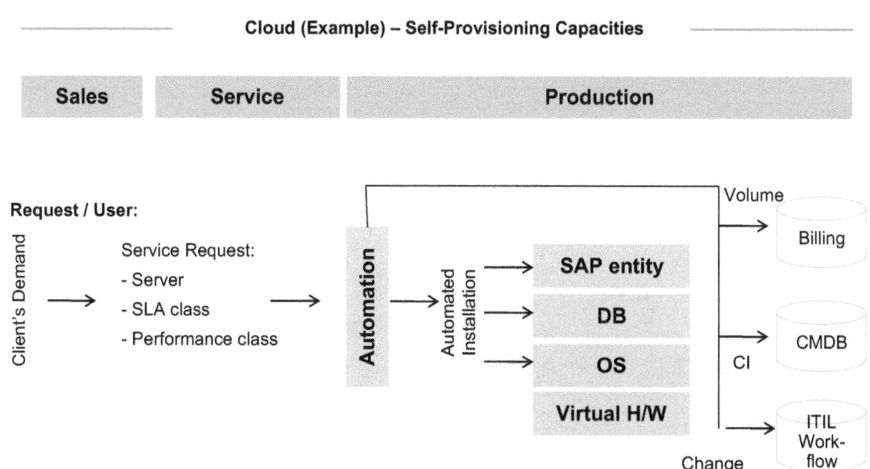

Fig. 13.1 Radical automation in cloud-based capacity provisioning (cf. Detecon 2013)

"right first time" user request, the services need to be standardized and shaped in a transparent, user-friendly manner. Old provisioning processes also have to change at their core, since no cloud-on-demand process would be possible without these also having automation and standardization. Virtual platforms are the basis for this achievement. The background physical hardware capacities are shared between clients (shared storage, shared memory, shared CPU performance).

Processes can be this fast only because requested server capacity is no longer tied to physical hardware. A certain basic capacity needs to be held "shared" in reserve. To keep the step costs for expanding these basic capacities in check (e.g. adding one or more units of VMware Linux or AIX Multicore hardware), the provider needs meaningful capacity plans and a relationship of trust with the client. A certain critical mass of physical hardware is also necessary, since modern production can only be possible with the economies of scale promised by shared platforms.

Client and provider should establish a shared forecast as part of a defined planning process. Unexpected deviations from the forecast are only harmless if they stay within a certain corridor, as SLAs and general responsiveness can only be guaranteed in that range without incurring major surcharges. When the capacity adjustments for the channel have been forecast sensibly, the model still stays highly flexible and incurs no excessive fixed costs. This model is also effective in handling so-called "Capacity-on-Demand" forecasting frameworks as part of outsourcing contracts (cf. Fig. 13.2).

SAP systems, databases, and the infrastructure they are built on (servers/OS, storage, backup) are comparatively easy to harmonize and standardize. Some of the principles named above can therefore be realized in traditional IT operations if one proceeds carefully—initial cloud readiness in SAP operations can be achieved without too much of a culture shock. The actual virtualization platform or choice of administration and automation solution is not the key problem. More attention

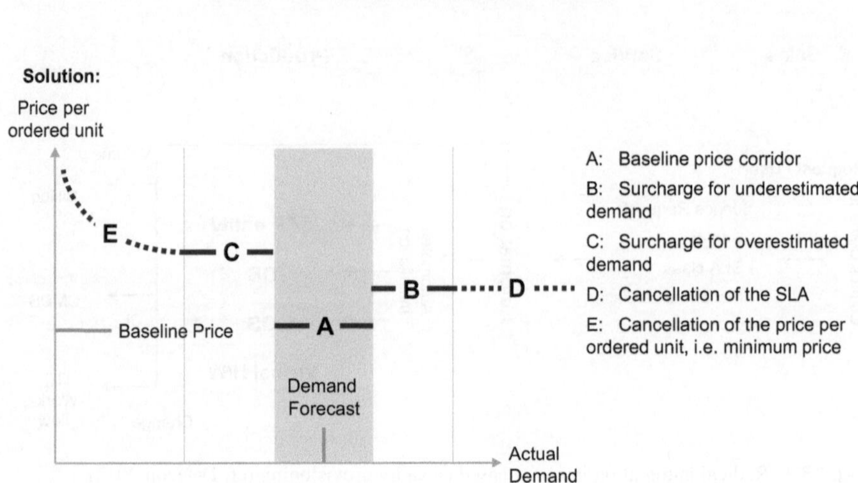

Fig. 13.2 "Capacity-on-Demand" model (cf. Detecon, T-Systems, DTAG 2009)

rather needs to be paid to adjusting products, organizations, processes, and ERP systems. We can go so far as to talk of a basic change in the company's culture. Approval procedures in particular need to be streamlined to accelerate the system. This can be an uphill challenge, since many IT departments use extensive distribution of labor, requiring approval from multiple entities along the way. Clearing a new server order can be slowed down to such an extent that it might take 100 days or more before the server is actually on line. Redesigning these processes will often be met with resistance. Automation and rationalization will make people worry about their jobs, which makes it essential to support the transition with effective change management measures.

The topic will get a particular boost when standardized cloud offerings are easily available and cheap, while traditional offerings need money and patience. These incentives must be made transparent for the client by distinguishing clearly between cloud offerings and traditional models in the pricing model and SLA (throughput times). The usual outcome is a satisfyingly educational effect on the client, who will typically opt for the standard offerings and bypass non-standard versions. This allows the provider to again increase and actively manage the degree of standardization (e.g. the ratio of standard to non-standard servers).

Standardization is a key lever that influences far more than the costs of providing capacities. Rather, it affects a wide range of cost drivers. Oftentimes, particularly lean operating models can be introduced with little fanfare by using such new service offerings. Transitioning complex backup processes from production to quality assurance or development systems would, for instance, lead to horrendous storage costs. If, however, the client is offered cheaper backup processes as a standard SLA class in the cloud offering, it makes it easier to migrate the entire

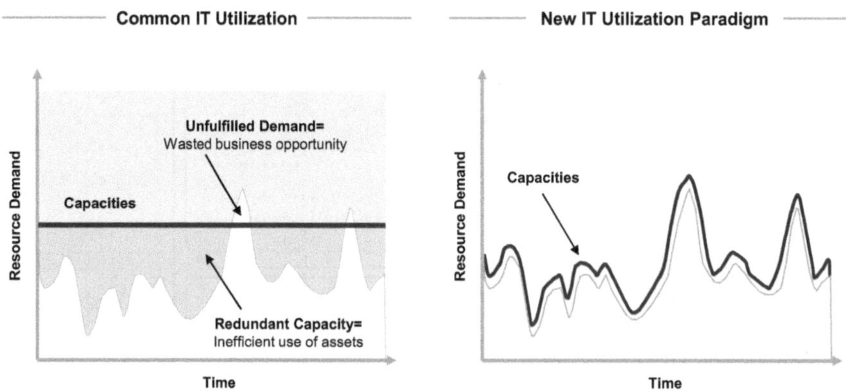

Fig. 13.3 Flexible provision of computing capacities via virtualization (cf. T-Systems and Detecon 2010)

data processing portfolio to the new standard with the next update. The same goes for database consolidation or newer and cheaper technologies that will be easier to launch when they come as part and parcel of an attractive cloud offering.

Many dedicated servers are running at less than 20% of their capacity. Virtualization allows companies to increase this utilization rate considerably. Temporary peaks in demand would have led to enormous costs in earlier times, since resource and hardware capacities had to be chosen to cope with the expected peaks. Virtualization again allows higher levels of performance to be made available at a fraction of the cost. In the case of bottlenecks in capacities, e.g. when a web shop experiences a rush, capacities can be ramped up flexibly without the risk of losing momentum due to poor performance or disenchanted users (cf. Fig. 13.3).

13.2 Vision and Structure of a Software-Defined Data Center

There can be no question about the motivation for and the benefits of using cloud computing. Whenever workloads are flexible and dynamic, the cloud has become a deal-winning argument. Unfortunately, many data center landscapes in business have fragmented over time, running a wide range of proprietary applications on custom-built hardware components. Largely isolated technological silos have grown up side by side (networks, storage, Windows servers, Linux servers, etc.), a situation that can have a dramatic effect in terms of holding back the new service paradigm. When we speak of standardization or automation, the key is to not limit it to individual silos. However, this can be one of the toughest challenges going forward.

For corporate IT, preempting the future is essential when it comes to the right balance between private and public cloud usage. However much IT strategies might

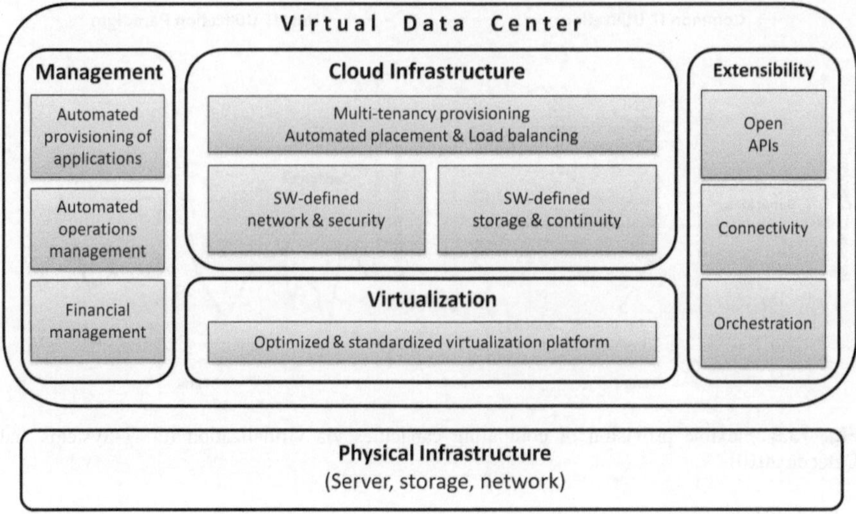

Fig. 13.4 Building blocks of a software-defined data center (*Source*: VMware)

differ from company to company, no actor in the industry will be able to ignore the question, unless the company has already handed over all of its IT to outsourcing partners. Among other factors, a look at the architecture and operations of the company's established data centers can already become the first step into a successful life in the cloud.

The ultimate objective has to be a fully software-defined data center that can share workloads dynamically between locations or external providers. A software-defined data center in this sense (cf. Herrod 2012) has its entire infrastructure virtualized as an abstract service, controlled completely by software.

The wholesale virtualization of servers, which VMware's vSphere and similar offerings have allowed many companies to introduce, represents only one possible foothold in such a scenario. Figure 13.4 shows the building blocks of an effective architecture, as used by VMware's vCloud Suite.

The main elements of such an architecture cover:

- **Virtualization**: Standardizing the technology design and operational processes as the fundamental services.
- **Cloud Infrastructure**: Alignment with service-oriented production, covering aspects of multi-tenant capabilities, optimized resource utilization and flawless workload distribution. Software-defined management of network connective with relevant security features. Ensuring the availability of services even after catastrophic incidents (think: business continuity). Self-service offerings for complex services (using templates and multiple virtual servers).
- **Management**: Cloud infrastructure tends to put special emphasis on the "Infrastructure-as-a-Service" concept, but a second component is needed to take the evolutionary leap towards offering a "Platform-as-a-Service". The availability of services is generally handled in an automated and proactive form. Pricing and service accounting also fall under this heading.

- **Availability**: Providing open interfaces for automating the entire environment. Standardized forms for linking virtual data centers (internal and external). Managing processes for providing cloud services.

Architecture of this type permits the simple and highly integrated automated delivery of SAP systems as described above. SAP is cooperating closely with VMware, e.g. by integrating productivity solutions like SAP NetWeaver Landscape Virtualization Management (cf. Cappell and Bernhoff 2012) with VMware's ecosystem.

Why does it make sense for companies to invest in software-defined data centers? Apart from cost advantages and the agility and quality of the service, the key is to capture early competitive advantages by getting hold of new application architectures and being able to handle massive amounts of data (think: "Big Data"). Companies thus pave the way for a real transformation of IT to support new business models; a common ambition of cloud computing that is all too rarely realized, e.g. by outsourcing workloads dynamically. There are technical obstacles (lack of standardization, threat of provider lock-in as a result of proprietary architectures, or the dependence on a service provider), but there are also other important items on the agenda for IT managers looking for cloud partners, including matters of SLAs, compliance, and security.

Companies like VMware have contributed massively to getting services into the cloud with their service provider programs. The approach consists basically of offering market actors standardized access to virtual data centers. The user is given guaranteed capabilities (depending on the service provider's chosen level) in a virtual setting that would ideally be recognizable from the user's own data centers. This increases the subjective feeling of trust in the cloud solution. There are also providers, like T-Systems, that have been certified by VMware and audited by impartial auditors (cf. T-Systems 2012). This adds a level of objectivity to questions like security and compliance. The notorious question of provider lock-in is answered by standardization, just as the free choice of provider overcomes the local restrictions and regulations concerning the geographies of data.

The flexibility of standardized service provider programs was used very well by Star Alliance in 2012 to get an online competition for the fifteenth anniversary of the airline alliance up and running in minimal time (cf. Ostler 2012). The challenge was to produce a special website robust enough to handle up to 21,000 users at peak times and a total data volume of 150 terabytes. With only 6 weeks to create it and with the project scheduled to run for only 5 weeks, building up a dedicated infrastructure for such a one-off action would have been unreasonable, so Star Alliance chose Wusys as a vCloud-powered partner to host everything on the basis of standard VMware technology. The system was managed, monitored, and run by IPsoft. With the high degree of standardization in this approach, the project was completed successfully in the planned timeframe and on budget.

Another example is AutoScout24 and its choice of a hybrid cloud concept (cf. Srocke and Ostler 2012). AutoScout24's own IT capacities are expanded at the point of need by adding external resources for additional or resource-intensive processes (e.g. imports in the workshop portal). The service provider is T-Systems, using a certified vCloud data center service. At the same time, T-Systems is also an integral part of business continuity: The vCloud is ready to bridge even a complete outage of AutoScout24's internal IT.

These two examples show the variety of reasons for companies to use standardized cloud offerings. They should encourage readers to look for more creative and innovative business concepts and to launch their data centers into the cloud to preempt the needs and challenges of tomorrow. Clearly, this also includes the constant introduction of innovative technologies to open up new opportunities for value creation.

The path towards software-defined data centers has been taken by many companies. After the virtualization of servers and storage, the time has come for the next big leaps in network management, creating new opportunities for the location-independent management of data centers (or rather: services). One major challenge is that IP addresses are still used to determine the identity and the physical location of a server. Virtual switches were a first step towards greater efficiency in the linking of virtual systems, but significant technological hurdles remain. Another step on the route towards industrial IT and software-defined data centers is clearly the separation of IP addresses from physical addresses. When virtual machines are being relocated from an in-house network to a provider network, there needs to be a plan for allocating IP addresses. In a software-defined data center, however, all of this is handled by the software (and not "simply" changed by automated scripts in line with design guidelines).

Achieving greater network transparency has been made possible with the "VXLAN model" developed in an alliance featuring VMware, Cisco, and other companies. The model has been put forward for standardization (cf. Mahalingam et al. 2011) and can be compared to the evolution of phone networks. Whereas in the past a phone number was tied to a residential or office landline, the rise of the cellphone has removed that local component. For data centers, a similar opportunity is created by the option to identify virtual systems solely by their IP address. With "MAC-in-UDP" encapsulation, VXLAN creates a layer 2 abstraction and detaches the virtual system from the physical network. The data center handles this with dedicated management software.

We can expect more innovation related to the concept of software-defined data centers. There will be even more savings in terms of investments and, in particular, normal operations—another reason for tackling the redesign of data centers.

13.3 Summary: Designing and Running the IT Factory

This chapter has looked at the IT factory from two different vantage points: From the point of view of business operations, that is, the question of how specifications, processes, and KPIs make for a highly automated solution, and the question of how and why clients will adjust their data center strategies for automation and standardized cloud services.

Providers like T-Systems have come to realize that modern IT production platforms need, above all else, to be automated and standardized to achieve a reasonable level of cost savings. Standardization involves processes, infrastructure, applications, and services at the same time—that is, lean principles, the refocusing on what is important, and the move away from manual services. The final purpose of automation is a complete service without manual intervention from one end to the other. Given their complexity (and costly operation), SAP services are a favorite example in this area. Apart from political and organizational considerations, we can expect the architecture of data centers to have the greatest impact on their flexibility, agility, and productivity.

One of the buzzwords of last year was the software-defined datacenter, inspired mostly by VMware and promoted with its technology partners. At its heart, this concerns two aspects: data centers (provider-based or in-house) managed completely by software to eliminate the (expensive) manual interventions described above, and infrastructure operating smoothly irrespective of its location. The latter factor is interesting for providers (for spreading the workload across locations) and for internal IT managers (for outsourcing services or coping with demand peaks). Innovative technologies here become a driver for new use cases and business models.

The automated rollout of server infrastructure has become the state of the art for most modern data centers. The deployment of entire services in the form of virtual appliances and templates can hide the complexity of the implementation process. In network services in particular, new technologies can be expected to give IT and the value it creates (or the costs it saves) another boost in the near future.

References

Cappell, C.-H., & Bernhoff, P. (2012). *SAP & VMware – a strategic partnership*. Retrieved January 2, 2013, from http://www.youtube.com/watch?v=vWxPKSN3BtI&feature=youtu.be

Detecon. (2013). Excerpt from a presentation on “Cloud Readiness” consulting methods at Detecon.

Detecon, T-Systems, & DTAG. (2009). Sample “capacity-on-demand” model (schematic presentation of an actual capacity planning and pricing model at DTAG).

Herrod, S. (2012). *The software-defined datacenter meets VMworld*. Retrieved January 2, 2013, from http://cto.vmware.com/the-software-defined-datacenter-meets-vmworld/

Mahalingam, M., Dutt, D., Duda, K., Agarwal, P., Kreeger, L., Sridhar, T., et al. (2011). *VXLAN: A framework for overlaying virtualized layer 2 networks over layer 3 networks*. Retrieved January 2, 2013, from http://tools.ietf.org/html/draft-mahalingam-dutt-dcops-vxlan-00

Srocke, D., & Ostler, U. (2012). *AutoScout24 setzt auf Hybrid Cloud*. Retrieved January 2, 2013, from http://www.searchcloudcomputing.de/plattformen/hosting-und-outsourcing/articles/376591/

T-Systems. (2012). *Top-Allianz für Cloud-Dienste: T-Systems bietet Kunden vCloud Datacenter Services von VMware*. Retrieved January 2, 2013, from http://www.telekom.com/medien/loesungen-fuer-unternehmen/129770

T-Systems, & Detecon. (2010). Illustration of optimum utilization management for cloud solutions, revised from a sales presentation on Cloud 7.0 at T-Systems.

14 Focusing on Core Competencies and Divestment

Marc Wilczek

For a company to make its mark competitively, it needs a strategic advantage, that is, the ability to do something better or more cheaply than others. Resource theory states that such advantages are, above all else, a product of internal capabilities (resource-based view of the firm, cf. e.g. Pfeffer and Salancik 1978; Porter 1980; Wernerfelt 1984; Barney 1991; Rumelt 1991; Peteraf 1993). Applying this theory, Porter (1985) has described companies in terms of their value chain, distinguishing between primary functions and support functions. The former contribute directly to value creation (for instance: production), while the latter only have an indirect contribution at best, but can make the existence of the primary functions possible in the first place (for instance: procurement, HR, or finance).

Following the idea of the value chain, Prahalad and Hamel (1990) have come to term the company's particular strengths that go beyond individual products its "core competencies." These core competencies are not immediately replicable by competitors, can be applied to a diverse range of products or markets, and directly affect the customer's perceived benefits regarding a product or service. They form the seedbed in which added value is created for the customer as the final link in the value chain. Core competencies are the sum of individual capabilities or production technologies, the product of the organization's years of collective experience and expertise. They are unique qualities with real added value for the customer. To avoid narrowing their effect down to internal silo thinking, the company needs communication and collaboration that goes across the boundaries of a certain product. With such unbounded core competencies in place, any company—even if it works with a mixed bag of products and a diversified range of businesses—can achieve economies of scale and economies of scope. In the end, these are the engines for exceptional success and competitive advantage (cf. e.g. Panzar and Willig 1977; Teece 1980; Panzar and Willig 1981).

M. Wilczek (✉)
T-Systems International GmbH, Heinrich-Hertz-Str. 1, 64295 Darmstadt, Germany
e-mail: Marc.Wilczek@t-systems.com

F. Abolhassan (ed.), *The Road to a Modern IT Factory*, Management for Professionals,
DOI 10.1007/978-3-642-40219-7_14,

In processes of transformation, core competencies come into their own. From the point of view of IT service organizations, they are an essential factor on the road towards becoming efficiency leaders. By focusing on its own home turf, the company has the ability to produce better services at lower cost than the competition. Using the insights gained from a portfolio analysis (cf. Chap. 15), the company can concentrate on those areas that are strategically significant and offer an advantage in the market. Apart from purely quantitative considerations of whether the area in question is responsible for absolute or relatively high profit or contribution margins, an area can be strategically significant if, for instance, it enables the company to access other fields of business and thus paves the way for economies of scope. Certain effects can also feed on or filter down through the complex structure of the company's business. When, for instance, activities affecting Product A have a direct impact on the sales of Product B, so-called *spill-over effects* come into play. When the effect on sales becomes visible, but is delayed, it is called a *carry-over effect*. Given the many interdependencies and correlations between fields of business, no single field should ever be seen in isolation. The fields of business deemed strategically significant should be subjected to a make-or-buy decision (cf. Chap. 19) to determine whether the service in question can be produced more efficiently in-house or whether it is a candidiate for outside sourcing.[1]

When a certain field of business is not strategically significant or promises no competitive advantage, the company should withdraw from it completely and without hesitation. This frees up assets (tangible, intangible, or financial assets), adding new liquidity to the business that can be reinvested more efficiently in new projects or in the remaining core fields. Divestment is the natural counterpart of investment and should be used when markets contract or companies reduce the vertical integration in their business.

Activities that remain in-house and are not procured from third parties by outsourcing or out-tasking should be produced in the most efficient manner possible by using all of the internal synergies available. For global IT service organizations, this has been called the "de-bracketing" of activities, i.e. the centralized clustering of activities that can be used for several product lines or processes at a time. In practice, this can refer to a central helpdesk to support end users irrespective of the specific product of the company that they have bought. The same goes for other cross-operational functions, such as capacity and utilization management, quality assurance, incident management, or supplier and vendor management (which in itself clusters the purchasing power of the company for negotiating favorable SLAs with suppliers).

[1] Helpful in this context are traditional investment appraisal tools, and, in particular, a net present value (NPV) analysis while simultaneously considering internal hurdle rates (derived from an internal rate of return calculation). The results are typically subjected to a sensitivity analysis which assesses the impact of uncertainty factors, outlining this in the form of a corridor between a best and worst case scenario.

In the 1980s, Jack Welch (CEO of General Electric from 1981 to 2001) became famous for his ambition to either make his company one of the top two brands in each of its fields of business or to withdraw completely from the market and concentrate on other activities. "Fix it, sell it, or close it" was the motto under which GE's portfolio was subjected to a massive spring clean and refocusing over a period of only a few years (cf. Hostettler 2010a). Looking back, Welch (2005) stated that only three factors are critical for success in any given commodity business: Good quality, low prices, and good service. Companies that have internalized this creed can be enormously successful even in commoditized markets, as companies like Wal-Mart and Dell have famously demonstrated. At the same time, Welch encouraged companies to pursue "de-commoditization" wherever and whenever possible. They could do so by rising above the crowd through innovation, better processes, or additional services, thus escaping from the constant downward pressure on prices and becoming successful players for the long term. One should not underestimate how important this is: A recent study by the University of Mannheim revealed that 40 % of all executives in industrial goods companies incorrectly estimate their company's relative prices compared to the relative value for the customer. The subjective belief that prices need to come down leads them to squeeze their profit margins unnecessarily, engage in avoidable price wars, and promote the slow collapse of their business models (cf. Homburg and Totzek 2012).

In the IT and telecommunications industry, Prahalad and Hamel (1990) compared GTE and NEC to show how NEC prevailed over GTE in just a few years by focusing on its core competencies, simultaneously becoming one of the top-five players in the telephone, semiconductor, and mainframe sectors. In their paper, Prahalad and Hamel reveal that NEC managed to do so by anticipating the eventual convergence between computer and communication technology, and benefitting from this early insight. The source of the company's success was a combination of concentrating on only very few activities and of excelling in these particular activities.

Another related example can be found in the automotive industry. Believing that more diversification was the answer to the increasing competition in the car market, Edzard Reuter (CEO of Daimler-Benz AG from 1987 to 1995) became the proponent of his vision of an "integrated technology business", which many people would later come to call delusions of grandeur. In response to the experience of the oil crisis and the green movement of the 1970s, he saw opportunities for growth in reaching out into new fields of business, leading to a gamut of new acquisitions, including AEG, MTU, Dornier, and Kässbohrer (cf. e.g. Bea and Haas 1995; Freitag et al. 2007; Hank and Meck 2010).

The time for a radical change of direction came under the guidance of Jürgen Schrempp (CEO of Daimler-Benz AG from 1995 to 1998 and DaimlerChrysler AG from 1998 to 2005). Schrempp saw the shareholder as the center of the company's universe (shareholder value principle) and forced through an organizational shake-up. Following Welch's idea, his plan was to become the undisputed leader in the automotive sector by concentrating on core business and jettisoning loss-making business areas.[2] Returns and market capitalization were the new yardstick by which everything was measured. To whatever extent the company might have benefited from this turnaround in the late 1990s, all of the gains and the entire vision of a global corporation were lost soon after. Forced to inject significantly more capital into the ventures with Mitsubishi and Hyundai, the aftershocks of the "marriage made in heaven" with Chrysler were felt. Sales figures were on the decline, and losses skyrocketing. Public opinion turned against Schrempp: The initial praise gave way to harsh criticism. Named one of the top managers of 1998 by Bloomberg Businessweek, he was awarded the unflattering title of worst manager only 5 years later.[3] Dieter Zetsche took over the reins in 2006, streamlined the portfolio, gradually withdrew from most ventures, and led the organization and the brand back to its roots. In 2007, the name of the company was changed simply to Daimler AG.[4]

References

Barney, J. (1991). Firm resources and sustained competitive advantage. *Journal of Management, 17*(1), 99–120.

Bea, F. X., & Haas, J. (1995). *Strategisches management*. Stuttgart: Springer.

Daimler. Retrieved December 28, 2012, from http://www.daimler.com/dccom/0-5-1324891-49-1324904-1-0-0-1345593-0-0-135-0-0-0-0-0-0-0-0.html

Freitag, M., Brors, P., et al. (2007, April). Daimler Chrysler: Die Quittung. *Manager Magazin*, 34–45.

Hank, R., & Meck, G. (2010). Wer heucheln kann, ist schon ein gemachter Mann. *Frankfurter Allgemeine Zeitung (FAZ)*. Retrieved December 18, 2012, from http://www.faz.net/aktuell/wirtschaft/unternehmen/edzard-reuter-wer-heucheln-kann-ist-schon-ein-gemachter-mann-11055622.html#Drucken

Hillenbrand, T. (2005). Der Verheerer von Möhringen. Spiegel Online. Retrieved December 18, 2012, from http://www.spiegel.de/wirtschaft/analyse-der-verheerer-von-moehringen-a-367178.html

Homburg, C., & Totzek, D. (2012). Rules for successful competitive pricing in business markets. IMU Research Insights, Vol. 2

Hostettler, S. (1999). The best & worst managers of the year. *Bloomberg Businessweek*. Retrieved December 27, 2012, from http://www.businessweek.com/1999/02/b3611001.htm

Hostettler, S. (2004a). The 25 top executives of the year. *Bloomberg Businessweek*. Retrieved December 27, 2012, from http://www.businessweek.com/magazine/toc/04_02/B38650402best.htm

[2] Cf. Bea and Haas (1995), p. 68.

[3] Cf. N.N., http://www.businessweek.com/magazine/toc/04_02/B38650402best.htm; http://www.businessweek.com/1999/02/b3611001.htm and http://www.manager-magazin.de/unternehmen/karriere/0,2828,280715,00.html, all retrieved on December 27, 2012; Hillenbrand (2005), http://www.spiegel.de/wirtschaft/analyse-der-verheerer-von-moehringen-a-367178.html, retrieved on December 18, 2012; N.N.; http://www.sueddeutsche.de/wirtschaft/daimler-und-chrysler-hochzeit-des-grauens-1.464777, retrieved on December 18, 2012.

[4] Cf. Daimler, http://www.daimler.com/dccom/0-5-1324891-49-1324904-1-0-0-1345593-0-0-135-0-0-0-0-0-0-0-0.html, retrieved on December 28, 2012.

Hostettler, S. (2004b). Jürgen Schrempp: Schlechtester Manager des Jahres. *Manager Magazin*. Retrieved December 27, 2012, from http://www.manager-magazin.de/unternehmen/karriere/0,2828,280715,00.html

Hostettler, S. (2010a). Ex-General-Electric-Chef Jack Welch im Interview: Politiker sind bloß neidisch auf Manager [first published in the print edition of the SZ on May 29, 2008]. *Süddeutsche Zeitung*. Retrieved December 27, 2012, from http://www.sueddeutsche.de/wirtschaft/ex-general-electric-chef-jack-welch-im-interview-politiker-sind-bloss-neidisch-auf-manager-1.195889

Hostettler, S. (2010b). Hochzeit des Grauens. *Süddeutsche Zeitung*. Retrieved December 18, 2012, from http://www.sueddeutsche.de/wirtschaft/daimler-und-chrysler-hochzeit-des-grauens-1.464777

Panzar, J. C., & Willig, R. D. (1977). Economies of scale in multi-output production. *Quarterly Journal of Economics, 91*(3), 481–493.

Panzar, J. C., & Willig, R. D. (1981). Economies of scope. *The American Economic Review, 71*(2), 268–272.

Peteraf, M. A. (1993). The cornerstones of competitive advantage: a resource-based view. *Strategic Management Journal, 14*(3), 179–191.

Pfeffer, J., & Salancik, G. (1978). *The external control of organizations: A resource dependence perspective*. New York: Harper and Row.

Porter, M. E. (1980). *Competitive strategy*. New York: Free Press.

Porter, M. E. (1985). *Competitive advantage*. New York: Free Press.

Prahalad, C. K., & Hamel, G. (1990). The core competence of the corporation. *Harvard Business Review, 68*(3), 79–91.

Rumelt, R. P. (1991). How much does industry matter? *Strategic Management Journal, 12*(3), 167–185.

Stadler, C. (2004). *Unternehmenskultur von Royal Dutch/Shell, Siemens und DaimlerChrysler*. Munich: Franz Steiner.

Teece, D. (1980). Economies of scope and the scope of the enterprise. *Journal of Economic Behavior and Organization, 1*(3), 223–247.

Welch, J. (2005). *Winning*. New York: Harper Business.

Wernerfelt, B. (1984). A resource-based view of the firm. *Strategic Management Journal, 5*(2), 171–180.

Utilization 15

Tom In der Rieden

This chapter considers the utilization of resources and how it can be measured and improved, since higher utilization rates are the most cost-efficient means of increasing efficiency in IT over the medium term without the need for major investments. The focus lies first and foremost on material assets: The facilities, equipment, hardware, and software used in IT.

15.1 Surveying Resources and Finding an Optimum Utilization Rate

The first step is to know which material resources are available to produce the services of the company or internal service organization. This can rely on obvious data sources, such as a dedicated Configuration Management Database (CMBD), if available. This data may, however, be too detailed for the purpose and it typically includes no actual data on the utilization of the resources.

A better way is therefore to distinguish by production sites (typically data centers) and categories of resources, such as floor space, air conditioning, rooms, power supplies, network infrastructure, storage, server capacities, or cloud resources, etc.

The current utilization of these categories is then measured, and an ideal utilization rate is defined. Although one would be tempted to put that ideal rate at 100 %, this is never seen in reality. For instance, a 100 % utilization of power supplies in normal operations would mean that typical demand peaks, e.g. when powering on new facilities, would lead to the immediate collapse of the power grid at the company. Nor is 100 % floor space utilization possible for equipment—after all, one needs aisles and corridors to get around.

T. In der Rieden (✉)
T-Systems International GmbH, Mecklenburgring 25, 66121 Saarbrücken, Germany
e-mail: Thomas.In-der-Rieden@t-systems.com

F. Abolhassan (ed.), *The Road to a Modern IT Factory*, Management for Professionals,
DOI 10.1007/978-3-642-40219-7_15,

This means that an ideal utilization rate needs to be found on a case-by-case basis without trying to impose uniform standards. The trick is to follow established benchmarks. To obtain meaningful benchmarks, one can consult trusted external experts or one can turn to a specialist benchmarking agency for the right figures.

It pays off to invest in such benchmarks, as they can help avoid costly and time-wasting mistakes about possible or desirable goals for different parts of operations, given the actual circumstances. This insight also helps concentrate interventions and investments in the right places, i.e. where improvements are most likely. If the floor space of a data center is used to 75 %, a benchmark of 70 % tells us that this is not a poor performance. If, however, the benchmarked businesses achieve an 80 % utilization rate, action should be taken.

When such data is available for comparison, the optimum utilization rate can be defined for each of the defined resource categories. This optimum rate should be considered the 100 % target for the time being and acts as a baseline for all improvement initiatives.

New technologies are regular drivers for change. Therefore, benchmarks should be revised at suitably long intervals (e.g. every 2 to 3 years), as they may have changed in the meantime. More modern servers may produce less heat and more compact designs do not take up so much expensive floor space. In that case, the defined 100 % target can be adjusted to account for these new results.

15.2 Defining Actual Utilization

The next step tries to measure the resources' actual rate of utilization. Typically, it is calculated as the ratio between used and unused resources. When trying to determine to what extent a resource is "used", one should always keep in mind that it is meant to be a commercial calculation: A resource is used when it means that it is set off against production costs.

Again, it is important to apply suitable benchmarks to find out whether the current values are average, better, or worse than elsewhere.

In the case of network ports, to take one example, one would compare the number of physical LAN ports in use with the total number of ports. This example might not be a good fit with recent developments, as modern virtual infrastructure means that many ports/VLANs (virtual LANs) are virtualized and their number defines the limits for the infrastructure. There are often several (V)LANs per client, e.g. one used for managing the client's infrastructure, one for the client's data, and one as a back-up and recovery system. In practice, however, VLANs are rarely used when calculating network utilization. In the case of storage, one compares the amount of space that has been used with the available storage capacity. An exception applies for servers in service centers that are run on behalf of clients: Here, the number of commissioned servers is compared to the total number of servers, but the test and management servers used by the provider for test or management purposes are also included in the client figure (as their usage should

Table 15.1 Measuring utilization with company-wide parameters

Resource type	Sample utilization indicator
Network	LAN ports used/LAN ports installed
Mainframe	MIPS used/MIPS installed
Server	Servers used/servers installed
Storage	TByte used/TByte installed
Cloud storage	TByte used/TByte installed
Data center infrastructure	kW used/kW installed

also be optimized). For mainframe resources, the comparison is between available and used MIPS (Million Instructions per Second).

Special rules apply to cloud systems, where different benchmarks need to be used for the parameters and other involved companies may need to be considered. For instance, the provider of a storage cloud for external clients cannot compare performance with the providers of server clouds. The units of calculation also differ in some cases: For servers, the comparison here is between the computing power that has been purchased and the total capacities. The number of actual servers is irrelevant, since the same physical machines may be used for multiple client commissions.

15.3 Setting Targets and Tracking Progress

When sufficient meaningful measurements and benchmarks are available, the performance of the units in question (e.g. network management in a given data center) is compared to the values for similar organizations (cf. Table 15.1). Depending on how the company is performing for the parameter in question, new targets are defined.

- When the performance of a data center/location is below average in one area (e.g. usage of LAN ports), the target is to reach the average level. Areas that achieve below-average performance are typically the prime targets for intervention.
- If the location or data center already produces average performance, the next target should be to reach the upper quartile of the comparison group.
- If the location or data center is already in the upper quartile, it should try to take the lead in the group.
- If the location or data center is actually in the top spot, the result is excellent—but the target must be to retain that lead (Fig. 15.1).

Performance should be measured on a monthly basis. The entire monitoring process and the criteria it employs should be clear and standardized for the entire organization, especially if different data centers/locations are to be compared.

Monitoring should make use of automated tools wherever possible. Again, the rule of simplicity applies: When such tools are missing, but their creation or procurement would cost valuable resources or time that could be used better

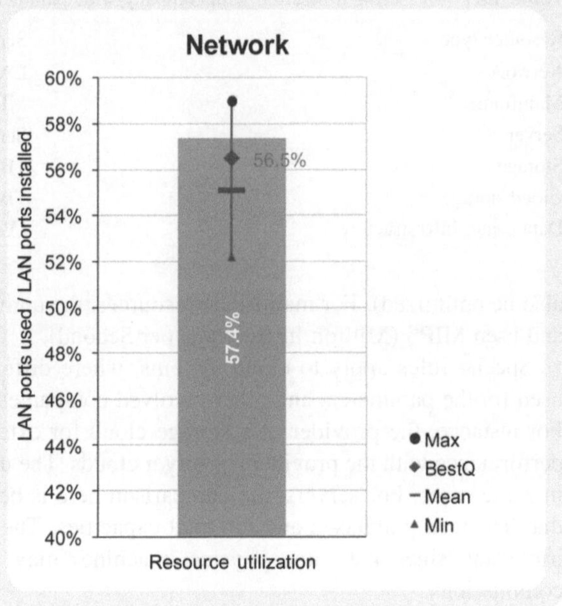

Fig. 15.1 Despite the apparently low rate of utilization of LAN ports, the benchmark comparison shows performance for this sample company is above average. The focus should not lie on improvement measures in this area when there are other areas that are performing less well [*Source*: In der Rieden (2012)].

elsewhere, a simple Excel spreadsheet also does the job. This is not the place for technological one-upmanship. The priority is to have relevant and meaningful monitoring data at the touch of a button.

15.4 Interventions and Their Targets

The most important targets for intervention are to be found in areas that do not reach the benchmark. While the options discussed in Chap. 3 are more or less short-term "first response" measures, the key here is to find medium-term solutions that will have an effect over a period of up to 24 months. This means that more far-ranging solutions are also an option, which need medium-term planning and investment. Every measure should have a specific percentage improvement as a target, to be reached by the next monthly monitoring cycle (e.g. improving floor space utilization by 10 % every month).

If the targets are not reached, the person in charge needs to identify and remove the obstacles along the way. This might not be possible at the level that he or she can influence, so the process may have to be escalated.

It helps to start any improvement intervention in the locations/data centers with the worst utilization score. Often, individual locations have unique weaknesses that hold back the overall performance of the company's IT organization. A typical example is the combination of old and new data centers: While most new locations would be performing in the "green light" zone in all benchmarks, the older infrastructure often performs poorly—more often than not simply because of the data centers' small size, which leaves little room for efficiencies. An option in this case is to consolidate the data center infrastructure: Old, expensive, poorly utilized centers are closed down in favor of a few large and energy-efficient centers.

When considering such changes, the company should keep an eye on its business offerings: Does every customer need access to every service at every location? Or might it not be commercially sensible to develop a global and cross-regional structure, with specialist locations for specific activities? Concentrating resources on these activities would lead to better utilization, since not every resource needs to be offered by every location. The suitability of this consolidation strategy needs to be decided with an eye on the unique circumstances at the company in question, but most IT organizations with multiple locations have some leeway in this respect.

Seen in this sense, utilization rates become a tool for managing scarce investment resources: When a location is underperforming, no further investments should be made before the utilization target has been reached. If, by contrast, a data center is operating under a high workload, an expansion may be a sensible option if the new capacities would also be well-utilized or if higher utilization is only possible with new technology.

One way to achieve improvements with minimal effort is to copy best practices from properly utilized infrastructure to other infrastructure with lower utilization rates if this is technically possible. This can work for simple cabling systems, for rack arrangements, or for cloud architectures. The trick is the slow and steady standardization of products and processes in all locations, as it will offer an immense reduction in maintenance, support, and admin effort.

15.5 Optimizing Labor

This chapter will conclude with some statements about the optimization of human resources. Apart from the cost advantages mentioned, copying best practices can also offer benefits on the personnel side: It makes IT staff more mobile in the company, because people can cover tasks at virtually any location if the architecture and tools used there are similar to their familiar areas. In this way, the IT organization can avoid having to let qualified personnel go for financial reasons, even though such staff might be hard to find again when the markets recover. It also improves staff satisfaction and the loyalty of qualified personnel. They know that there are optimum processes and tools to do more in less time, opening up resources for creating new value beyond their routine work.

As a rule, people's workload—i.e. HR utilization—should be measured and improved consistently by introducing activity-based time management. Monitoring utilization by activities allows teams with similar activity profiles to be compared in terms of their workload and performance. It also reveals how much actual labor goes into any given IT product.

Teams with high workloads can be relieved without adding new personnel by taking on board people from teams with lower utilization. In some cases, this needs a medium-term timeframe, as training might be required. However, it is a way to not only ensure that utilization across teams is optimized, but that people are more satisfied with their work.

In the end, incentive and reward structures can help the company reach its targets. It can make sense to include the utilization targets for specific resources as performance targets for the people in charge of them. These performance targets given them an easily measurable—financial—incentive to commit to the utilization drive.

16 Towards Standardized Portfolios: End-to-End Challenges in Modern IT Production—From the Portfolio to the Production Process

Henryk Biesiada and Bernd Debus

16.1 Standardizing Offerings with Defined Market Portfolios

The current IT service market is subject to a disproportionate pressure on prices. The need for custom solutions on the part of clients means more cost-intensive production that can hardly be achieved at market-viable rates. More and more IT service organizations are having to turn primarily to selling standardized services at the best possible prices. However, this new approach is often undermined by their existing portfolio layouts, which are too often still bound to their traditional business of providing one-off solutions to match the specific needs of their clients. The obvious disadvantage is that this stands in the way of the core elements of industrial IT production, with the production process still remaining highly reliant on manual input—and its costly nature.

It is a major challenge for modern IT service organizations: They need to re-envision their portfolios to allow industrialized batch production suitable for delivery to multiple clients. The traditional production of one-off solutions is losing ground. At the same time, IT service organizations need to respond to the market's expectations and not lose sight of the unique needs of the individual user.

A contradiction in terms? What might appear a tangled knot at first sight can indeed be untied, as the auto industry of the last few decades has shown impressively: As models and marques of cars have proliferated, the number of generic, brand-neutral parts in them has multiplied in step.

Applying this paradigm to the design of a typical IT service portfolio, IT production would appear to require the following set of basic interventions.

H. Biesiada (✉)
T-Systems International GmbH, Mecklenburgring 25, 66121 Saarbrücken, Germany
e-mail: Henryk.Biesiada@t-systems.com

B. Debus
T-Systems International GmbH, Fasanenweg 9, 70771 Leinfelden-Echterdingen, Germany
e-mail: Bernd.Debus@t-systems.com

F. Abolhassan (ed.), *The Road to a Modern IT Factory*, Management for Professionals,
DOI 10.1007/978-3-642-40219-7_16,

First, the basic services need to be established by aligning the portfolio with the actual demand in the market. The new technical opportunities arising from the continuously accelerating cycles of innovation in both hardware and software seem to play a more and more marginalized part in this respect.

This should be followed by identifying the individual custom services that the market actually demands: these should be given a fixed definition in the overall portfolio. The insights gained from this analysis can help define the basic service components—that is, those components that are offered to all customers alike—and the most cost-efficient production processes for them.

The production of these generic services, expanded with more custom offerings, represents the cost-optimized production process in its entirety, a process that should then be screened in detail for its end-to-end capabilities and its flexibility for responding to the market's demands for change or alteration.

The following illustration (Fig. 16.1) represents an ICT market portfolio from the client's vantage point. It splits the solutions on offer into two categories.

Application services cover industry-specific software development and implementation, with release management plus application optimization and trialing as horizontally integrated services.

Infrastructure services refer to the running of applications, basic data processing center or network services, and user device services.

This distinction allows clients to access those service components that are indeed relevant to them and to commission custom services tailored to their unique requirements. Clients can navigate the streamlined portfolio easily and pick-and-mix the required services at the point of need—and change them at any time. Clients requiring stationary workstation services can, for instance, opt for the "Managed Workplace Services" module. If, at a later date, they decide to add mobile components, they can simply upgrade to the "Mobile Enterprise Services" modules, as all service components have been designed for direct interoperability.

A well-designed market portfolio promises the cost-efficient and timely delivery of services and responsiveness for all potential changes.

When IT service organizations are able to distinguish coherently between client-specific service offerings and actual technical service delivery, they are ready for the move into industrial IT production. The payoff is substantial, as the following will show.

16.2 Standardized Internal Portfolio Structures

We have so far considered the need to align market portfolios with the clients' requirements. It is just as important to remember the implications of portfolio design for the production process itself and for its costs.

Economies of scale come within easy reach by carefully managing the number of technical options or reducing the number of suppliers: this promises higher purchasing volumes and thus greater room for negotiating volume discounts. At the same time, it often helps improve the utilization of the available production facilities.

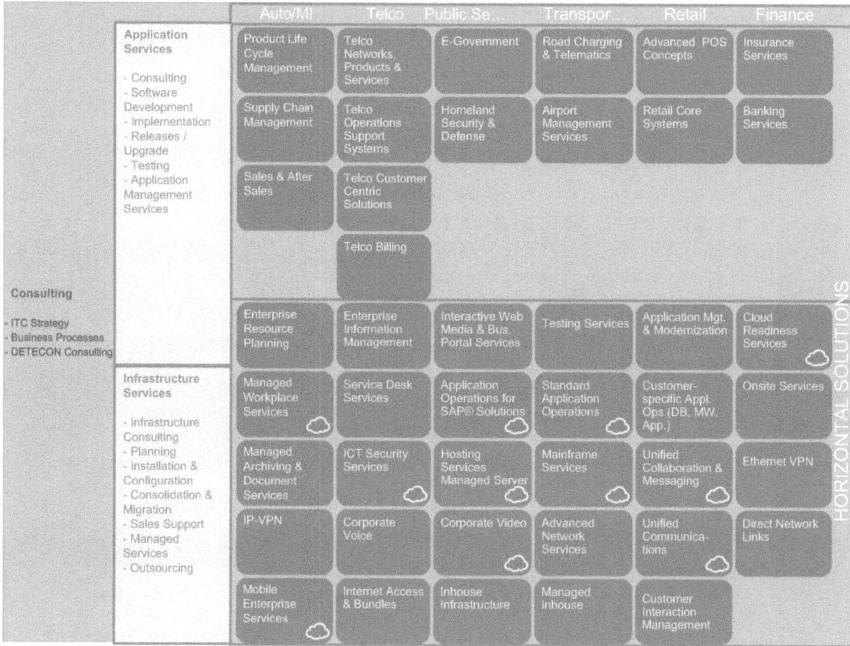

Fig. 16.1 ICT market portfolio aligned with the client's perspective (*Source*: T-Systems)

By adhering to a strict dual- or multi-supplier approach for purchased components, a degree of competition can be introduced into the procurement process to give the buyer even better standing in price negotiations.

Training and development efforts can also be brought down by reducing the range and variety of workflows and operating instructions: this can often open up opportunities for substantial automation. More flexible staffing systems become a much more viable option, paving the way for true lean production. By taking this further into the other elements of the lean production philosophy, such as just-in-time production, "standard work" processes, and performance management systems, sustainable savings lie within reach.

Workflow standardization also means less diversity in the production process and, by extension, higher quality. These levers should be kept in mind when designing new offerings, as they help reap the full benefits of industrialized IT production.

To develop offerings as effectively as possible, three categories of elements should be considered when doing so. These include, in the first place, "Offering Elements" that can be sold as solutions for the customer by bringing together different "Standard Delivery Elements" (SDEs). The costs and the quality of these SDEs should be known to help combine them appropriately in the above-mentioned Offering Elements.

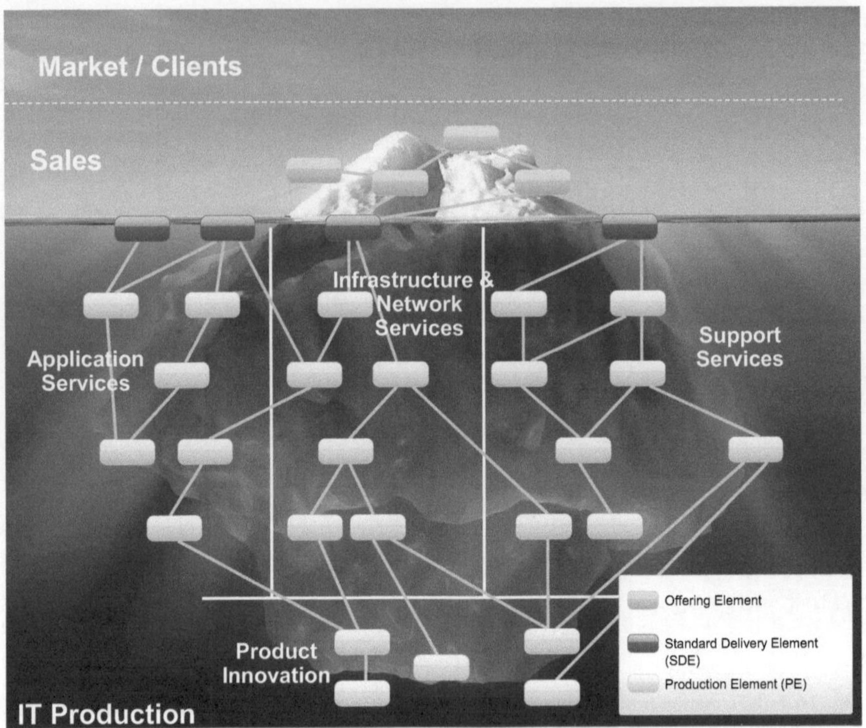

Fig. 16.2 Offering elements are only the tip of the iceberg for IT production (*Source*: T-Systems)

SDEs are, in turn, made up of individual "Production Elements" (PEs). When a greater number of generic PEs is used, the number of custom variants is again brought down for an optimized production process.

The above illustration (Fig. 16.2) outlines how these elements link up with each other.

This structure makes it easy to allocate each object in a portfolio and the related responsibilities to the various processes and organizational units of the IT service organization. The Offering Elements come into play on the customer-facing side, the SDEs ensure the effective link between production and sales, and the Production Elements help bring in the benefits of industrial IT production by increasing the use of generic components while reducing the number of technical variants. With this structural groundwork in place, the organization is ready to progress further on its route towards fully industrialized IT production.

16.3 From Production Portfolios to Production Processes

Proceeding in parallel to the ongoing standardization of the production portfolio, the operational processes need to evolve from a manual to an industrial basis to seize all the potential savings in reach. However, this step from manufacturing-driven processes to industrial production poses unique challenges for service providers in this sector of industry.

The first step is to detach oneself from the ambition to develop everything that is technically possible and switch to a focus on the most cost-efficient design of only those solutions that are actually necessary to deliver the required services. This feeds into a more commercially-minded approach in the technical areas, aiming for the continuous economic improvement of operations. Last but not least, modern methods of operations research need to be seized and applied in industrial IT production as they are elsewhere.

The success of this venture will depend on overcoming the common tendency to reject and undermine these changes, a tendency frequently found among technicians and engineers when they are asked to replace technically refined processes with simpler, generally automated methods. After all, this means deliberately removing an essential part of their profession's purpose.

We can conclude that a capable market portfolio will mean substantial cost advantages compared to more traditional ways and means of delivering services, when and if the above-mentioned factors are considered. Looking at the production processes used in more established industries can often be a source for invaluable ideas and insights about where and how optimization is possible.

16.4 Scouring Portfolios for Make-or-Buy Options

The purpose of reviewing the IT service portfolio is to refocus the service organization on only those production processes that are indeed strategically meaningful and that promise a real competitive advantage. These areas of the business should be subjected to a make-or-buy check (cf. Chap. 19) as the basis for a sound decision as to which parts of the portfolio can be removed, if any ("stop") and which of the affected Offering Elements should be optimized ("maintain"). This optimization can be attempted by involving other parties, up to a complete hand-over of the relevant activities ("buy"). Alternatively, the relevant Offering Element will still be produced by the IT service organization itself ("make"), and ways need to be found to restore the commercial viability of this in-house production. Whatever the outcome, this method represents a well-structured means of deciding whether to start a make-or-buy project for selected Offering Elements and, if so, which path to choose: "stop", "make", or "buy". Each option has a unique set of actions that need to be taken.

When subjecting the portfolio elements of the IT service organization to a make-or-buy check, the primary factors to consider are the market, costs, and quality. Its stated purpose is to produce a market-oriented, cost-efficient, standardized, and

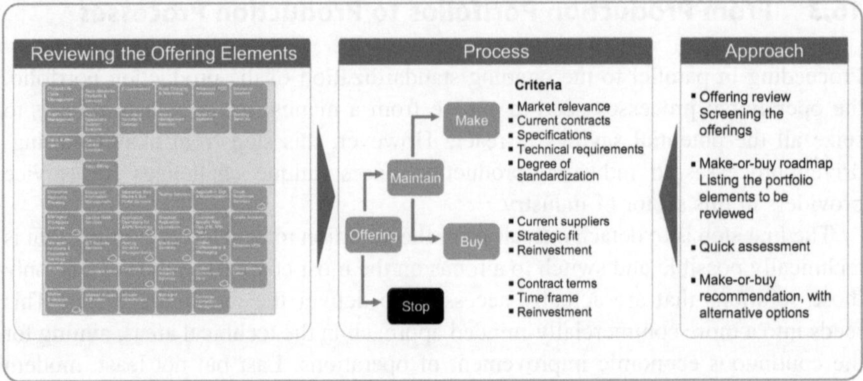

Fig. 16.3 Outline: make-or-buy analysis for Offering Elements (*Source*: T-Systems)

therefore competitive product portfolio. It is a great means of exploring all of the service elements, increasing transparency about inherent risks, and anticipating needs for intervention in good time. A regular check-up of this nature will also reveal the unique opportunities and options, such as promising growth areas, and help achieve a future-proof portfolio (Fig. 16.3).

A make-or-buy check can take two forms: The first is a systematic review of all of the elements of a portfolio (**Offering Review**) with the purpose of gaining a handle on the portfolio in the form of a **Make-or-Buy Roadmap** listing all of the elements that deserve a closer analysis. The strategic significance of the elements is a key criterion in this regard: If the element is essential for the IT service organization, it should—generally—be produced in-house. Another criterion considers the element's market relevance. Offerings that are highly relevant for clients should only ever be handed over to external partners after full consultation with clients. Other points to consider are the offering's specifications and technical requirements. Can the chosen partner deliver on these functional and technical requirements at the required level of quality? Highly standardized elements often offer a good basis for outsourcing to a partner, as they make a modular pick-and-mix definition of the offering easier. The service organization should also scrutinize its contracts to check whether outsourcing is actually an option or whether it would only be possible with additional effort or costs. Finally, time is a factor to be considered: If method implementation is time-consuming, it might not be an economical or effective choice.

The second approach is the **Quick Assessment.** This selects specific Offering Elements that obviously require urgent improvements to find clear recommendations in terms of a make-or-buy decision or other alternatives.

Data Center 2.0: Energy-Efficient and Sustainable

17

Rainer Weidmann and Hans-Rüdiger Vogel

17.1 Sustainability and Responsible Businesses

With a long history dating back to the eighteenth century, the term sustainability originates in the unlikely area of forestry (cf. von Carlowitz 1713). Over the centuries, it has been the object of many new definitions and interpretations, as Edmund A. Spindler explores in his history of the concept.

Current literature tends to use a definition that resembles the concept of sustainable development espoused in the 1987 Brundtland Report of the United Nations. In essence, a business can be called sustainable if it can operate permanently without damaging its own foundations (cf. Lexikon der Nachhaltigkeit, Aachener Stiftung Kathy Beys).

The concept of 'sustainability in IT' arrived as part of the 'Corporate Social Responsibility' (CSR) paradigm and goes far beyond mere energy efficiency (Green IT). Instead, it concerns the interplay of (corporate) IT and society at large (business, environment, and social responsibility).

- **Business**
  Even before considering any sustainability factor, IT production is always subject to enormous cost pressures which are only reinforced by continuing globalization. IT production sites are being chosen with an eye on many factors that were previously of little or no relevance. In the last 15 years, energy costs have developed from a minor item to one of the core concerns in the commercial calculation. This is not least the result of increasing, politically motivated levies on energy prices that cannot be compensated for with long-term contracts. To stay competitive, existing production sites are now being forced to rethink

R. Weidmann (✉)
Detecon International GmbH, Dingolfinger Str. 1-15, 81673 Munich, Germany
e-mail: Rainer.Weidmann@detecon.com

H.-R. Vogel
Detecon International GmbH, Frankfurter Str. 27, 65760 Eschborn, Germany
e-mail: Hans-Ruediger-Vogel@detecon.com

F. Abolhassan (ed.), *The Road to a Modern IT Factory*, Management for Professionals,
DOI 10.1007/978-3-642-40219-7_17,

their efficiency measures in terms of power consumption and general dimensions.

- **Environment**
  It was modern computing that made it possible for people to understand global environmental mechanisms and changes in the form of highly complex simulations in the first place. At the same time, computing has itself become one of the forces influencing the environment. Global climate change, the concreting-over of land, and the use of natural resources are all relevant for IT production. Creating transparency at this level by publishing CO_2 figures or engaging in compensation measures shows a company's commitment to sustainability and can help prevent image problems later on. At the same time, technological evolution and, in some cases, legal requirements call for the continuous improvement of the relevant KPIs over the entire life of a data center.
- **Social responsibility**
  Social responsibility and public acceptance are key. The effect of failures to obtain social acceptance for a technology can be witnessed at first hand in the current energy industry and the fate of nuclear power. Initiated by political pressure, the move away from nuclear power has created major new challenges for energy providers who were unprepared for this decision. In some cases, it means radically rethinking long-established business models.

In the interplay of these three forces, IT—in the form of large data centers run by providers or co-location companies—used to remain generally 'invisible'. However, the curtains have been lifted by actors like Greenpeace and its "How dirty is your data?" study or by the industry's own marketing in the area ("Green Data Center"). This has brought about a new presence in the political arena and calls are becoming louder for the industry's direct inclusion in political climate protection initiatives.

Apart from the cultural side of IT production in the twenty-first century (digital life, consumerization of IT, etc.), the sustainability principle also concerns commercial aspects with a major impact on the face of IT production. Namely:

- **Increasing energy costs**
  Renewable energy is constantly becoming cheaper as a result of better technology and increasing competition in the field. At the same time, the current energy revolution is creating new pressures in the form of the cost of new power distribution systems or fiscal levies. These have a direct impact on energy prices, which can be expected to rise over the medium term. This increase cannot be cushioned by engaging in long-term supply contracts, since they often exclude the impact of new levies imposed by government. The only viable means of response lies in the determined use of energy-efficient components and holistic planning with an eye on the efficient use of power. Additionally, the local use of renewable energy sources and the effective exploitation of waste heat are among the factors that are gaining relevance for the developers of data centers.

- **Changing cultural values**
  The increasing visibility of IT production in modern society is giving rise to an increase in critical opinion concerning sustainability in the industry. In modern, networked societies, a negative image, such as poor sustainability performance or even insufficient transparency can soon lead to an exodus of customers and commercial losses. The indirect costs of a negative image are hard to quantify in practice. Frequently, they are not given the attention they deserve. A positive choice would be to conduct an impact analysis on 'sustainability in IT production' in the same manner used for regular business continuity planning.

The following laws, regulations, codes, and organizations are only a tiny selection of the many forces that affect IT production in the area of sustainability:

- **EU Code of Conduct for Data Center Efficiency** (2008)
  The code of conduct was published by the European Commission to improve the energy efficiency of data centers. The basic idea was to create shared standards for European data centers, with further details provided in a best practice paper published in 2010.
- **Erneuerbare Energie Gesetz** (**EEG**) (Renewable Energy Act, Revision of 1 Jan 2012)
  The target for 2020 is to achieve a share of 35 % for renewable energy, set to increase to 80 % by 2050. The EEG's subsidies are financed by levies on energy prices. The act is currently being revised for tighter regulations.
- **Kyoto Protocol** (UNFCCC)—United Nations Framework Convention on Climate Change (2005)
  In its original form, the convention bound its signatories, including the states of the European Union, to reduce their CO_2 emissions by 8 % below the baseline of 1990 in the period from 2008 to 2012. As part of the EU, Germany had committed to a reduction of 21 %. In the Doha session of 2012, the Convention was extended until 2020, although specific reduction figures will not be set before 2015.

  In order to fulfill its CO_2 reduction commitments, the European Union and its member states will have to tighten current regulations and introduce new legislation.
- **European Union Emission Trading System** (**EU ETS**) (since 1 Jan 2005); EU directive 2003/87/EC.
  This system has been designed as a tool of the European Union to fulfill the member states' commitments under the Kyoto protocol. Originally intended for the operators of power plants and other large-scale CO_2 emitters, it is being expanded to more and more areas of industry in response to the on-going debate about climate change.
- **Renewable Energy Certificate System** (**RECS**) (2002)
  The RECS was the first international system for trading certificates for power from renewable sources. The certificates are traded between the 15 European member states irrespective of the actual production of renewable energy. The power sold to the end consumer does not have to come from renewable sources,

as long as the relevant amount of power from renewable sources has been produced and certified within the RECS area.

- **European Energy Certificate System (EECS)** (2009)
  The EECS is another system for reviewing and certifying the renewable origin of power. Essentially, it uses the register of origin kept by the RECS and implements EU directive 2009/28/EC. In 2013, the EECS will replace the RECS.
  Neither the RECS nor the EECS are true green power certificates, since they both allow power to be 'relabeled' by purchasing additional certificates.
- **Rat für Nachhaltige Entwicklung (RNE)** (Council for Sustainable Development, since 2001)
  The 15-member RNE was founded by Germany's federal government in 2001. Its members are public figures recruited for 3 years to work on questions of sustainability. The Council has published the:
  - **Deutscher Nachhaltigkeitskodex (DNK)** (German Sustainability Code, fourth revision, 2011)
    Applicable to Germany only, it defines 20 KPIs for sustainable business management.
    At an international level, there are further standards and guidelines, such as the **Global Reporting Initiative (GRI)** or the **European Federation of Financial Analysts Societies (EFFAS)**.

17.1.1 Opportunities

The first reaction is typically to see the increasing political and public pressure as a threat to the established business model. However, this response can worsen the situation, create hardened fronts, and cloud our awareness of the opportunities created by the new circumstances.

The IT industry still has lots of potential, as the following examples reveal:

- There remains considerable potential for efficiency in IT systems themselves, and in the production and distribution of power. These hold out the promise of new business opportunities in the IT industry just as they do in the traditional manufacturing industry.
- The political decision in favor of renewable energy in Germany and the public debate it caused about the distribution of power and the security of power supplies in general has created a new field of business in Germany's IT production sector. Future data centers are making the switch from being pure power consumers to producers, feeding heat and power into their local grids. This can take many commercial forms, from partnerships with local utilities and the construction of CHP plants or local heating networks to the establishment of entire new business units. Any surplus wind or solar power that is not needed for the primary purpose of charging the uninterruptible power supply battery banks can then be sold. In response to these trends, T-Systems began to give sustainability a new presence by introducing innovative technologies in its Munich data center in 2007. This included the first fuel cell integrated into

data center operations. A high-temperature biogas fuel cell (MCFC, Molten-Carbonate-Fuel-Cell) made by MTU CFC Solutions delivers 250 kW in power. The heat given off is transformed into cool air for the data center by means of a two-step absorption refrigeration system. The technology allows one server unit (approx. 250 m^2) to become autonomous and CO_2-neutral at an exceptional 90 % efficiency. After this dimension of sustainable energy production had been explored, the company launched the DC2020 project at Munich in cooperation with Intel. The new approaches are maintained and monitored with empirical precision to understand how energy efficiency can be improved on the user side of the data center. This completes the circle from energy production to energy consumption—the data center system seen in its entirety.

17.2 DC2020: Results from T-Systems' Labs

Server and storage capacities are growing at exponential rates. New networking and communication models call for ever more processing power. This trend shows no signs of abating (cf. Lange et al. 2011). Apart from the direct power consumption of the IT components, data centers need to consider other factors, such as the power needed for air conditioning, cooling, lighting, facility security and so on. One important lever for the energy consumption of data centers (and, by extension, their CO_2 emissions) lies in energy efficiency, with optimized hardware and optimized infrastructure. Infrastructural energy efficiency is measured with the PUE score (Power Usage Effectiveness) as an important efficiency indicator (cf. The Green Grid 2007). The PUE score determines the relationship of total energy consumption to the energy consumed by the actual IT components alone. It represents power consumed by additional devices that are needed to operate the facilities. The greater the PUE score, the more energy is not used for running the IT hardware itself, but for keeping the data center cool and operational. Current PUE scores tend to fall around the 2.0 mark. However, comparing different centers' scores is not a trivial task, since interpretations differ concerning the right measuring points and periods, and the components that are considered part of overall power consumption. A PUE calculation should include all power consumers that are part of data center operations. The final score should be an average, calculated over a defined, longer period of time (a year). Even then, the PUE score alone does not say much about the energy efficiency of the data center, as improving the energy efficiency of IT equipment would necessarily have a negative impact on the entire facility's PUE performance. This means that total power consumption should never be ignored.

The purpose of the "DC2020 — Datacenter2020" project was to conduct systematic research into which levers there are on the side of air conditioning in particular to optimize the energy efficiency of entire data centers. The results of the project can be explained in a few words (cf. DC2020 2009–2011; Patterson et al. 2011): Basically, there has to be a strict separation between cool and hot air (intake and exhaust air) in the IT facilities. This can be done by sealing off the raised floors completely and adding enclosures, combined with intelligent air flow regulation that keeps the amount of surplus air on the intake side as low as the system allows. From an energy consumption point of view, it does not matter whether the cold or hot air ducts are enclosed. What is important, however, is achieving the biggest possible spread between both air temperatures of more than 12 K. This allows the heat exchangers to operate at maximum efficiency. When the number of servers and other components in the racks is then increased for even higher energy density, the exhaust air will automatically become hotter. Coordinating the interplay of IT and data center infrastructure in this sense promises major savings. The knack lies in finding the right level of utilization. Maintaining CPU operations at significantly above 60 % capacity helps achieve the required exhaust temperature. Taking this a step further and raising the intake temperature from the current approx. 71–80 °F (following ASHRAE's recommendations, cf. ASHRAE 2008) can lead to a total reduction of 25–30 % in energy consumption and CO_2 emissions. Data centers can do so by introducing the new concepts outlined here, such as the use of free cooling without artificial refrigeration as long as the outside environment is colder than the IT facilities. The chosen temperature in the facilities therefore determines the period of time during which free cooling is possible: The higher that temperature, the longer the facilities can use power-efficient free cooling. With other technology such as adiabatic cooling adding to this, data centers in locations like Munich have to rely on forced refrigeration for less than 100 h/year—meaning immense savings. A truly future-proof data center design should ask itself whether conventional refrigeration systems actually need to be included or whether an alternative, zero-CO_2 cooling concept like ground or surface water cooling could be introduced. Such questions should be asked before settling on a location, since the right environmental conditions are not available everywhere.

17.3 A Look Ahead: Blueprint DC2020

How will the data centers of the future be run? What needs to be done to achieve real sustainability and green IT? Energy efficiency demands an annual average PUE score of 1.3 or better, considering all devices that consume power. Achieving this means planning for energy efficiency from the very beginning, considering in particular the consumption of natural resources and the new insights gained from the DC2020 project. An intake temperature of 80 °F and free cooling operations for over 90 % of the year should be considered the basic standards for modern data centers. The higher mean temperature and the acceptance of a broader range are excellent conditions for using the waste heat produced by the data center to heat neighboring buildings, be they office blocks or swimming pools. Nor should the design of such data centers be bound to overly rigid plans, but should be able to respond flexibly to changing circumstances. If one considers the fact that modern IT hardware is able to withstand an intake temperature of up to 104 °F or power of up to 5 kW exerted on an object the size of a sugar cube, designs and cooling facilities can become far more flexible, responding to the specific needs of each project.

Other liquid cooling systems (not necessarily relying on water) for direct CPU cooling can be considered in the design of the data center architecture. The new modular, flexible technologies allow the designs to cover both high-density and low-density applications, e.g. for archive or tape applications. In the end, different infrastructure requirements and solutions can co-exist under one roof.

Data centers are increasingly becoming the lynchpins of the modern information society. This makes their availability paramount. So-called twin-core centers with redundant, mirrored data mean that IT hardware crashes can occur virtually without any noticeable effects. Data remains highly available on a 24/7 basis. In order to not lose sight of the costs of this level of availability, more emphasis needs to be placed on modularity and flexibility. All designs, from grid connection to uninterruptible power supplies, air conditioning, or the layout and use of data center space, need to anticipate all possible modifiable components. Basic supply systems and central components need to be laid out to guarantee this level of flexibility from the beginning without any need for major reconstruction at a later date. Preemptive planning and flexibility, in particular, means including different cooling methods (direct CPU cooling) and different energy supply methods (DC power for IT components to avoid wasteful power conversion) in the very first plans.

These design paradigms are held together by intelligent and automated power management, which acts as a central coordinator and finds the optimum, energy-efficient spot for all data center components depending on the given (energy consumption) state of the system. Intelligent Data Center Infrastructure Management (DCIM) needs to be designed in such a way that energy demand and consumption are balanced in the most efficient way possible. This DCIM integrates all levels from the facility utilities down to CPUs and memory. Such processes make it possible to maintain intelligent load management even across multiple locations.

17.4 T-Systems' New Magdeburg Data Center

Many of the new ideas and standards are currently being put into practice in a new data center complex in the town of Biere (near Magdeburg, Germany), with 150,000 m^2 of floor space being readied for operations in 2014. In particular, the twin-core concept is being implemented by linking up with the existing data processing facilities at Magdeburg to achieve a new level of flexibility and modularity.

The plans are to construct a section of 5,400 m^2 of total IT floor space in a first phase, expanding to to a total of 34,200 m^2 after the final construction phase has been completed. All expansion phases are virtually identical copies of the first phase. The new data center has been designed with an outspoken commitment to energy efficiency. It is expected to need approx. 27 % less power than conventional facilities. The predicted PUE score lies between 1.2 and 1.3.

The design of the data center has been chosen specifically with the requirements of cloud computing in mind. This is reflected in the physical layout of the facilities and arrangement of the production equipment (servers). The twin-core concept means powerful network connections and infrastructure to allow fast and reliable access to the data and applications for cloud computing. The facilities will connect to the Germany-wide Telekom gigabit backbone net with fully redundant fiber optic systems. There is another fully redundant connection system linking the two data centers in Magdeburg, meaning that the entire twin-core center will have quadruple redundancy for its connection with the Telekom backbone—promising a new dimension of availability for cloud services.

References

Aachener Stiftung Kathy Beys: Lexikon der Nachhaltigkeit. Retrieved December 14, 2012, from http://www.nachhaltigkeit.info/artikel/erste_verwendung_durch_die_vereinten_nationen_1728.htm

ASHRAE. (2008). *White paper: Environmental guidelines for datacom equipment*. Atlanta, GA: The American Society of Heating, Refrigerating and Air-Conditioning Engineers (ASHRAE).

Bassen, A. (2011). DNK–Deutscher Nachhaltigkeitskodex des Rates für Nachhaltige Entwicklung.

Cook, G., Van Horn, J., & Greenpeace International. (2011). How dirty is your data?

DC2020. (2009–2011). *Whitepaper DC2020 No. 1–3*. T-Systems International GmbH und Intel GmbH. Retrieved from http://www.datacenter2020.de

Eberhard-Harribey, L. (2006). Corporate social responsibility as a new paradigm in the European policy: how CSR comes to legitimate the European regulation process. *Corporate Governance, 6*(4), 358–368.

Lange, C., Kosiankowski, D., Weidmann, R., and Gladisch, A. (2011). Energy consumption of telecommunication networks and related improvement options. *IEEE Journal of Selected Topics in Quantum Electronics, 17*(2), 285.

Rat für Nachhaltige Entwicklung. (2012). Der Deutsche Nachhaltigkeitskodex (DNK).

Patterson, M. K., Weidmann, R., Leberecht, M., Mair, M., and Libby, R. M. (2011). An investigation into cooling system control strategies for data center airflow containment architectures. *Proceedings of the ASME 2011 Pacific Rim Technical Conference & Exposition on Packaging and Integration of Electronic and Photonic Systems*, InterPACK2011, July 6–8, 2011, Portland, OR.

Spindler, E. A. (2012). Geschichte der Nachhaltigkeit – Vom Werden und Wirken eines beliebten Begriffes.

The Green Grid. (2007). *WP#6-The green grid data center power efficiency metrics: PUE and DCiE*. Retrieved from http://www.thegreengrid.org/Global/Content/white-papers/The-Green-Grid-Data-Center-Power-Efficiency-Metrics_PUE-and-DCiE

von Carlowitz, H. C. (1713). Sylvicultura Oeconomica.

Zisler, S., & Vattenfall Europe Hamburg AG. (2007). European Energy Certificate System – Herkunftsnachweis für Grünstrom.

Sourcing Strategies 18

Birgit Wahl and Carsten Glohr

When companies want to partake of the relative cost advantages in other locations, they can decide to relocate or to use suitable sourcing strategies and models.

These models establish the foundations on which service providers and service clients cooperate. The cooperation can take the form of captive models like spin-offs, joint ventures, and mergers or non-captive models like offshoring to Asian suppliers. Additional dimensions like nearshoring vs. offshoring or single-sourcing vs. multi-sourcing add further variety to these models.

Few factors have such a strong impact on outsourcing success as the choice and definition of a fitting sourcing model. There is a wide range of possible models that differ in terms of certain criteria:

- Costs (operating costs, set-up costs, or transition costs)
- Flexibility and agility (e.g. ramp-up time and scalability)
- Controllability and strategic match
- Practical feasibility (e.g. access to resources and stability of the skill pool)
- Risks (business, transition, security, compliance, or stability risks)

A wrong choice of sourcing model can have a lasting impact, even leading to the complete failure of the entire outsourcing campaign.

We can distinguish between various basic alternatives (Fig. 18.1):

Centralized Multi-Sourcing Model:

In the case of centralized multi-sourcing, the client would work with several centralized or local partners, who are chosen and directed by the centralized service management unit. The local partners are therefore chosen by the company head office (in loose coordination with the regional units). The advantages of such multi-sourcing lie in the competition between providers, the reduced dependence

B. Wahl (✉)
T-Systems International GmbH, Fasanenweg 5, 70771 Leinfelden-Echterdingen, Germany
e-mail: Birgit.Wahl@t-systems.com

C. Glohr
Detecon International GmbH, Sternengasse 14–16, 50676 Cologne, Germany
e-mail: Carsten.Glohr@detecon.com

F. Abolhassan (ed.), *The Road to a Modern IT Factory*, Management for Professionals, DOI 10.1007/978-3-642-40219-7_18, © Springer-Verlag Berlin Heidelberg 2014

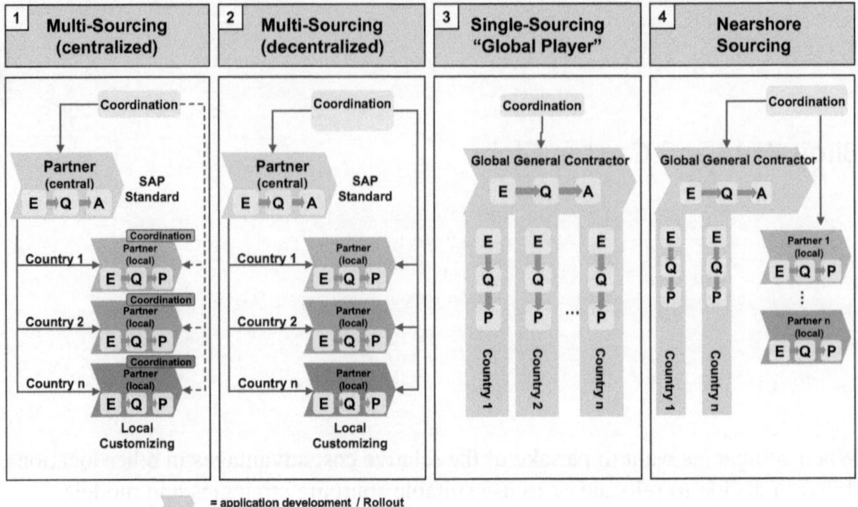

Fig. 18.1 Models with outside participation, i.e. non-captive models (cf. Detecon 2010, 2011)

on single providers, and the customer focus that this brings. In single-sourcing, with its strong reliance on single partners, this focus can too often be lost along the way.

Decentralized Multi-Sourcing Model:

In decentralized multi-sourcing, a regional unit would pick the local partner itself, with centralized partner management only overseeing consulting services and best practices. This can make the approach more flexible and more easily accepted, but a centralized approach to managing the sourcing partners allows more professionalization and greater overall transparency about the outsourced business, which is essential for economies of scale. However, it often also means more complex coordination and communication.

Single-Sourcing Model:

In single-sourcing, the client would look for a large, global provider to act as its strategic partner, which often refers to commissioning one of the big players of the industry as general contractor for the delivery of the required services. The provider is often headquartered in the developed economies, but has a broad global reach that covers the client's locations. Apart from that global reach, the provider would often have cheap near- or offshore capacities to offer. Whenever there are gaps in the partner's capacities, the partner will act as the general contractor and commission other suppliers in the partner's own network without the client generally being aware of this. The strategic partner takes over all coordination of the local agents. The main advantages of the model are:

- Fast "time-to-target" execution.
- Massive headcount capacities.
- The provider's reputation.
- Minimal internal management efforts when the partner acts as general contractor.

At the same time, the client has fewer opportunities to exert an influence. This is made worse when the client is smaller in relation to the provider and is thus not given the recognition the former deserves. This lack of equality can soon lead to a termination of the partnership.

Infrastructure Sourcing:

In infrastructure sourcing, the model has the greatest chance of achieving economies of scale or consolidation. A pure near-/offshore specialist here becomes a strategic partner. Although such partners still tend to differ from global full-service providers, they often hail from the emerging markets and can therefore offer significant cost advantages. However, these advantages are often associated with massive linguistic or cultural differences between providers and clients.

The management of near and offshoring as part of a global single-sourcing model will now be discussed in more detail.

18.1 Near- and Offshore

Defining the near- and offshore lies in the eye of the beholder. From a European point of view, nearshoring works with the cheap labor reserves of Central and Eastern Europe, not forgetting Turkey. By contrast, offshoring uses locations in Asia, usually India or China.

From the point of view of the American market, Mexico and Brazil used to be the main nearshore locations. Chile is working hard to catch up with them. At the same time, top Indian IT companies have made a splash in the U.S. markets, as no language barrier has to be considered. However, no real offshore delivery model is possible here without a major onsite component, as the time difference makes direct cooperation impossible.

The Asian markets use only nearshore concepts, as the language, cost, and time zone factors all apply. However, the region is also very sensitive where prices are concerned and not all countries in Asia continue to offer real competitiveness.

The terms "onshore" and "onsite" also need to be understood in this respect. Onshore refers to services that are provided onsite by people from near- or offshore locations. Onsite services are also provided there, but using local labor resources.

In the recent past, onshoring concepts have come up in consulting and project management work. People are trained in nearshore locations and then used onsite at the client in high-wage countries (fly-in). Wage costs are a great bargaining counter that even balances out the additional travel expenses.

Another visible trend is the growth of nearshoring in the delivery model. The cultural fit, language, and time zone factors come into effect here as they offer the opportunity for less complexity in integration and cooperation. In many cases, too few standardizable services can be provided offshore without losing efficiency.

In data center operations, the proportion of offshoring is still far lower than in application development or operations, which is certainly also due to the fact that not all IT service providers offer data center capacities (as capital-intensive services).

18.2 Delivery Models

The value chain of a service is broken down into its constituent elements, which are allocated to a delivery model:

- Onsite/Onshore
- Nearshore
- Offshore

The following criteria are relevant:

- Proximity to the customer, integration, and the need for coordination (governance models for clients and providers)
- Susceptibility to standardization
- Costs
- Quality

For standardization purposes, every service needs to be broken down, described in detail, and allocated to a delivery model. The supply chain needs to have as few transitions as possible, typically keeping to no more than two to four such points. In general, near- and offshore capacities should lie around 60–80 %.

When the offer is prepared, the services stated in the service catalog need to be reconciled with the client's requirements. The aim should be to keep the standard delivery model as far as possible, not least to maintain nearshore and offshore capacities.

Important restrictions on the side of the client include data protection and data security requirements, the languages needed for interacting with the client, and the various time zones where business takes place. Using translation tools for client communication has proven to be a poor choice. Languages, time zones, and cultural fit are becoming increasingly relevant factors in the selection process. All top offshore providers use the entire range of onsite, nearshore, and offshore capacities in their delivery models.

Central and Eastern Europe is a favorite destination not only of European IT companies, but also of the large players in the global offshoring industry.

In the above-mentioned model, a single location is proposed. When combining different services into one offer, multiple locations are linked up. Each additional location makes coordination more complex and thus increases the costs of the model. If more than seven or eight locations are used in a single model, these costs for communication and coordinate grow exponentially. Section 18.5, "Defragmentation", shows how the delivery model can be balanced to account for both the point of view of the client and the service itself.

18.3 Global Delivery Networks Moving from 1:1 to n:m

The early history of near- and offshoring was characterized by 1:1 relationships. One onsite location worked with one near- or offshore counterpart.

This binary relationship was soon replaced by a combination of different near- and offshore models in a complex sourcing strategy. This balances the advantages and disadvantages of "pure" near- or offshore models, although it means more interfaces in the supply chain. It needs a high degree of standardization of processes, tools, and management methods to function.

This does not promote aspects of lean production or automation that are driven by local know-how or optimization. As a result, locations link up globally and form a n:m delivery model. Modern communication methods, global networking, and shared standards make this possible—expanding knowledge-based approaches to networked organizations with modern forms of communication like those used in social networks (Webex, chats, communicator, tele-presence,. . .). The amount and speed of information and knowledge make it important to move from database-driven knowledge sharing to more interactive forms.

Also needed are dedicated structures for coordinating, planning, and executing work—virtual forms of organization, such as centers of excellence and communities, grow up in response.

The n:m network also needs a shared notion of quality, behavior (sense of urgency), and escalation mechanisms for routine and special cases. At the frontlines facing the client, the global network should not really be noticeable.

An exchange program is used to get to work on the shared cultural preconceptions. People are moved at all levels in the global network. Exchange programs of this nature need clear targets, as they are not meant as pure incentives for employees, but as a way to coordinate the interfaces between locations and achieve real efficiencies. It will then be just as natural for locations in Budapest (Hungary), Cyberjaya (Malaysia), and Puebla (Mexico) to cooperate as Munich and Hamburg do. In a global n:m network, organizational management needs a two-dimensional leadership structure that responds to global and local needs alike.

18.4 Optimizing Existing Locations

Cost savings are the top driver. With this in mind, the existing locations in a sourcing alliance are subjected to regular benchmarking in terms of the following:

- Costs
- Productivity
- Utilization
- Quality
- Skills.

New locations are considered and an expansion of the established network is tested—which can also mean the downsizing or closure of existing locations.

This does not always have to mean going into new countries, but also choosing cheaper regions in existing countries. The global near- and offshore network will change every year as a result. The example of CEE shows this very well. Many IT companies started operations in the capitals of countries like the Czech Republic, Slovakia, Hungary, or Romania. Nowadays, these capitals are only home to the main offices, whereas production has moved to other regions—in Romania from Bucharest to Iaşi or from Prague to Brno in the Czech Republic.

Six to nine months would pass between the analysis and the start of production. A prerequisite for success is the ability to work in a networked, virtual set-up.

Existing locations need to be prepared to achieve a 10–16 % increase in efficiency every year. On top of other traditional measures, this can be achieved with the following approaches:

- Reducing the number of skill classes per service by means of standardization and automation.
- Reducing the training and onboarding costs in a learning organization.
- Bundling services ("Size matters"), cf. Chap. 18.5 below.

18.5 Optimizing Services with Defragmentation Strategies

Defragmenting services and clients happens in response to organic growth in new or existing near- and offshore locations or the inclusion of new personnel in outsourcing.

Defragmenting is a cyclical process aimed at optimizing the volume for each service or reducing the number of delivery units needed for a client. It operates via the following key factors:

- Economies of scale achieved by bundling volumes
- Minimizing interfaces by reducing the number of locations

The apparent contradiction between high volumes per location and as few locations as possible per client commission cannot be resolved immediately. The defragmenting methods should be used repetitively, since the right volume and sweet spot will change as a result of automation and standardization.

Approach:

- True-Up (analytical phase)
- See & Prove (quick wins and assessment for the future allocation and targets for "Size Matters")
- Way Forward (implementing and modifying the sourcing matrix to prepare for future ventures)

Reallocating services to new locations also means clear targets for efficiency improvements.

18.6 Transition and Transformation to the Near-/Offshore

For the client, the successful transition is an important step. The transformation process is, however, just as important for reaching the commercial targets.

Transitioning services to the near- or offshore brings immediate savings in people-driven services. After the situation has stabilized, the actual transformation process begins, which is either a regular continuous improvement process (standardization, automation, and lean management) or designed specifically for the client in question.

When multiple clients overlap for a single service, continuous improvement is usually chosen as the lever. Corresponding efficiency programs:

- Cost savings
- Productivity increases "more with less"

The leverage of prior year effects aims at values of 7–14 %, depending on maturity and volume growth. Goals specifying which effects are to be achieved via which levers and clear targets for monthly progress are important for this to succeed. The efficiency targets need to be cascaded down through all areas.

People-driven business models need to aim at substantial increases in targets. The purpose is an actual productivity increase: that is, every member of staff has to produce more output in a given period of time. Their productivity is therefore measured by logical units and process steps:

- How many logical units, such as storage, servers, SAP systems, Exchange users, or database systems per month are handled by each member of staff?
- How many incident/problem tickets per month are handled by each member of staff?

As in all monitoring of this type, it is essential that the data is recorded in full for every employee to produce a meaningful result at the end of the month. Potential targets for optimization can be found by benchmarking the various locations and links in the value chain.

18.7 Demand and Resource Management

Near-/offshore locations are expected to maintain high utilization rates. This makes reliable capacity plans essential. Such capacity planning has the following modules:

- Annual demand planning
- Rolling 6-monthly forecasts

1. Annual demand planning

   Demand planning uses volume planning in terms of the current business volume and any transitions and efficiency improvements. These plans are broken down to the level of services and relevant skill classes in the 6-monthly forecast and translated into resource planning.

   The following adjustments in the workforce are then introduced into integrated resource planning by production and HR:

   - Efficiency improvements
   - Transition to new services
   - Defragmenting
   - Fluctuation
   - Parental leave (not to be underestimated in younger organizations)

   This results in a need for more recruitment, skill shift programs, and the transfer of capacities.

2. Rolling 6-monthly forecasts
   The forecast is coordinated on a monthly basis between the near- and offshore locations and the commissioning business units. It is important to aim for almost 95 % precision to be able to increase utilization to 90 %. This is possible when controlling, management, and lateral functions are kept very lean. The overhead should be less than 5 %.

   A further 5 % is needed to cover flexibility, short-term project planning and fluctuation in volumes, skill shift programs, and the transfer of resources.

   The necessary skill shifts and transfer of resources between the units is controlled via a capacity and skills management environment.

   Efficiency improvements of 7–14 %, depending on the service cluster, need to be approached systematically in the resource transfer. A simple increase in volume cannot compensate for this. The people released as a result of efficiency drives should be retrained and allocated to new services.

   This results in utilization measurements of over 90 % as the target for the billable units.

   The skill shift also happens across services, since the service cluster will see a transition to higher-value skills, which in turn makes services more expensive. Demand is managed via regular planning and on-going forecasts as discussed in Chap. 19.

Reference

Detecon. (2010, 2011). *Schematisches Szenario aus verschiedenen Detecon Projekten zum Thema Sourcingstrategie*, Projektleiter C. Glohr.

Creating Value with Make-or-Buy Decisions 19

Carsten Glohr and Henryk Biesiada

There are now few larger companies who have not outsourced significant parts of their IT. This makes questions about which IT services should be produced internally and which should be bought from the outside very important. When making this decision, many companies rely on rather vague statements, such as looking at what is part of their core competencies and what is not. However, a good "make-or-buy" decision should not be based on such "superficial" competency considerations. Rather, it deserves a sound basis of concrete criteria.

19.1 The Right Level of Vertical Integration

The first step for successful outsourcing is taken very early on—when deciding the right degree of value contribution. The question here concerns the objects (e.g. services, processes, services, or organizational units) that are suitable for outsourcing. For that purpose, it helps to package the different value-adding elements. In practice, service-oriented packages have proven most suitable (cf. Fig. 19.1).

The IT service modules should be clearly delineated from each other and have as few interdependencies between them as possible to avoid any potential friction at the interfaces. The services earmarked for outsourcing should have clearly measurable quality indicators (SLAs) and reference frameworks (for billing models) to keep the outsourced IT services manageable.

A service is suitable for outsourcing if this action would offer great potential (cost reductions, quality improvements, or greater flexibility) with moderate risk and sound feasibility (Fig. 19.2).

C. Glohr (✉)
Detecon International GmbH, Sternengasse 14–16, 50676 Cologne, Germany
e-mail: Carsten.Glohr@detecon.com

H. Biesiada
T-Systems International GmbH, Mecklenburgring 25, 66121 Saarbrücken, Germany
e-mail: Henryk.Biesiada@t-systems.com

F. Abolhassan (ed.), *The Road to a Modern IT Factory*, Management for Professionals,
DOI 10.1007/978-3-642-40219-7_19,

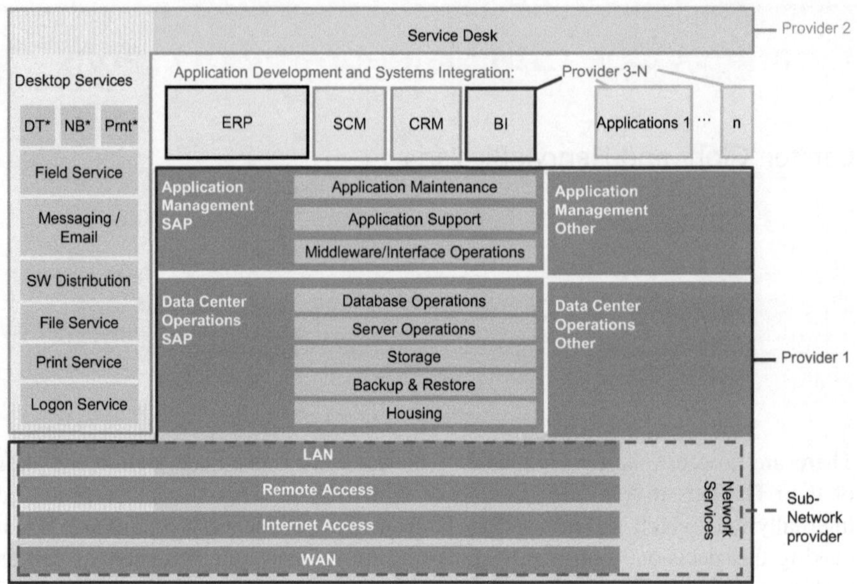

Fig. 19.1 Common service packages in a multi-sourcing scenario (cf. Detecon and Glohr 2012)

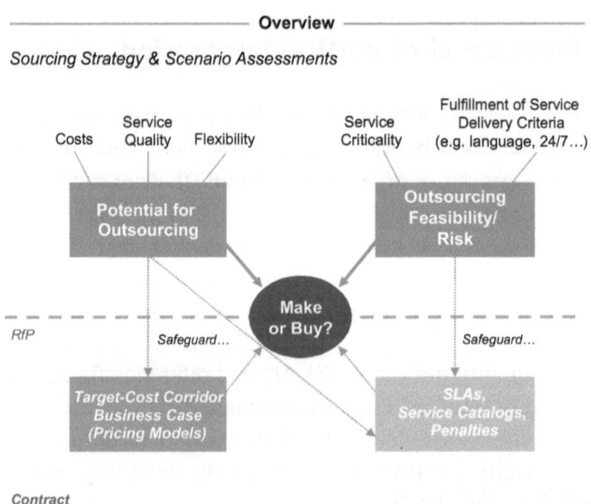

Fig. 19.2 Criteria for defining the suitable level of vertical integration as part of the sourcing strategy (cf. Detecon and Glohr 2012)

Oftentimes, companies ignore the significance of this early decision. Many failed outsourcing initiatives are due to a poor choice of provider, but also to rash, subjective decisions and the lack of a sound degree of vertical integration. Mistakes made at this early stage are hard to remedy later on in the outsourcing process. This means that the right packaging and demarcation of candidates for outsourcing demands absolute professionalism and experience.

The standard approach for selecting suitable sourcing candidates is outlined here in the form as used and developed further in many projects. The result is appropriate vertical integration and a sensible packaging of the service modules. They can be sourced on a selective basis, using multiple providers as part of a multi-sourcing model.

19.2 Outsourcing Feasibility and Risks

The main pillar of the standard approach is a multi-level decision-making process. It begins by assessing the risk/criticality and the ability to outsource the service modules in question. These considerations then feed into the aggregate factor "feasibility" (cf. Fig. 19.3).

The factor of risk/criticality establishes how critical the application or service is for the company. To this end, the analysis considers which business processes are supported by the application or service, which consequences a disruption might have, and how many users would not be able to work if the service were lost. A check of the service's aptitude for outsourcing rates whether the prerequisites for outsourcing are in place. These include the presence of complete documentation, the modularity and ability to package the application, the availability of the necessary know-how, and the ability to influence possible compliance considerations. If the competencies are limited in the organization (e.g. a lack of COBOL programmers), but still easily sourced in the market, the outsourcing would appear possible. The check should also test whether the remaining parts of the organization are prepared for the impact of the outsourcing. One important aspect in this respect is the extent to which the company uses formal processes (e.g. for testing, deployment, application development, etc.) and whether these can be adapted for sharing the work with the outside provider.

Both checks are then brought together for the umbrella factor "feasibility". The aggregate results are seen individually for each service module and can be visualized in a dedicated portfolio.

The outsourcing of application services in particular holds many risks (but often also great potential) and is often viewed very controversially in the market. By contrast, the more replaceable infrastructure services (computing services, desktop services, storage, network services) also benefit from a case-by-case assessment for each application. This can mean checking 50 or more applications separately.

19.3 The Potential of Outsourcing

The decision also considers the potential optimization in the service modules, in terms of service quality and costs. The results are aggregated in the overall criterion "outsourcing potential" (Fig. 19.4).

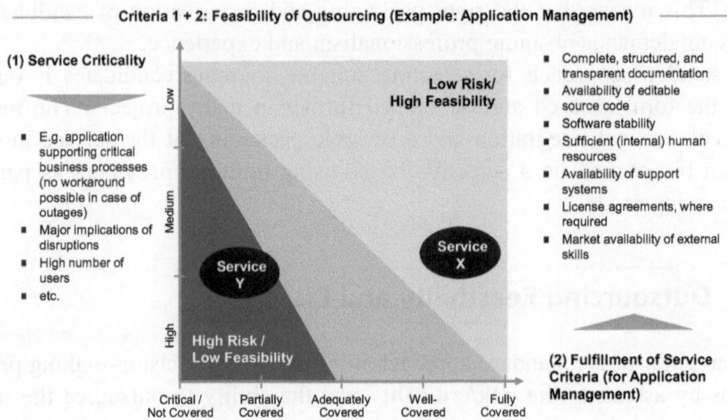

Fig. 19.3 Sample criteria for the feasibility of outsourcing—application services (cf. Detecon and Glohr 2012)

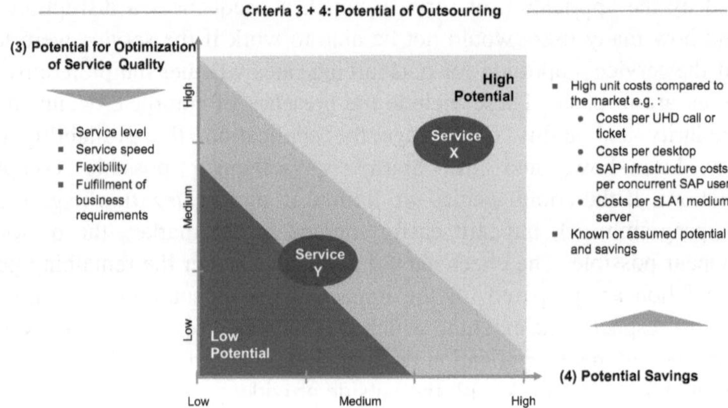

Fig. 19.4 Criteria for the potential of an outsourcing decision (cf. Detecon and Glohr 2012)

The top-line criterion "potential" is calculated by analyzing and assessing important optimization points in terms of the cost and quality of service.

Potential on the side of service quality can often be found in smaller, but globally active businesses who do not have the means to guarantee 24/7 SLAs, but can buy this ability in the markets.

Potential for cost optimization can (a) be estimated roughly or (b) calculated precisely with detailed unit cost benchmarking. Real benchmarking can be labor-intensive, but both approaches have their justification. More precision at the start offers greater certainty at later stages and allows a more precise quantification of the potential in the sense of its profitability. Comparing market prices with cost forecast allows a calculation of the net present value (NPV) or return on investment (ROI) for the decision. If the potential is only assessed by rule of thumb, not all is lost.

In that case, the effort will, however, be higher in later tendering processes. The danger here is that the hoped-for savings are not actually reflected in the bids and that all efforts go to waste as a result.

The assessment can also consider side-effects, such as the transition of fixed to variable costs etc.

19.4 Defining the Level of Manufacturing Penetration

The right degree of manufacturing penetration is then defined by bringing together the top-line factors "feasibility" and "potential" for each service module. The results of this can be visualized in a consolidated portfolio, giving different weighting to the dimensions to match the given priorities.

Services that offer high feasibility and high potential (in the zone "Go" of Fig. 19.5) are then put to tender in the next phase. Services with medium risks and potential (zone "Check") can be taken to the market as a separate test balloon and eventually outsourced if the bidders offer good terms. The decision whether or not to outsource the service remains open. Services with low potential and high risks (zone "No-Go") stay in-house.

The approach allows a sound, professional, and transparent decision to be made, which creates an important basis for a successful outsourcing strategy.

This methodology concerns the review and adjustment of the right vertical integration in an existing IT service portfolio. A special case is a make-or-buy decision for prospective IT portfolios. This can be required when a company intends to go international or when a service provider wants to build up partner structures to serve new clients. The decision can be made to "go it alone" or already establish external and internal partner structures for future business relationships.

It often becomes necessary to add a regional dimension to the packaging of services and to look at the suitability of the available supplier models, since the nature of offshore specialists, global players, vendors, integrators, technology specialists, or local providers can differ considerably. A look at the strategies of potential future partners is important to establish a partnership between equals. The level of vertical integration and a suitable partnership model is chosen for each service and region. We will look at two examples for external and internal partnering.

19.5 International Network Services: An Example of External Partnering

In international network services, providers have long relied on working with external service providers. This model is an interesting "make-or-buy" case for telecommunications companies, since their history often gives them a strong position in one region, but also forces them to make massive investment to access the markets in other regions.

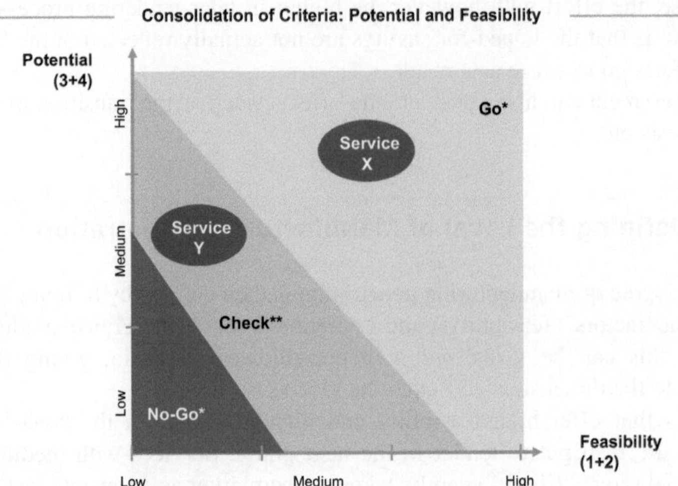

Fig. 19.5 Consolidated portfolio for selective make-or-buy decisions (cf. Detecon and Glohr 2012)

In the internal market for network services, prices above the market average can mean commercial losses as a result of the excessive overall costs. Recovering competitiveness means achieving a real reduction in costs and prices, while keeping or improving quality.

In the telecommunications business in particular, the complete outsourcing of operations is often an obvious option, but it does not have to be the right option. A mix of short-term intervention (e.g. renegotiating existing contracts, moving to a cheaper access provider) and medium-term realignment as a "service integrator" who buys service and infrastructure capacities from local partners can have a lasting impact on the cost structure.

Quality can thus be kept at a high level, and the company can gain or recover a competitive edge.

Fundamental, long-term improvement potential can be found in optimizing network design, in reducing the costs of network access, in establishing consistent checks for spending on external suppliers ("Third-Party Spend Management"), and in creating more appealing market offerings with a broader service portfolio. For instance, the normal portfolio can now include value-added network services—using the "buy" mode, i.e. in cooperation with partners.

The successful execution of this concept would create substantial savings and add attractive new items to the company's portfolio.

19.6 Optimizing ICT Services: An Example of Internal Partnering

Internal partnering can be another way to reduce costs and stay competitive. This refers to the bundling of units in larger, global ICT organizations that often provide complementary portfolios for complementary market segments.

As a sourcing option, internal partnering can activate substantial synergies and is often a suitable choice in terms of the decision described in Sect. 19.1, as it helps reduce costs, improve quality, and gain flexibility with moderate risk and relatively good feasibility.

The ideal expansion of portfolios and customer groups can be achieved in internal partnering, which allows the company to offer a full range of services under one coherent umbrella brand. A typical situation is that one unit in the IT service organization would offer a broad sweep of IT services for a specific customer segment, while another unit produces specialist communications services for a complementary customer group. Putting these units under one roof lets them form a unified market presence and offer integrated ICT services. Frequently, there is also unhelpful and unconstructive competition between the units that can be overcome with such internal strategic partnerships.

Typical challenges in such units lie in the pressure on prices in services, the unhelpful pricing structure, gaps in the portfolio, or the constant need for cost optimization that can only be achieved by growth. Growing into an ICT full-service provider with a higher-value portfolio needs the harmonization of its units. The advantages of internal strategic partnerships are the win-win outcomes that they offer for all people involved. They allow the company to engage with the market as consolidated full-service providers. In turn, they enable the company to reduce costs by means of growth and efficiency improvements. Potential utilization risks in the individual units with specialist portfolios are compensated for by the bundling of both business lines and strengths. In the ICT industry in particular, this also creates an opportunity for holistic certification know-how—another boost to the company's market presence.

This is also a future-proof solution for employees, since it opens up new prospects for the development of their skills.

The internal clustering of complementary units creates viable units with a consolidated, market-oriented portfolio and considerable punch.

Reference

Detecon, & Glohr, C. (2012). Presentation "IT Outsourcing Advisory" (The method was developed and used in several consultancy projects at Detecon).

Optimizing Procurement Portfolios and Supplier Management

20

Peter Schnitzenbaumer and Thomas Wind

20.1 Suppliers Becoming Part of the Value Chain

Customers expect IT service providers to deliver standardized and cost-efficient solutions, at the same time tailored to their unique needs and made to exceptional quality standards. Modern IT providers, caught up in global competition, are concentrating more and more on their core competencies in response. This takes some depth out of their business and, in turn, makes them part of a longer, often global value chain. They are integrating many other products and services in the package delivered to their clients, which they buy from outside suppliers further down that chain. Their customers' expectations can therefore only be fulfilled if they stay on top of quality and costs from end to end along this entire supply chain. Professional supplier management has therefore become an important tool for optimizing service and product quality at IT service organizations. Used effectively, it becomes an excellent way to become more innovative as a business.

20.2 Challenges in Supplier Management

When a car's brakes malfunction, the driver would not blame the producer of the brakes themselves, but the maker of the car behind whose wheel the driver is sitting. Apart from the costs for necessary recalls, such incidents can have a major impact on the producer's brand image and lead customers to take their business elsewhere.

P. Schnitzenbaumer (✉)
T-Systems International GmbH, Alfred-Herrhausen-Allee 7, 65760 Eschborn, Germany
e-mail: Peter.Schnitzenbaumer@t-systems.com

T. Wind
T-Systems International GmbH, Mecklenburgring 25, 66121 Saarbrücken, Germany
e-mail: Thomas.Wind@t-systems.com

F. Abolhassan (ed.), *The Road to a Modern IT Factory*, Management for Professionals, DOI 10.1007/978-3-642-40219-7_20, © Springer-Verlag Berlin Heidelberg 2014

The situation is the same in industrial IT. When a router stops working, users will not complain to the hardware maker, but to the IT service provider. Even apparently minor faults can have immense repercussions in the IT industry, as the case of a major European bank losing all IT for several days has shown recently.

In "mature" industries—such as the automotive industry—outside parts and services account for three quarters or more of the final product. In IT, there is still far more vertical integration, but the direction is clear in the evolution of modern industrial IT production. An IT service provider working for large international clients would therefore choose a strategy of focusing on core competencies and outsourcing other parts of its value chain to other suppliers. This will automatically lead to more relevance for supplier management aligned with the goals of the business, going beyond simple procurement to cover the systematic management and handling of all suppliers of the IT service organization with due consideration for technological/functional, qualitative, commercial, and legal factors over the entire life of their business relationships.

This new outlook brings about many new challenges for supplier management. Put simply, we can distinguish between external challenges relating to the right supplier constellation and internal challenges resulting from the corporate structure.

On the external side, the degree of dependence on individual suppliers is one such challenge, as it can mean that the IT service organization is heavily dependent on often one-sided supply or delivery relationships with sub-optimal terms and conditions. Another source for tension can lie in the fact that one's suppliers might become direct competitors or the suppliers of competitors in other constellations.

Working with many different suppliers—be it a group that has grown over time or a deliberate selection—can increase the coordination efforts for selecting, managing, and looking after the chosen suppliers. Apart from these higher handling costs, this multi-source approach also makes bundling the procurement activities harder—if it is possible at all—and can slow down standardization and automation.

On the inside, many organizations face the problem of lacking a clear sense of the scope, purpose, and objects of supplier management and that there is often no appropriate organizational place for it with the right interfaces. Few companies have established procurement as a dedicated unit with effective integration in the other corporate processes (plan—build—run) as part of a comprehensive sourcing strategy. When this essential procedural and functional integration with the other relevant parts of the business is missing, effective management and support structures become virtually impossible. A common cause is the absence of established and working governance models to regulate the relationships and the roles of the various areas. Missing or ambiguous functional profiles or responsibilities mean that supplier management becomes a patchwork. For it to work, it needs to go beyond "traditional" procurement functions and cover other areas, phases, and technologies. Its scope should cover all of the supply-side functions from selection and integration to collaboration and supplier reviews.

Complex IT service organizations would benefit from a matrix-like organization, with supplier management both acting as a central function and being integrated into the various production business units. Central supplier management takes over coordinating interdepartmental activities, but supplier management functions need to stay integrated in the business units, especially to stay close to actual operations and to remain in touch with the specific suppliers in the various categories. Such an organization would reconcile the different perspectives and needs of all stakeholders in the sense of "one face to the supplier".

20.3 Establishing a Lasting "Zero Outage" Culture

To achieve the Zero Outage standard that the market expects industrial IT services to uphold, supplier management plays a major role in making sure that the services delivered by all suppliers in the value chain actually meet that standard. The corporate strategy for an IT service organization therefore has to expect a zero error culture at all of its suppliers, which means consolidating all of the activities into comprehensive supplier quality programs to achieve these exacting standards in service delivery, as well as to identify and remedy all potential and actual weak spots. Suppliers need to be integrated into the global process standards to make perfection the yardstick in one's work.

Integrating suppliers in this manner demands the fundamental agreement of a shared notion of customer service and quality, as well as the tasks, objects, and approaches to reach the set targets. On the operational side, work begins immediately in the design phase by running through a detailed list of criteria, covering process harmonization in incident, problem, change or risk management (e.g. in terms of establishing 24/7 support and reporting structures or defining a support model for sustainable quality improvements). Such support models would cover both reactive and proactive services, because holistic quality management gives more preference to preemptive error avoidance than later error correction. Practice has shown that defining and introducing a governance model is the basis for successful cooperation in this respect. In addition to governance factors, a defined and fully coordinated set of KPIs would name specific quality indicators to which every supplier is held accountable, used for regular reviews and a comprehensive quality monitoring dashboard with such quality parameters as the "mean time to repair" or "problem management solution rate in time" (Fig. 20.1).

For a quality-focused harmonization of the agreed service levels, the contractual terms of suppliers should be revised and adjusted no later than the pilot phase and before actual operations begin.

Supplier certification with these criteria gives both sides in the equation a fixed quality standard to work with, a standard that both sides know needs to be maintained just as much as the technological/functional portfolio and the commercial standards to win and keep a profitable business partnership.

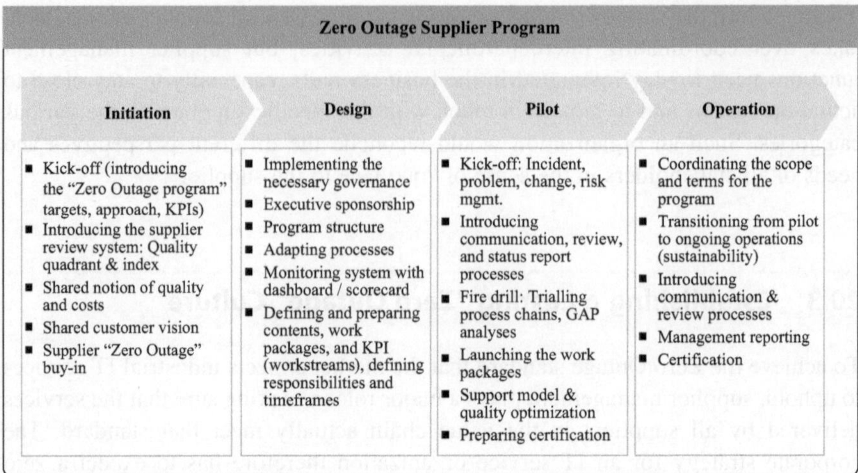

Fig. 20.1 The "Zero Outage supplier program" in brief (illustration by the authors)

20.4 "More for Less" via Consolidation and New Forms of Cooperation

Apart from the primacy of top delivery and service quality, service managers are also expected to bring down procurement costs. In a buyer's market, opportunities for savings in procurement can primarily be found by using the competition between suppliers; in turn, a seller's market means changing the nature of demand. A balanced market means finding win-win outcomes for the demand and the supply side alike. To achieve any savings, what one needs is excellent data for the procurement categories in question, as well as intelligence about current and potential suppliers, market developments, and competitive terms. With this basis in place, savings targets can be introduced that should be ambitious, but also realistic at the same time. Here in particular, supplier management needs the perfect integration of buyers and the operational side, e.g. by forming teams based on procurement categories or by individual suppliers and supplier groups. Capacity management should be included as a central process of any IT service organization. While buyers play the lead role in the actual procurement processes, central supplier management should be involved to coordinate these activities across business divisions.

Producing better quality while continuing to bring the costs down might at first seem like squaring the circle, but the apparent contradiction becomes much less daunting when one considers the wider impact of the transformation towards standardized and automated IT production. An optimized procurement portfolio is built on the general portfolio of the IT service organization, which would be moving away from vertical integration and towards the target of more than 80 %

standardization. Such degrees of standardization and off-the-peg solutions not only makes high quality an easier proposition, but also help to reduce costs in IT production. With the modular nature of the delivery components, this approach also promises the required flexibility. The individual elements should be chosen to be as non-proprietary, service-oriented, and functional as possible to match the needs of the markets and customers. Coupling resources and production modules with their platforms allows standardized offerings to be adjusted and tweaked to meet the unique requirements of clients, applying a defined set of key indicators to track product availability and capacities in combination with the delivery of support services. This continuous process in turn becomes a basis for extensive automation and optimization in the production modules, so as to allow fully standardized offerings.

For large, internationally active IT service organizations, it's common to find as many as 200 or more suppliers involved in core activities. This calls for a consolidation in the supplier landscape when trying to optimize the procurement portfolio, which should proceed with a view to the suppliers' range of services/technological fit, delivery and service quality, costs, and terms and condition. A smaller number of suppliers means less effort goes into managing them and larger orders, which means economies of scale for the remaining choice of suppliers. Larger volumes also mean lower unit costs, again feeding into better prices and terms. The ultimate vision is a consolidated set of suppliers, chosen in line with the strategic principles of industrial IT production, but also picked cleverly enough to maintain competition and avoid excessive dependence on single suppliers. Doing so needs the ability and the will to replace suppliers who do not match the defined criteria, even if—or especially if—they have been long-standing partners for large-scale orders.

20.5 The Rise of Strategic Alliances

The transformation to industrial IT production will not only change the number of suppliers and the procurement processes needed to handle them. It will affect the forms of collaboration. Standardized finished products need standardized semi-finished products from suppliers, although this refers less to individual components and more to complete packages or system components. Again, other "mature" industries are leading the way with their multi-tier supplier structures (system suppliers, sub-suppliers to system suppliers, etc.). This development will see the stronger integration of "tier 1" suppliers in IT production, beginning in particular with specifications management and solution design. The purpose of IT service organizations is to gain a product and service portfolio matched to their service portfolio and level of integration by using specially selected suppliers. This will add more procurement alternatives, which might become dedicated product variants as part of the "own brand" offerings of the organization.

The assumption has to be that strategic alliances will become more and more important for IT service organizations. In such alliances, one or more market and customer segments or R&D activities are covered with selected suppliers.

The disadvantages of withdrawing from parts of the value chain will be weighed up by engaging in a longer partnership with a provider who possesses a complementary set of competencies. As in other sectors of industry, the motives for engaging in such strategic alliances lie in the broader or new market access they offer, in the economies of scale to be had where unit costs are concerned, and in the reduction of fixed costs. Rising costs in R&D are also easier to sustain among multiple partners when one considers the ever shorter product lifecycles and the increasing risk of losses. Important criteria when picking partners for strategic alliances include their legal independence—by contrast to outright mergers—and the sharing of commercial success. Depending on the corporate strategy chosen by the IT service organization, supplier management will have to contribute to mastering the factors that are relevant in this respect, such as the focus on transparent cooperation targets, the selection of the partner, the timing of the cooperation, and the design of suitable incentive systems.

Traditional procurement partnerships between IT service organizations and their suppliers are far from a thing of the past, but they are being expanded or replaced outright with other forms of cooperation in a more and more industrialized IT sector. They will be built around each actor's core competency strategies for the various links in the IT value chain. Top managers will soon find that cross-functional supplier management of their IT organizations occupies one of the top spots of their agendas.

People Management during Transformation 21

Michael Rubas, Peter Schnitzenbaumer, and Petra Trost-Gürtner

21.1 Forces Shaping IT Production

Three forces shape the future way of working in industrial IT production: Globalization, the pressures of cost and quality, and demographics. With its clients and markets operating globally, the IT factory also needs to think globally: wherever they are in the world, IT needs to be available "on tap" and at a dependable level of quality. Clients expect not only global delivery, but also the local availability of specialists.

The burden of costs and the pressure of higher quality expectations concerning business infrastructures and operations call for answers to very basic principles, such as make-or-buy and off-/onshoring. The sweeping automation and standardization in IT production affects jobs and organizations directly, as old jobs are removed and new jobs created, calling for people with other qualifications to fill them. The foremost areas affected by this trend are production and management. Henry Ford's factories lived off their ability to produce cars in the most efficient manner possible, assembling and finishing cars in the shortest possible time. Design, fuel consumption, safety, or inter-car communication were simply not an issue. Just like the welders and mechanics on the assembly lines have been replaced by more and more robots, industrial IT production will need fewer people

M. Rubas (✉)
T-Systems International GmbH, Dachauer Str. 651, 80995 Munich, Germany
e-mail: Michael.Rubas@t-systems.com

P. Schnitzenbaumer
T-Systems International GmbH, Alfred-Herrhausen-Allee 7, 65760 Eschborn, Germany
e-mail: Peter.Schnitzenbaumer@t-systems.com

P. Trost-Gürtner
T-Systems International GmbH

F. Abolhassan (ed.), *The Road to a Modern IT Factory*, Management for Professionals, DOI 10.1007/978-3-642-40219-7_21,

in actual production and more people developing and adjusting standard products to customers' specific needs.

A third factor is demographics, with the labor force in the Western Hemisphere shrinking and the age distribution of companies changing rapidly. This situation is reinforced by the fact that Western industrialized nations are not producing enough research scientists and ICT engineers in their universities, a lack of talent that needs to be compensated for with personnel supplied from or in other countries: a new challenge for HR management.

21.2 Impact on the Organization and its People

Total Workforce Management (TWM) is a must-have for HR managers wanting to shape the transformation in their companies. With TWM, they have absolute transparency about the headcount, labor costs, and skills in their own organization and the service partners they are working with. They can use these insights to develop new scenarios that take account of the role of globalization, automation, demographic trends, or make-or-buy decisions, be it within the organization itself or at external service providers. When the scenarios are in place, they are fine-tuned for efficiency and practical feasibility, before people are retrained or recruited at home or abroad to implement them for real.

People's skills play a major role in change. According to the definition given by ISCO (International Standard Classification of Occupations), the term "skill level" refers to the complexity and scope of the tasks and responsibilities in a job. Most IT organizations distinguish between five such skill levels, beginning with simple duties in call centers, etc. on level 1 and reaching the highly complex responsibilities of project leaders in transformation projects on level 5. After near- or offshoring, this pyramid can take on a diamond shape in the global organization, with the higher echelons (skill levels 3–5) being the reserve of high-wage countries and the lower levels covered in the offshoring destinations. Automation, standardization, and make-or-buy decisions mean that there are fewer and fewer low-level activities, while new jobs are being created further up the chain in such areas as ICT architecture or product/project management. For HR managers, navigating through these upheavals and getting the company's people to come along for the journey can be one of their most intricate and sensitive tasks. They have an extensive toolbox for global production training or introducing the future mode of operations, beginning with the definition of specific criteria for the recruitment and selection of prospective employees in modern diagnostic procedures. The war for talent is calling for such innovative approaches to recruitment, as high potentials need to be recognized and retained for the company. Young talent is not only a source for the managers of tomorrow. In IT in particular, such recruits and their sophisticated and creative outlook become an invaluable source for innovation on the road to new business models.

In near- and offshore destinations in particular, companies need to engage in proactive people marketing to make themselves known as attractive employers and make onboarding easier for the new people they are looking for. Shifting and transposing jobs to new locations needs a durable organization to continue to uphold global quality standards while aiming for cost reductions of up to 80 percent. A clever choice of destination in terms of the local competition, salary levels, and labor force needs to be shored up by educational partnerships with local colleges and universities, clear onboarding plans, and remuneration and benefits chosen to match the expected skills and performance.

Apart from the general conditions in the workplace, communication and cooperation should be regarded as levers of motivation with a major impact on staff satisfaction. Work in this area needs a clear plan that shows every single employee where he or she stands in the big picture. Be it in regular and intensive appraisals, in everyday team work, or in dedicated management calls, the job of communication is to make sure that people not only understand the transformation they are expected to introduce, but to bring it to life every day. Over the years, studies have repeatedly shown that the job satisfaction and performance of employees correlates directly with the responsibilities they are given. Skill shifts and new skills alone already call for more responsibilities to be given to people to make sure that they actually use all of their new or expanded skills for the good of the company. In the transformation process, this means, in particular, a new scope for managers who not only communicate and spread the changes into their units, but have to embody these changes as visible figureheads.

Change can be painful for a part of the workforce, not least when established processes are outsourced and shipped abroad. A successful change strategy will ensure that such decisions are communicated at the earliest possible point and that the people affected are involved from the beginning. They need to be offered alternatives for the jobs that are taken away, which means retraining as well as clearly defined programs for outplacement, part-time employment, early retirement, or straightforward financial compensation. People management cannot hope to have the right answer for everybody, but it can find something for many and should create new prospects for the people who remain in place.

For HR and its managers, any transformation is a major challenge and source of pressure. In larger corporate structures, transformation budgets can easily involve seven-figure sums, making errors costly and their effects immediately visible across the entire company. The success of change is directly correlated to people's desire to cooperate. Getting them to do so is one of the foremost challenges for HR management.

21.3 People in the IT Production of Tomorrow

Companies' established sites will remain the home of product development, ICT architecture, and portfolio management. The people working at these sites need to provide a much higher level of skills, which should be reflected in the financial rewards offered to them. The changes will affect managers first and foremost, as their qualifications are subject to sweeping changes. What used to be process management in the sense of overseeing the running of a production line is now becoming skills management with responsibility for people, technologies, and costs. Young people choosing careers in the IT industry—whether at its traditional or its new locations—have a much broader requirements profile to fulfill, beginning with a solid academic background, preferably in the natural sciences or technology via the ability to express themselves in the corporate language—English, in most cases—to real social skills that are essential for getting people from different cultures to work together in the first place.

21.4 Perfection Through Change

"To improve is to change; to be perfect is to change often." When Winston Churchill[1] uttered these words, he did not speak about industrial IT production, but he meant that same belief in perfection that the IT of the future needs to live up to. As IT has come to not only simplify, but indeed govern and shape the everyday lives of people, mistakes and errors can have catastrophic, in the worst case even global repercussions. The ambition has to be "zero faults". In the pursuit of that ambition, employees need to come to see change not as a threat, but as a means of perfection. Every day, people management therefore needs to bring to life and communicate the motto proposed by Gail Sheehy[2] "If we don't change, we don't grow. If we don't grow, we aren't really living."

[1] Winston Churchill (1874–1965), British Prime Minister and recipient of the Nobel Prize for Literature (1953).

[2] Gail Sheehy (1937–), American biographer, whose publications include biographies of Hillary Clinton, Michael Gorbachev, George W. Bush, George Bush, and Anwar Sadat.

Part V

Innovation Ecosystems

Innovation as the Fuel of Commercial Success

22

Marcus Hacke, Stefan Diefenbach, and Dirk Wellershaus

22.1 Innovation as the Fuel of Commercial Success

Companies that want to remain successful in their chosen markets need new ideas to become more efficient (doing things right: reducing the costs/prices of products and services) or more effective (doing the right things: growing their markets with new products and services) (Rickmann et al. 2012). This calls for new ideas to be developed and introduced constantly to safeguard the company's ability to grow and remain profitable for the long term (Liehr and Wolf 2009). These ideas are the innovations that are essentially important: this means that an idea about how to reduce costs can be as inherently valuable as a new business model or a new sales channel (Hauschild 1997). As trivial as this point might sound, many companies find it difficult to choose the right ideas and, above all, to put them to commercial use.

This is the job of in-house innovation management at many companies, established as the function that coordinates, budgets for, and decides about the creation, prioritization, and development of ideas, as well as the practical details of their execution. This can include in-house campaigns, the introduction of demonstration or pilot projects, workshops with clients, and many other activities. Their purpose is twofold: the simple transfer of know-how and the establishment of the company's public profile as an innovative player in the market (Specht et al. 2002).

Studies have shown that technological decision-makers are generally not satisfied with the innovation skills of their companies. They complain about a lack of replicable processes and about the absence of the resources needed to push these issues productively (Andersson et al. 2012).

M. Hacke (✉)
T-Systems International GmbH, Hahnstr. 43d, 60528, Frankfurt am Main, Germany
e-mail: Marcus.Hacke@t-systems.com

S. Diefenbach • D. Wellershaus
T-Systems International GmbH, Am Propsthof 49, 53121 Bonn, Germany
e-mail: Stefan.Diefenbach@t-systems.com; Dirk.Wellershaus@t-systems.com

F. Abolhassan (ed.), *The Road to a Modern IT Factory*, Management for Professionals,
DOI 10.1007/978-3-642-40219-7_22,

When it comes to the development of actual products or solutions, innovation management as an organizational unit faces the unique problem of getting its contributions actually recognized: Good ideas have many parents (many of whom are not part of innovation management) who can claim their success for themselves. Innovation managers therefore often have to justify their work in terms of how in-house innovation management contributes to the process. At the same time, the general cost burden makes many companies less willing to engage in long-term work with uncertain commercial promise, with upfront investments affecting their balance sheets long before any results become evident (Hischke et al. 2009).

Companies are much more receptive to innovations that go beyond integrating new technologies in their products, that is, innovations that open up new prospects for their core business. In most cases, picking the right technology for products and services is a much easier call than e.g. the specific expansion of the services on offer in response to a specific demand in the market, a process that may need new methods or fully scalable processes for providing and supporting the services sold (Andersson et al. 2012).

While companies are becoming reticent about investing their assets in risky development work, the market is putting more pressure on them in the form of shorter product lifecycles with increasingly complex products, services, or processes (Dapp 2011; Velu et al. 2010).

Mostly the aftershock of the entry of Asian competitors into the formerly Western-dominated market, this trend gave rise to the concept of agility, following a Congressional Committee on ways to improve the competitiveness of the American manufacturing industry (Goldman et al. 1995). The term agility here refers to companies working in virtual networks to respond immediately to changing circumstances. Such networks are easily reconfigured, and can accelerate the development of technologies and ideas to market readiness (Kidd 2012).

22.2 Opening up Innovation Process for Greater Agility

Businesses have found a way to take part in pioneering developments while keeping their own risks to a manageable level. The industrial landscape is changing into a knowledge economy, which is mostly the effect of many more people, researchers and organizations working together across the globe by using new technologies for information, communication, and knowledge management (Velu et al. 2010). This follows humanity's social urge for voluntary collaboration and interaction, for being part of communities, and for sharing and exchanging the results of labor (Dapp 2011).

Traditional approaches and structures are becoming less and less viable as a result of the closer ties linking people across geographic or commercial boundaries. At the same time, "groupthink", i.e. the tendency of homogeneous groups to think alike as a result of their centralized make-up (Janis 1972), and the fear of disclosing valuable information can help explain why some innovations have failed to produce the effect they were meant to produce in the past. This has led to the idea of agility.

For companies to become more innovative by means of interactive value creation (Reichwald and Piller 2009), their internal innovation-linked processes need to allow the contribution of external resources (open innovation). This improves interdisciplinary range and brings together diverse competencies, broadening the potential scope for new solutions (Dapp 2011). The boundaries between sectors of industry are becoming permeable and fluid, again opening up new options for shared products or shared business models (Velu et al. 2010), for spreading risk (e.g. in specific development partnerships with both parties taking a share of the investment burden), and for using synergies (Dapp 2011).

Open innovation is, at the same time, a major challenge for companies, since it demands interaction beyond their organizational confines. Companies need to learn to deal with the consequences in terms of transparency and confidentiality, which means rethinking the old ways of innovation management (Liehr and Wolf 2009). For instance, companies need to put incentive and reward systems for external contributors in place in an internal, but open and highly interactive organization (Dapp 2011).

There are many ways to put this vision of "open innovation" ecosystems to work, such as crowdsourcing, the integration of conceptual input and practical contributions from ecosystem partners. For these ways to work, they need to be practical and effective in terms of the organizational, technological (e.g. web 2.0 technologies), and procedural constitution of the company (Liehr and Wolf 2009).

22.3 Ecosystems as the Frame of Reference for Shared Innovation

Openness to "foreign" ideas and cooperation is spreading rapidly, primarily as the result of global competition and the pressure to innovate (Dapp 2011). This is leading to more and more such ecosystems, purpose-bound communities that bring businesses closer to research and science institutions, to technology partners, and to client companies in particular, and that help maintain the constant flow of information between formerly isolated actors.

Innovation ecosystems allow their actors to focus their combined capacities on developing ideas and transforming them into scalable and successful business concepts (for more details, cf. Arnold et al. 2012). One element essential to all of this is the individual parties' shared notion of the purpose and their motivation to contribute their specific influence or input (from a systemic point of view) to the value creation process.

An ecosystem of this type generally consists of four components or perspectives on the market's needs, aimed at achieving shared commercial success (cf. Fig. 22.1).

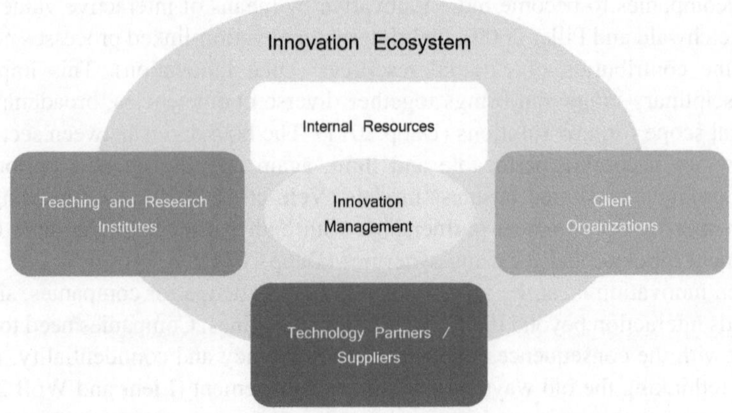

Fig. 22.1 The four components of an innovation ecosystem (illustration by the authors, 2012)

22.3.1 Client Organizations

One essential source for innovation in the ecosystem lies in (further) developments of products or services by IT service organizations working with technology businesses in response to the practical application of a technology in a client project (be it as regular business operations with established clients or a pilot project as a test balloon for new technologies at potential clients).

About half of all technology companies are reactive innovators (Andersson et al. 2012). The ambition should be for them to become active innovators, understanding the needs of the client and developing ideas about how innovative solutions could be used by the client. This should give them a presence as innovators in the industry.

This balancing act between maintaining secrecy about one's ideas ("closed innovation") and being open to clients ("open innovation") is discussed as a potential win-win situation in Chap. 23.

22.3.2 Technology Partners/Suppliers

Many technologies are being developed at highly specialized businesses. They may mature into industry standards. When a company expands its role in this respect from pure supply to strategic cooperation, both partners can benefit greatly from the new, mutual work on innovation. In the mobile communications sector, network operators, the producers of devices, and the developers of operating systems are working closely with each other to include the network's capacities in application development or support the operating system's abilities with the physical network. Such partnerships are often not without their friction and tensions, since the different actors in them will be primarily pursuing their own interests.

Influencing the technology roadmap of a technology partner by feeding in the concerns and needs of one's clients can be a key to success (Andersson et al. 2012). For IT service organizations, it is essential to agree on the immediate and constant availability of new developments or the use of state-of-the-art technology in the ecosystem (so-called "evergreening"). This is to prevent the ecosystem, which is intended for the long term, from being undermined by one of the partners engaging in another, potentially more responsive alliance.

Certain circumstances can work against close cooperation in such an ecosystem. Chief among them are internal factors, such as the conflict between a supplier partnership oriented on cost efficiency and true strategic cooperation over many years. Many decision-makers in the industry also believe that technology businesses lack the incentives to contribute their innovations when no tangible commercial benefits are visible (Andersson et al. 2012).

The aspects that need to be considered for reliable innovation partnerships are reviewed in more detail in Chap. 24.

22.3.3 Teaching and Research Institutes

Researchers are the vanguard of science. That means that the technologies, processes, and innovations of the near and far future are the natural habitat of teaching and research institutes. These actors can shoulder the risks of commercially unsuccessful developments, since academia does not, in essence, work for profit. Businesses accompany academia from the outside, but can engage with this world where a topic promises some commercial gains. They also benefit from engaging with scientists whose often highly specialist know-how and competencies can be integrated into their production processes and whose talents they can track and, where need be, secure for themselves.

Chapter 25 considers the question of how companies in research-intensive industries can expand their own innovative capacities by adding specialist expertise from the academic world.

22.3.4 Internal Resources

To inspire people to innovate and to use their knowledge and creativity, companies need to make room for talented people to focus on innovation (establishment of an innovation culture, cf. Specht et al. 2002).

This draws attention to the "war for talent", finding the potential recruits in the new generation of employees. It is becoming essential for companies to have the most creative and most innovative people as active members of their ecosystems. This does not have to mean employing them as part of the regular workforce. They can also be part of other actors in the ecosystem, where they can put all of their creativity to use for the best possible results.

People are beginning to pay attention to the community or ecosystem they are part of. For many, being a respected and autonomous actor in a dedicated network is a great incentive.

Chapter 26 explains that the practical challenge for the coordinators of such ecosystems consists of establishing and managing the shared governance, communication, HR, and process superstructure to allow all partners to see and seize their unique benefits from it. The discussion also touches on what effective in-house innovation management looks like in practice.

22.4 IT Service Organizations Integrating the Ecosystem's Output

The greatest current challenge in the field of innovation is making the best possible use of trends like cloud computing, big data, unified communications, or mobility for one's customers. This means integrating technology into new services or processes to respond to specific customer requirements, while maintaining the greatest possible profitability of the capital invested for the purpose. Usually, this is only possible when the likelihood that an innovation will become a success is evident and immediately recognizable (Velu et al. 2010).

This means involving the client actively, finding and developing the right talent, and intensifying relationships with technology partners. The ability to develop ideas in tandem with clients and partners instead of closing the shutters in direct competition will become essential for commercial success, as will the ability to take in feedback, observations, and experiences and use these in the sense of a learning organization (Velu et al. 2010).

"Open" value creation means far more and far closer ties with external actors and thus considerably more complexity. Companies need to learn to cope with the faster flows of communication and interaction and to use them purposefully (Dapp 2011). To be able to do so, they need interaction skills with the right organization, communication, and incentive structures, put to work in flexible and effective processes (Bughin et al. 2008).

Another key competency is the ability to bring people together from areas that are seemingly unrelated and network them in the correct, target-oriented manner. The coordinator needs to rein in any perceived need to intervene to the appropriate minimum and promote transparency in the network, not least about his or her own activities. This will lead to a successful network culture (Dapp 2011).

Any IT service organization that wants to fulfill its customary role in coordinating such an ecosystem needs to develop these competencies. Switching from inward-looking to outward-looking innovation will become a point of distinction for the organization (that is, the ability to bring open innovation to life in all of its aspects), as will a focused and forward-looking sense for integrating innovative elements or arranging the many players in the ecosystems meaningfully with the shared purpose in mind.

References

Andersson, H., Kaplan, J., & Smolinski, B. (2012). Capturing value from IT infrastructure innovation. *McKinsey on Business Technology, 27*, 14–23.

Arnold, H., Erner, M., Möckel, P., & Schläffer, C. (Eds.). (2012). *Applied technology and innovation management*. Berlin: Springer.

Bughin, J., Chui, M., & Johnson, B. (2008). *The next step in open innovation*. Brussels: McKinsey Technology Initiative Perspective.

Dapp, T. F. (2011). *Die digitale Gesellschaft – Neue Wege zu mehr Transparenz, Beteiligung und Innovation (DB Research – Trendforschung – Aktuelle Themen 517)*. Frankfurt: Deutsche Bank Research.

Goldman, S. L., Nagel, R. N., & Preiss, K. (1995). *Agile competitors and virtual organisations*. New York: Van Nostrand Reinhold.

Hauschild, J. (1997). *Innovationsmanagement*. Munich: Vahlen.

Hischke, S., Mühlner, J., Salwinczek, C., Wolf, M., & Engel B. (2009). Zukunft der Dienste und Netze: Mit Marktwissen zum Erfolg digitaler Innovationen (Einleitung). In S. Hischke, J. Mühlner, C. Salwinczek, M. Wolf, & B. Engel (Eds.), *Nationaler IT Gipfel – Arbeitsgruppe 2 – Konvergenz der Medien*, 7–12.

Janis, I. L. (1972). *Victims of Groupthink*. New York: Houghton Mifflin.

Kidd, P. T. (2012). Agile manufacturing: A strategy for the 21st century (Agility Forum - online publication). Retrieved December 21, 2012, from www.cheshirehenbury.com/agility/index.html 2012

Liehr, T., & Wolf, M. (2009). Innovationsmanagement: Balance zwischen Kreativität und Disziplin – Der Prozess der Neuprodukt-Entwicklung auf Basis voridentifizierter Bedürfnislücken im Markt. In S. Hischke, J. Mühlner, C. Salwinczek, M. Wolf, & B. Engel (Eds.), *Nationaler IT Gipfel – Arbeitsgruppe 2 – Konvergenz der Medien – Zukunft der Dienste und Netze: Mit Marktwissen zum Erfolg digitaler Innovationen*, 103–127.

Reichwald, R., & Piller, F. (2009). *Interaktive Wertschöpfung – Open Innovation, Individualisierung und neue Formen der Arbeitsteilung*. Wiesbaden: Springer Gabler.

Rickmann, H., Diefenbach, S., & Brüning, K. T. (2012). *IT-Outsourcing – Neue Herausforderungen im Zeitalter von Cloud Computing*. Berlin: Springer Gabler.

Specht, G., Beckmann, C., & Amelingmeyer, J. (2002). *F&E Management – Kompetenzen im Innovationsmanagement*. Stuttgart: Schäffer-Poeschel.

Velu, C., Barrett, M., Kohli, R., & Salge T. (2010). *Thriving in open innovation ecosystems: Toward a collaborative market orientation* (Working Paper Series 4/2010). Cambridge: Cambridge Judge Business School.

Customers as the Engines of Innovation 23

Holger Dörnemann

In July 2010, Zeit Online published an article on "how companies benefit from innovative clients" (cf. Jung 2010), underlining the growing role of the user in the invention and development of products. The examples chosen by the author were picked from the consumer goods industry, but research and numerous case studies tell us that the high-tech sector, especially the software industry, can use the client as an engine for innovation and commercial success (cf. Bughin et al. 2008).

Coming from the Latin for "renew", innovation is a versatile term that encompasses both ideas/inventions and products/services. For companies, it means the constant work of translating ideas into finished products (or parts thereof) as a way to maintain their long-term success.

This chapter considers the case of a software enterprise to see the importance of involving the client in innovation and to understand how this can become a win-win situation for both sides. Managing innovation has been a key element of the work of companies like VMware from the very first day of their operations. Many so-called "disruptive technologies" like vMotion (the live migration of virtual servers e.g. as part of maintenance on the physical servers) or fault tolerance (continuous failover without data loss after hardware crashes) would not be possible without substantial contributions from clients (cf. Austin 2012a). At the same time, clients are also a source of constant feedback on current developments (e.g. vMotion without a Storage Area Network).

The following discussion concentrates on the interplay between producer and client. However, a functioning innovation ecosystem, as described in Chap. 22, means that the same level of attention needs to be paid to all actors in the equation.

H. Dörnemann (✉)
VMware Global, Inc., German Office, Freisinger Str. 3, 85716 Unterschleißheim, Germany
e-mail: HDoernemann@vmware.com

F. Abolhassan (ed.), *The Road to a Modern IT Factory*, Management for Professionals, DOI 10.1007/978-3-642-40219-7_23, © Springer-Verlag Berlin Heidelberg 2014

23.1 Managing Innovation Processes

The difficulty for businesses clearly consists of the need to find the right innovation strategy when product lifecycles are shrinking rapidly and the market demands more growth and turnover at the same time. Ideas need to mature efficiently and effectively into finished products in ever shorter periods of time, products that have a lasting impact on the client's value creation and not only offer clever new technologies. This means that the customer has—as always—the upper hand in determining the success or failure of a new or changed approach. No company can sustain a long series of failed developments. Greater inclusion of the client in the development process itself is therefore an immediate solution. In the end, it is up to companies to reduce the risks of self-evident market or technology challenges as soon as possible. The question has to be: Which forms of cooperation with the user are possible, and how can they be managed and controlled?

The starting point is to consider which information a company actually needs to get new market opportunities via innovation. In his 2003 publication, Thomke distinguishes between two basic types of information that are required for conducting any innovation process (cf. Thomke 2003):

- Information about *requirements* to tell us what people are looking for when purchasing a new product.
- Information about *solutions,* i.e. the technical means and potential capabilities for the user.

We have to ask how information about requirements that the client "possesses" and information about possible solutions, the primary currency of a developer organization, can be brought together most efficiently to be turned into marketable products. In the past, many companies have approached this balancing act in a quite traditional way and compiled requirements from customer surveys or market research. The respondents—that is, the actual users—played a mostly passive part. There have been many cases of software products that seem to have been developed with no regard for the user's needs. This discrepancy is mostly the outcome of closed developer groups believing that they know what the client needs and leaving it too late to verify this belief. In the end, clients find themselves in a situation where the provider tries to impose a problem on them to sell a solution. After all, there must have been a problem, else the producer would not have had to make a new product in response.

At the same time, recent history has seen some open source projects become major successes without companies to back them. They have created new opportunities, new market ideas, new business models, or even whole new companies. The focus here lies on the clients or, more accurately, the users. Information about requirements and about solutions meets in the middle for the greatest possible intersection of both spheres. Probably the most well-known software product that has grown up in this client/consumer seedbed is Linux. Theorists frequently term this approach "co-creation" (cf. Bughin et al. 2008). Sourceforge is a popular platform for software projects with publicly accessible source code—and it quickly reveals which ideas are accepted by the "market" and which fall by the wayside: About two in three

Sourceforge projects are either inactive or only pursued by a few enthusiasts. Does the future of the software industry nonetheless lie in open source projects that only have to be "polished" to become full products?

The real experience of software companies is the middle ground, at least for the short to medium term: Protecting intellectual property and tapping into the vast know-how of the wider community. For companies that want to give their products and offerings a good and fast start in their markets, working together with as many clients as possible is becoming a more and more relevant means of finding out about customer needs. At the same time, they cannot release their intellectual property into the wild, and they need to safeguard the potentially business-relevant information and commercial interests of the client. Not every client would or will speak openly about his or her strategy. All of this can have a lasting (and sometimes negative) impact on the co-creation process.

23.2 Closed Innovation vs. Open Innovation

In his work on "Open Innovation" (Chesbrough 2003), Chesbrough introduced the twin terms "closed innovation" and "open innovation". Closed innovation suggests that innovation rests on the work of (a few) in-house creatives, i.e. that information about solutions is the leitmotif. The advantage is evident: Full control over intellectual property. By contrast, Chesbrough described open innovation as a new paradigm according to which companies make more use of external knowledge and ideas. The leitmotif is give-and-take: sharing opportunities and risks with internal and external know-how.

Reichwald and Piller have visualized both concepts in an illustration (cf. Ill. 1 in Reichwald and Piller 2005) that has provided the model for illustrating VMware's approach in Fig. 23.1.

The challenge for producers is first and foremost to find a suitable strategy that, on the one hand, channels the flow of information about requirements and, on the other, shares relevant information about the possible solutions. In a closed-innovation world, the producer plays the role of a mediator who collects and compiles information from clients. The advantage is the large amount of feedback from user groups, surveys, or internal information from the customer-facing end of the business. At the same time, the difficulty lies in using that information and feedback for the "market". For outside observers, it might seem surprising that VMware's many regional units produce weekly reports for product development, which include a brief breakdown of clients' feedback on product traits or specific requests. For Germany alone, this is a full-page spread of condensed comments every week. Despite this vast array of issues under consideration, R&D regularly feeds back information for the teams out in the field and the end customer. Both the producer and the client benefit from this: Customers' needs are recognized early on and existing solutions are revised to track the changes in the users' world. What this needs, however, is a feedback process that actually works. Without high-quality,

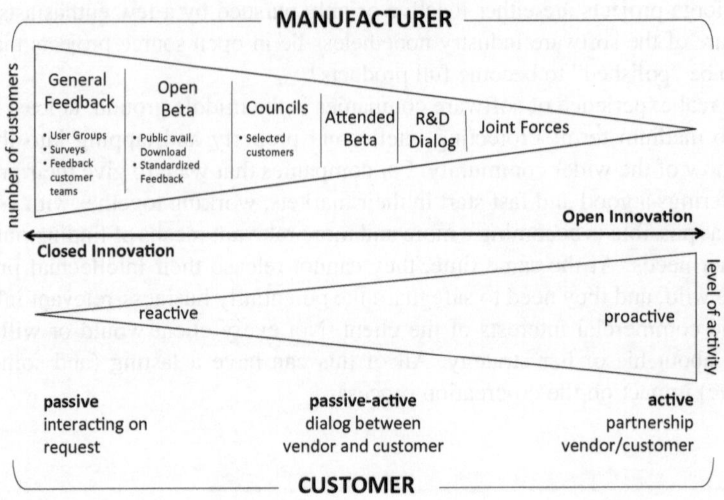

Fig. 23.1 Closed vs. open innovation

meaningful feedback from developers, the weekly reports would soon be regarded as useless busywork.

23.3 Research and Development Programs

Customer feedback becomes proportionately more useful when the customer becomes an integral part of the innovation process. This also means considerably greater coordination and support effort on the part of VMware, and only parts of the client base can be covered at this level of interaction. Since it also needs a considerable effort on the part of the client, there is a relatively stable balance between the number of clients in scope and the number actually willing and able to get proactively involved. The participating companies are motivated by the usual suspects: Improved agility or quality, reduced costs, better market image. However, such co-creation lives above all off the contributions of individuals who are driven by the wish to express themselves, enjoy their work, and experience appreciation.

There are four basic programs in VMware's research & development section:

1. **Beta Program**
   The essence of a beta program is to improve product quality and gain feedback about new functionality. Such programs are in widespread use, either as public downloads for the broader interested public or in more focused intensive programs with individual clients.
2. **Customer Council**
   The purpose of this program was to integrate user information into the short- and medium-term product roadmaps, so as to get VMware's products better aligned

with the needs of its clients. Its elements led to a stronger relationship between VMware and the clients' side of the equation. Councils were conducted before actual beta tests and thus had the opportunity to influence the final shape and specifications of the product.

3. **R&D Customer Connect**
   This program focused on direct interaction between R&D personnel and clients. The developers gained insights and invaluable feedback about how solutions are being used in real life. This gave them a better sense for the users' business and their technical constraints. The closer relationships led to new areas of use and technologies designed for the "rough and tumble" of everyday business and not the ivory tower of research.
4. **Activate**
   As part of the Activate Program, sponsored reference projects were conducted with the clients: these allowed the clients to introduce (new) technologies into their IT environments and gave VMware reference points for whether and how the products are used and experienced in real life.

23.4 New and Innovative Models for Client Involvement

VMware is expanding the traditional ways of working with clients by investing in new opportunities to harvest innovative ideas from the wider community about how to make improvements to products and solutions. This means tapping into the vast know-how available in the field. Three means of doing so can be discussed as examples:

Flings: VMware has established labs.vmware.com as a platform for discussing new ideas with potential users. Users can download and debate "flings" (as in: romantic flings) from developers to understand the potential of contributions by individual developers or developer groups at the earliest possible date. Flings that garner a lot of attention and feedback can become part of finished products. Some of these flings are not indeed proposed by developers, but by other technical personnel at VMware. One development in Germany gained some attention in the worldwide community in 2012, although it had originated from the customer contacts of a pre-sales representative. In essence, it meant reducing investment costs by using old (written-off) hardware with lean Linux images for connectivity with virtual desktops.

Innovation Contests: The internally focused fling idea was taken further by VMworld 2012. The new concept invited innovative ideas from the community (cf. Austin 2012b), had them rated them by a jury, and then pursued further by the VMware developer team. Of the approximately 120 entries, about half concerned product specifications, most of which were already part of the roadmap (adding another layer of validation for them). The eventual winner was the contribution by the Canadian M. W. Preston. He proposed dynamic data centers in the sense of adding predictive resources (history and forecast) to the current (reactive) handling of dynamic workloads.

Open Source Projects: As discussed above, co-creation has lots of dormant potential for business. Serengeti is a recent VMware project that began its life as an open Source project on the github platform (github.com) and is being powered to a considerable extent by VMware resources. Serengeti addresses simple ways to structure virtual clusters for analyzing large data repositories (big data) by using means other than hard physical resources. It took only half a year for the technology to reach pilot stage at a German client, with another client also now reviewing its potential application. For customers, it is a real alternative to expensive bricks-and-mortar technology—and for VMware it is proof of the viability of the solution. Serengeti is being trialed in close cooperation and consultation with the client, bringing together local German and US resources. This is a step up from co-creation to joint-force realization.

23.5 Summary

The economy is changing at an ever-faster rate. The software industry is clearly one of the sectors with the greatest potential for innovation and change. Software companies, who used to rely virtually exclusively on their own ability to innovate, not least to protect their intellectual property, are trying out new approaches. The trend is clearly going in the direction of open innovation and putting the customer at the heart of things. Many VMware solutions have been inspired by users and client projects of all shapes and sizes. The speed with which such innovations need to be brought to market will only continue to accelerate. This can only be possible if companies learn to check and verify the needs of their clients by proactively getting them on board. VMware is investing in the use of "collective expertise" and has recognized that diversity and a profusion of different opinions are indeed the way to go, as group dynamic research has told us again and again (cf. Hill 1995). The Open Innovation Contest at VMworld 2012 has proven two things: first, that the audience responded more than willingly, and second, that many interesting innovations are out there. As an open source project, Serengeti also enjoys a great deal of attention and has already been recognized as an appealing option for future big data projects by many names in the industry. Clients are becoming the engines of the future of innovation.

References

100% Open. (2011). Open innovation defined. Retrieved January 3, 2013, from http://www.100open.com/2011/03/open-innovation-defined/

Austin, J. (2012a, April). Innovation at VMware – staying on the edge. Retrieved January 3, 2013, from http://communities.vmware.com/community/vmtn/cto/innovation/blog/2012/04/02/staying-on-the-edge

Austin, J. (2012b). VMworld 2012 Open Innovation Contest. Retrieved January 4, 2013, from http://www.youtube.com/watch?v=DuLf3vm5XG0

Bughin, J., Chui, M., Johnson, B., et al. (2008). *The next step in open innovation.* New Jersey: McKinsey.

Chaney, P. K., & Devinney, T. M. (1992). New product innovations and stock price performance. *Journal of Business Finance & Accounting, 19*, 677–695.

Chesbrough, H. W. (2003). *Open innovation: The new imperative for creating and profiting from technology*. Boston, MA: Harvard Business School Press.

Hill, L. A. (1995, April). *Orientation to the subarctic survival situation.* Harvard Business School Background Note 494-073.

Jung, D. R. (2010, June). Wie Unternehmen von innovativen Kunden profitieren. Retrieved from http://www.zeit.de/wirtschaft/2010-06/nutzer-innovationen

McDougall, R. (2012). Project serengeti: There's a virtual elephant in my datacenter. Retrieved January 4, 2013, from http://cto.vmware.com/project-serengeti-theres-a-virtual-elephant-in-my-datacenter/

Reichwald, R., & Piller, F. (2005). Kunden als Partner im Innovationsprozess. Munich: TU München.

Thomke, S. (2003). *Experimentation matters: unlocking the potential of new technologies for innovation.* Boston, MA: Harvard Business School Press.

Innovation Partnerships 24

Thomas Ehrlich

24.1 General Motives and Innovation Strategies

Sound innovative capabilities determine a company's market value and its ability to create new value. However, only replicable, long-term innovation strategies that offer uniqueness, economies of scale, and cost savings by skill sharing can be considered true successes. This chapter takes the point of view of technology businesses to consider the key elements of innovation partnerships: their motives, identification, management, the role of mirroring organizations, cooperation, and communication.

With an increasing presence of innovation in a company's business and its explicit positioning as an innovator, the key question becomes: How to capitalize on innovations? In well-established innovation partnerships, both partners will see innovation as a core process, add interactive skills (with shared roadmaps, forecasts, or communication platforms), and make their ambitions compatible with each other.

If this type of innovation alliance arises from a pre-existing supplier partnership, the move to an innovation partnership between equals can demand extensive change management efforts in both organizations. The ability of infrastructure providers to innovate depends essentially on an ability to innovate on the part of the technology companies whose core technologies they use as enablers for their business. In most cases, technology determines the business models. Innovation partnerships can take many forms in this respect, from product development in the sense of expanding companies' portfolios to prototyping, which is a common area in the automotive industry.

T. Ehrlich (✉)
NetApp Deutschland GmbH, Sonnenallee 1, 85551 Kirchheim bei München, Germany
e-mail: Thomas.Ehrlich@netapp.com

F. Abolhassan (ed.), *The Road to a Modern IT Factory*, Management for Professionals,
DOI 10.1007/978-3-642-40219-7_24,

Innovation is a viable counterbalance to increasing costs, diminishing margins, or industry environments that are subject to consolidation in the form of mergers or takeovers. An infrastructure CIO interviewed by McKinsey in 2012 gave the indispensability of innovation a vivid expression: "My technology strategy depends on products that have not yet been invented. This means that I need to understand what my strategically most important suppliers are working on and find ways to influence their product roadmap." A number of senior infrastructure executives surveyed for the same study even suggested that "constant innovation is the only way to fulfill the customer's expectations while also responding to the constantly increasing requirements in terms of commodity IT, data storage, and networks." (cf. Andersson et al. 2012).

Coherent, long-term innovation partnerships will affect virtually every part of the organization and are often associated with such activities as think tanks, pilot projects, beta tests, etc. These are usually bilateral forms of cooperation that provide inherent ecosystems (cf. Chap. 22.3 and innovation ecosystems) in which the discovery, development, integration, or utilization of intellectual property is promoted within a formal legal framework. Networks are the outcome, but also the basic precondition for such ecosystems that live off transparency and the ability to spread knowledge through all interfaces.

The will and ability to change are essential qualities of vigorous innovation partnerships, which can lead to radical about-turns in strategies that need the support of shareholders and stakeholders, C-level officers, board members, customers, employees, or the general public. Even technology companies like NetApp face three elementary questions when developing a new innovation strategy: "Make or buy?", "Loose development partnerships?", or "Coherent innovation partner strategies?" Some innovation partnerships completely forego the usual IP protection in favor of strategies that get external innovative forces on board in the sense of open innovation or co-creation. The more aggressive the innovation strategy of an organization, the more progressive its chosen innovation partners will be. At this end of the scale, the deliberate disclosure, handing-over, or linking-up of intellectual property can be an explicit target. This consciously accepts the implicit risks: the loss of control or the impact of certain forces that can actually work against the cooperative innovation purpose.

24.2 Identifying Innovation Partners

Before the actual scouting for an innovation partner begins, the first job is to define one's purpose. Two approaches can be used to that end: Evaluating existing partners, such as technology/application partners or service providers, or forming new partnerships to match the intended purpose. In companies for which the technological innovation strategy is, in essence, the framework for the business model itself, innovation management is traditionally the reserve of the CTO or CIO. This often includes the identification, assessment, validation, and integration of potential innovation partners. Innovation management should, in such cases, be considered an executive management function.

Innovation partnerships can mean a paradigm shift for traditional supplier partnerships. They work less by measurable key performance indicators, balanced scorecards, or benchmarking, and more by the sustainability and compatibility of "soft" factors of the corporate culture, such as the vision, brand identity, reputation, intercultural management, corporate social responsibility, or team concepts (cf. Gabler Wirtschaftslexikon (2013), "Corporate Culture"). For an effective alignment and a partnership that is scalable and reproducible, special indexes should be developed to cover such soft factors for a meaningful assessment of potential innovation partners.

24.3 Innovation Managers and the Scope of Cooperation

As the engine driving the innovation process, the role of the CIO or CTO is changing into one tasked with coordinating the tension between technology as a commodity and innovation as the source for new business. In essence, innovation managers need to introduce and establish a sustainable culture of innovation, as outlined in Chap. 24.4. All of this might need a "rethink" on the part of the C-level officers: From responding to developments to proactively shaping them. They become the mediator, lynchpin, and authority in charge. They not only get behind the potential innovations, but follow their implementation in beta tests, in portfolio management, or in the final production of products and solutions. When innovation partnerships are in the fortunate position of being able to draw on years of shared experience, e.g. from OEM or integration partnerships, the shared business model can focus on building opportunities and strengths. By contrast, newborn partnerships need to concentrate more on risk management before they can begin to come up with concrete innovations. The first and foremost risk factor in this respect is the potential loss of control by sharing or outsourcing intellectual property.

The right answer for both partners lies on the side of monetization: Who can turn how much of the innovation into monetary gains? Monetization can, for instance, take the form of distinct property rights or a sale to a third party. Innovation partnerships operating with an eye on the go-to-market aspect help develop market penetration, sales, margins, or technical/commercial competitiveness by combining the two sides' core competencies into a new or perfected portfolio. The following questions can be used to evaluate this facet:

- Are the partners prepared to go beyond their specific market segments?
- Are the parties prepared to take immediate decisions?
- Is the system multi-tenant capable?
- Are the core competencies of the partner appreciated?
- Can the partnership operate for more than 10 years on the back of long-term contracts with clients acquired together?
- Is the partnership credible in a third-party market?

24.4 Organizational Compatibility and Mirroring

As a business enabler and value creator, innovation is subject to a complex interplay of different forces: Sectors of industry, market segments, customer structures, product portfolios and much more. Networks like innovation partnerships can become much more productive if the rules are clear, the roles allocated, and the processes for setting targets and resolving conflict known. Potential problems should be cascaded down at every level, down to the innovation module at stake, where the partners are working side by side on the specific aspects of the problem or the pieces of its solution. Such a highly distributed, networked approach gives the system the required critical mass and the scalability it needs to go to market.

Trust and mutual appreciation as equal partners are crucial to successful cooperative innovation. Also elementary is the establishment and coordination of innovation teams that work in real partnerships. The question that needs to be asked is: Does the will exist for an inherent transformation? How strong is that will in the organization? How does the alignment affect the technology, production processes, sales, or support? Can existing service level agreements or IT infrastructure library processes be kept or expanded in parallel by both sides?

Explicit innovation targets and partners embedded directly in one's own value creation process help reduce the potential for conflict. Organizational mirroring gets all of the development partners in all of their central functions on a level playing field. This needs fluid structures, plus people with matching positions, competencies, and abilities. Where such people are missing, conflicts or disagreements have no resolution and might fester or escalate. Carefully arranged at both the contractual and the practical, operational level, mirroring organizations remove potential friction from the value creation process and make the entire set-up more responsive and scalable.

24.5 Economies of Scale and Collaboration

Services should, in the first instance, be seen as pure potentiality—the ability or willingness to deliver the service. This distinguishes them directly from material products. While they might seem related when the ideas for them are first born, services need to be developed at a potential level—making them highly scalable. The right sizing of the potential service in all of its aspects, i.e. the structures, technology, and personnel needed to deliver them, is therefore usually aligned at the earliest possible point with the maximum possible customer reach or market potential.

This makes economies of scale a fully predictable factor when modeling core, administrative, and support processes. They should be made possible at all procedural levels in the service economy, as the uno-actu principle reminds us that the production and consumption of a service usually happens at a single instance in time, if it is not tied to certain material goods, cf. Haller (2012). Product innovation, on the other hand, can be scaled to match demand as a result of the window of time between production and consumption. In both models, the optimum match of expertise and processes is a critical factor.

On a pragmatic level, the partners in the innovation partnership rely on technologies that enable collaborative work, improve team efficiency, and foster communication between them. Many of these technologies include common tools like videoconferences, shared workspaces, or whiteboards. Modern Web 2.0 technologies or social media like blogs, forums, and wikis promote the flow of know-how in intelligent "developer communities". In 2010, McKinsey already recognized instances in which the use of Web 2.0 concepts for a progressively innovative alignment with business partners correlates directly with a measurable growth in market share, cf. Bughin et al. (2010).

One intrinsic challenge in all of this is the ability to find, recruit, and retain talented and qualified personnel. High potentials possess technological affinity, managerial know-how, and the creativity needed to solve problems, making them the ideal candidates for any innovation initiative. How should recruitment and incentives be repositioned to reach these sought-after groups? The options are many and diverse: Giving engineers and developers more managerial authority, reducing their aversion to risk by getting behind both successes and failures, or using newcomers to the industry as sources for new ways of thinking. Business networks like LinkedIn offer HR organization tools that make locating such personalities a real option.

24.6 Processes of Communication

A comprehensive communication strategy is an integral part of any innovation strategy, as it brings together all of the internal and external communication processes in sourcing. For a coherent and continuous flow of information between the people in charge of different innovation processes, the marketing, PR, and HR teams of development partners should be brought on board as soon as possible in the process, the key messages aligned with each other, and a consensus established about which pieces of information should be released when to their audiences.

The parties should agree on a shared language, recorded in a basic agreement that they both coordinate and approve, and which covers the essential points to be published. It includes, among other elements, a management summary, the expected benefits, the basic facts and figures, and a set of FAQs. The key messages are prepared for each target group, meaning custom messages for executives, employees, media channels, social media multipliers, shareholders and stakeholders, customers and analysts. A coherent timetable is drawn up for the release of the various publications. Most innovation partnerships with a shared go-to-market strategy also prepare a dedicated, shared internet presence (brand, logo, communication) for the defined market.

Conclusions

With companies caught between the need to innovate and the burden of costs, strategically aligned innovation partnerships built around mirroring organizations have proven to be a suitable means of improving competitiveness, protecting quality standards, and benefiting from economies of scale.

References

Andersson, H., Kaplan, J., & Smolinski, B. (2012). Capturing value from IT infrastructure innovation. *McKinsey on Business Technology, 27*, 22.

Bughin, J., Chui, M., & Manyika, J. (2010). Clouds, big data, and smart assets: Ten tech-enabled business trends to watch. *McKinsey Quarterly, 7*, 2.

Gabler Wirtschaftslexikon. Retrieved January 7, 2013, from http://www.wirtschaftslexikon.gabler.de/Definition/unternehmenskultur.html

Haller, S. (2012). *Dienstleistungsmanagement: Grundlagen, Konzepte, Instrumente* (5th ed.). Wiesbaden: Gabler.

25 Transferring Innovation from Science and Research

Björn Froese

More and more high-tech companies are opening up in the pursuit of innovative solutions and involving other experts from outside institutions or research bodies to become more innovative. This chapter explores the trend towards new types of innovation networks that range from different actors engaging in cluster initiatives to companies dropping all former boundaries in crowdsourcing. The question it poses is how enterprises in research-intensive industries can add external sources from research and science to their own capabilities in the form of highly specialized expertise. It then looks at an ICT platform as an example of outsourcing: for many years now, this platform has successfully been bringing together many external actors at a high level in the search for innovative solutions.

25.1 Corporate Networks in Research-Intensive Industries

When companies recognized that differentiation of service offerings and the continuous improvement of the value-creation processes are strategic means for increasing revenue, they began to focus on the constant improvement and updating of these products and processes. The success of any innovation can, in this sense, be determined by examining its commercial gains (Hauschildt and Salomo 2011).

Traditionally, companies looked to themselves when searching for the source for such innovations. This meant that innovation was born within them and replicated in the company's local operations (Gerybadze and Reger 1998). The purpose was to establish the new product portfolio or the new process concepts as the status quo for the entire organization. This past form of innovation management saw companies as closed systems that tried to counter the danger of mis-investment by straightforward risk mitigation alone, such as stage-gate approaches or the use of well-balanced innovation portfolios (von Stamm 2003). Earlier innovation research

B. Froese (✉)
Detecon International GmbH, Dingolfinger Strasse 1-15, 81673 München, Germany
e-mail: Bjoern.Froese@detecon.com

F. Abolhassan (ed.), *The Road to a Modern IT Factory*, Management for Professionals, DOI 10.1007/978-3-642-40219-7_25, © Springer-Verlag Berlin Heidelberg 2014

consequently focused above all on the factors for the successful distribution of labor in this internal arrangement—cf. e.g. "House of Quality" (Hauser and Clausing 1988) or investigations of communication structures in companies' internal research (Allen 1988).

This traditional structuring approach, characterized by centralism and linearity, was dominant until the late 1980s (Gerybadze and Reger 1998), before being replaced by more collaborative models in the following two decades, beginning within organizations and then looking abroad to other institutions. The focus was first on reducing the complexity of the issue by creating a comprehensive umbrella system via individual subsystems (modularization) at the company (Baldwin and Clark 2004). The promising features of this concept were later recognized in terms of entire companies specializing their abilities and spreading the risks of innovation between them.

Another trait of the new approach to commercial innovation management is its new reach. Hauser and Zettelmeyer distinguish between long-term research, medium-term development of performance capabilities, and short-term work on specific outcomes (Hauser and Zettelmeyer 2004). The length of time for which an idea deserves to be pursued to allow real creativity beyond the level of piecemeal improvements is a common question (Timmons 1997), with circumstantial factors playing a major role in the assessment and with the same idea enjoying completely different levels of significance from business to business. High-tech companies that want to stay on top of even disruptive developments and trends therefore have a twofold challenge ahead of them: recognizing opportunities as soon as possible and understanding how they can be implemented effectively at the company.

The more the corporate innovation process opens up—from intra-company processes in the sense of interdepartmental cooperation or globalization to inter-company specialization and risk distribution—the more urgent it becomes for companies to know the best configuration for their innovation networks (Gemünden et al. 1996). When this concerns the realization of specific results that are obviously feasible, the self-evidently best option is simply to turn to companies specializing in the necessary product or process. When the company in question is part of a research-intensive industry, on the other hand, the company's R&D capabilities need to be complemented with partners who can pursue ideas with no immediate or evident commercial value. This makes universities or other scientific establishments, such as the Fraunhofer Institutes, essential partners for high-tech companies (cf. Gemünden et al. 1996, Hauser and Zettelmeyer 2004, who discuss the quasi anti-commercial incentives at work in the long-term pursuit of research results).

Nestle has researched the effects of cluster initiatives in research-intensive industries (Nestle 2011), describing the current trend towards uniting institutions that want to innovate together in local clusters (agglomeration): here, they can then use their complementary capabilities in the development and in the utilization of the innovation. This clustering helps instill a focus on the subject in question, creates a forum for even informal communication and learning, and reduces the transaction costs in the work of the cluster actors. Even small-scale constellations, e.g. those of public research institutions and for-profit companies, need an element of trust and the belief that neither partner will be so opportunistic as to work against the justified interests of the other partners. At the same time, the clustering of actors who normally stand in direct competition with each other can be an invigorating boost to innovation, as it allows the actors to differentiate themselves from their competitors only by producing absolutely top-class solutions when other factors have been equalized in the cluster. This also explains the structural policy behind incentives to create local agglomerations in times of global hyper-competition: raising local competitiveness to a higher level, together.

25.2 Open Innovation and Crowdsourcing

Clustering can be considered an attempt to reverse the decentralization of innovation resources caused by the sweeping globalization since the turn of the millennium by forming regional research clusters. However, there is also another—contrary—response: Using ICT infrastructure to outsource individual jobs in the innovation process to external actors and involve as many actors as possible with no regard for regional or institutional boundaries. This is commonly called *open innovation*, and it attempts to make use of the multitude of ideas and the specialist know-how of as many external sources as possible in the search for new solutions. Such external partners can be recruited from clients (especially lead users), researchers working anywhere in the world, or from any other source (for the following, cf. Ili 2012). Potentially, all phases of the innovation process are suitable for outsourcing, from the very first idea to the eventual market launch. We can distinguish between two types of information that can be managed by ICT resources, namely: information about requirements and information about solutions.

Information about requirements allows companies to understand the future preferences of current or potential customers. Oftentimes, customers themselves know how to change a product to fulfill needs or purposes other than those for which it had originally been intended. At the very least, they often have some insights about what they would expect and require from a new development or innovation.

Logically speaking, information about solutions concerns the response to a certain need. In product development, it refers to the means for fulfilling a customer's expectations. Such solutions can be developed by analogy, that is, by looking at structurally related problems from other domains. This makes it possible to look towards experts hailing from fields unfamiliar to the company.

Gassmann calls this approach the "real invention" of open innovation and sees *crowdsourcing* as a possible tool for opening up the innovation process beyond institutional boundaries (Gassmann 2013). In this sense, crowdsourcing refers to the ICT-driven sourcing of know-how or solutions from an unrestricted pool of off-site actors. This can use intermediary communication (web portals) to make the link between the question (seeker) and the answer (solver).

A commercially viable and appealing partnership depends on the incentives for the actors in it, the intellectual property (IP) rights concerning the developed solution, and the control over its exploitation.

Since eventual remuneration is usually limited to actors who produce solutions that are unique and innovative, the search for solutions needs a general level of up-front interest to get as many actors as possible involved in the crowdsourcing process. This makes it clear that crowdsourcing cannot be a one-off activity, but should rather be built on an existing community that cares about certain products or expert questions. A comprehensive communication strategy should be in place for this purpose (cf. Gassmann 2013).

The (exclusive) use of the solution can be ensured relatively simply with the traditional repertoire of contract law and intellectual property rights, not least because of the 'normal' monetary payment for solvers.

25.3 Case Study: InnoCentive

One popular example of a crowdsourcing platform that knowledge-intensive industries use to reach out to experts in research and development is InnoCentive (http://www.innocentive.com).

InnoCentive was founded in 2001 with venture capital from the Eli Lilly Group, a U.S. pharmaceutical company. It operates a private digital marketplace, generating income via the fees that InnoCentive seekers pay when choosing the solutions provided by solvers. The platform specializes in questions relevant to research-intensive industries, with payments for solutions ranging from $10,000 to $1,000,000. According to InnoCentive's published data, about half of the 2,000 posted problems (challenges) have been solved so far (Spreadlin 2012, CEO of InnoCentive).

There are currently more than 200,000 registered solvers, that is, experts interested in working on challenges, who are based in almost 200 countries around the world. Both seekers and solvers remain anonymous for the entire duration of the process, with InnoCentive acting as mediator and handling the exploitation rights for the proposed solutions.

According to Spreadlin, reaching out to worldwide talent via crowdsourcing is such an effective solution that attention should shift to a much more basic problem: the right definition of the problem or research question in the sense of a crowdsourcing challenge (Spreadlin 2012).

All of the new developments showcased here reveal how the traditionally isolated search for solutions in closed innovation is becoming a thing of the past. More and more companies are opening up to either hand-picked partners in research clusters or to the random expertise at a boundary-less level (open innovation).

Companies can stay in their home system and reach out to actors of another institutional type, such as public administration or academia. They need to remember that such institutions, which Ili terms "social systems" (Ili 2012), might be guided by incentives that differ intrinsically to those of a for-profit organization.

Scientists are thus seldom motivated primarily by monetary incentives. For companies wishing to bring the competencies of such foreign systems on board, the trick will be to understand their unique social incentive systems and to use them successfully, for instance by establishing a mutually attractive vision for a research initiative.

References

Allen, T. J. (1988). Communication networks in R&D laboratories. In Katz, R. (Ed.), *Managing professionals in innovative organizations* (2nd ed.).

Baldwin, C. Y., & Clark, K. B. (2004). Managing in an age of modularity. In M. L. Tushman & P. Anderson (Eds.), *Managing strategic innovation and change* (2nd ed.).

Gassmann, O. (2013). *Crowdsourcing – Innovationsmanagement mit Schwarmintelligenz* (2nd ed.). Munich: Hanser.

Gemünden, H. G., Ritter, T., & Heydebreck, P. (1996). Network configuration and innovation success: An empirical analysis in German high-tech industries. *International Journal of Research in Marketing, 13*, 449–462.

Gerybadze, A., & Reger, G. (1998). Managing globally distributed competence centers within multinational corporations. In T. A. Scandura & M. G. Serapio (Eds.), *Leadership and innovation in emerging markets* (Vol. 7).

Hauschildt, J., & Salomo, S. (2011). *Innovationsmanagement*. Munich: Vahlen.

Hauser, J. R., & Clausing, D. (1988, May–June). The house of quality. *Harvard Business Review, 66*(3), 63–73.

Hauser, J., & Zettelmeyer, F. (2004). Metrics to evaluate RD&E. In *The human side of managing technological innovation*. Oxford University Press.

Ili, S. (2012). Innovation excellence, symposium.

Nestle, V. (2011). *Open Innovation im Cluster*. Wiesbaden: Gabler Research.

Spreadlin, D. (2012). Are you solving the right problem? *Harvard Business Review*, September.

Timmons, J. A. (1997). Opportunity recognition. In W. D. Bygrave & A. Zacharakis (Eds.), *The portable MBA in entrepreneurship*.

von Stamm, B. (2003). Structured processes for developing new products. In *Managing Innovation, design and creativity*. Wiley.

In-House Innovation Management 26

Henryk Biesiada and Christine Ebner-Um

26.1 The Building Blocks and the Challenges of In-House Innovation Management

The last chapter has looked at the ecosystems that form the framework in which joint innovation can take place. It also considered the many challenges that one encounters when utilizing the rich know-how stored in an organization's many minds and getting these minds to work together to produce new innovations. These challenges include a unique challenge for global IT service organizations: to establish modern and effective innovation management that is not just a bridge between the organization's people, its external (technology) partners and providers, and research bodies as suggested by the idea of "open innovation", but which gets all of the integrative groundwork in place to instill a successful culture of innovation in-house.

This next chapter will go beyond the concepts introduced before and look at a real-life example of how effective in-house innovation management should be established and managed to live up to the business reality faced by IT service organizations.

Simple ideas management is no longer enough if we intend to seize all of the potential for innovation. An IT service organization's innovation management efforts should, in an ideal world, not only cover the innovation strategy and targets, but also the processes and structures that are needed for them. This means implementing and maintaining in-house systems in the sense of a reliable

H. Biesiada (✉)
T-Systems International GmbH, Mecklenburgring 25, 66121 Saarbrücken, Germany
e-mail: Henryk.Biesiada@t-systems.com

C. Ebner-Um
T-Systems International GmbH, Dingolfinger Str. 1-15, 81673 Munich, Germany
e-mail: Christine.Ebner-Um@t-systems.com

F. Abolhassan (ed.), *The Road to a Modern IT Factory*, Management for Professionals,
DOI 10.1007/978-3-642-40219-7_26, © Springer-Verlag Berlin Heidelberg 2014

infrastructure and efficient processes. By making sure of the right information and software systems, appropriate processes for planning, managing, and overseeing innovation efforts, and resources for processing data in terms of collating, checking, and pursuing innovative ideas, these ideas are given the guidance and support they need on their way to becoming real-life practice.

How can IT service organizations use innovation to get a head-start in the dynamic ICT business? The first thing they need is a corporate culture that promotes innovation. Both established roles and any necessary new roles should be adjusted to aid the innovation efforts. In its 'umbrella' role, innovation management needs to get all of the core processes of the organization to accept innovation as an inherent part of their purpose, and not as the job of any one area alone. Creating such an innovation-positive culture is, in this sense, one of the most complex and one of the most sensitive tasks that innovation management faces in IT service organizations.

Another internal challenge lies in the need to keep costs down while expectations concerning IT performance are growing. The operational business needs to be given technical solutions that help them develop innovations to market readiness. Keeping a global enterprise nimble and responsive also needs clear instructions, comprehensible rules, transparent targets, and people explicitly appointed to make innovation a tangible reality for the organization's people.

We can distinguish between four clusters of corporate functions that are essential for successful in-house innovation management:

- **Structure and governance:** How can interdisciplinary contacts be achieved, supported, and managed?
- **Communication:** Which internal communication measures are required to give the innovation process the support it needs?
- **People:** How should the workforce be organized? Which roles should be defined for the innovation process, and what is the job of HR managers in this respect? How can we involve people as soon as possible and as effectively as possible in the innovation process?
- **Processes:** Which steps do we need to turn a pool of unrefined ideas into a tangible outcome?

Successful innovation needs many factors to be in place in these clusters. Apart from new technologies, or their development, production, and the establishment of the right service offerings for them, innovation also needs to be brought to market with the right marketing strategy. This needs interdisciplinary cooperation to work effectively in the organization. The people involved need to know how to communicate and work with each other, e.g. research and development with the innovation team or production with marketing and sales.

Technological innovation can be as up-to-date as it wants: picking the wrong features or not preparing for the market launch will cost invaluable time and resources, which no IT service organizations with global ambitions can accept. This should be kept in mind when involving R&D, IT production, or distribution specialists in the innovation process from its very beginning.

Again, the close integration of all of the core functions into the innovation process is the right way to go. This doesn't just mean process design or workflows: All of the innovation activities need to have a clear, shared target in mind, wherever they might be located. If this shared target is, for instance, reaching market leadership with an innovative portfolio element, special attention should be paid by everybody involved to all of the criteria that are necessary to make it a success in the market, e.g. by considering its appeal for all of the potential customer groups. At an external level, this means effective coordination and cooperation between product management and sales/marketing.

The organization's strategy, culture, and general working atmosphere are internal levers with just as much relevance as legal considerations (patents, licenses, country-specific regulations). There is also the potential for conflict between the many interfaces of larger organizations: this needs to be seen as a major challenge for innovation managers. They need to find the right processes and alignment of the interfaces, not just between an innovation's original development and its product or application-specific evolution, but also between production and marketing. In this area, it helps to make use of coordination measures that cut across processes and departments, such as relying on multipliers, steering groups, or special, often interdisciplinary transfer task forces.

Interdepartmental communication should accompany innovations along the entire process chain to support their evolution and give them a public expression, both inwards into the organization and outwards into the wider public. Such professional communication support for innovations is becoming more and more important and should be regarded as a dedicated part of corporate communications. Innovation communication means including communication at every step in the innovation management process, beginning with the choice of the right media and platforms to reach out to all people involved. This choice can range from online or print media (intranet, flyers, bulletins, in-house magazines, blogs, or communities) to full-scale events or competitions. Later in the innovation cycle, this is expanded to include the public presentation and selling of the innovation.

No innovation is successful before the people it is meant for have understood and accepted it—being seen by customers as innovative or forward-looking is not enough. The job of communication is to get the company's people involved in the internal innovation culture from the very start and to make innovation a real and interesting experience for them.

Technical or functional competence is no guarantee for a successful marketing strategy or market presence for new products or services. Given the constant pressure to innovate in the ICT industry, it is more than essential to record and safeguard the new knowledge, since access to knowledge and information capital can make or break a company's competitive success. This means that HR management is no longer a purely administrative pursuit. For IT service organizations in particular, the danger is that they concentrate too much on the technical objectives in their innovation strategies or targets. Coming up with innovative ideas or designing and selling new products and services are processes done by human beings. Structures and tools are there to help these people. They are not able to replace them. At IT service organizations, HR management needs to work hand in hand with innovation management to have the right answers to the following questions: Has the workforce structure been considered when defining the innovation strategy or targets? Does workforce planning set aside dedicated resources for developing and pursuing innovations? Are there long-term prospects and opportunities for people's development hidden in the innovation process? Are the training opportunities on offer sufficient?

Here, a previously defined, fully integrated—both internally and externally—innovation management has the effect of determining success in the competition: All of the internal challenges need to be internalized and covered in the innovation mindset. IT service organizations who maintain working partnerships with clients or who work with the best (technology) partners and, possibly, research institutes in innovation partnerships, stand a good chance of getting quick and meaningful results.

26.2 The Innovation Process from First Ideas to Finished Output

At IT service providers, innovation means the sum of new inventions and their successful marketization. This requires a clear distinction between innovations that are immediately market-ready and innovations that need more than 2 years before they become tangible reality. Pushing 'quick-acting' innovations can make particular sense when trying to improve internal efficiency or external competitiveness, but not only there: In dynamic environments, yesterday's innovations might very soon be old hat. The same goes for slow-acting innovations. Here, too, the upfront investment has to be able to pay off before the innovation becomes obsolete.

The ideal innovation process has a lean governance superstructure and three distinct phases: Collect, Verify, and Execute.

All of a company's people are encouraged to take part in the process—everybody should become a contributor of ideas or other input. **Collecting** ideas can take the form of a structured system with dedicated platforms and tools. Uniform criteria, such as standard templates for filing innovative ideas, are essential for a quick follow-up, although there should be only a minimum of formalities reining in the ideas.

Verifying the proposed innovations is the second step in the process, which ends with a decision as to whether the idea is dropped, put on hold, or executed. Ideally, the verification should use a multi-level balanced scorecard, built around the corporate targets. Using such an approach has the advantage that it standardizes the process with a set of readily adaptable criteria. The following decisions can be taken at this stage:

- Revise: Concerning cases in which the available information is not sufficient for a final judgment about the idea.
- Reject: Cases that do not live up to the defined criteria.

- Split or combine: Cases in which the idea matches or complements another current idea (combining) or seems too complex for a single project (split).
- On hold: Cases in which the idea does match the criteria, but has to be postponed, in consideration of other priorities.
- Evaluate and transfer: Cases that match all of the criteria.

The last step in the process is the actual **Execution** of the idea by the right people, depending on the outcome of the verification process.

This process applies internally and externally, that is, also for cases in which the organization works with clients or cooperation partners on new ideas or solutions, on testing new prototypes, or on launching new products and services. IT service organizations that have the ambition to become true enablers of the innovation-powered growth of their business need a fast innovation cycle in place, integrated into a holistic ecosystem of innovation.

26.3 Factors Determining the Success of Innovating Ecosystems

In most cases, access to experts or to the right resources is not the greatest obstacle that needs to be overcome. The challenge is rather to manage the many interactions and collaborations within and between the numerous actors in the ecosystem. The effective integration and management of all of the available resources is necessary if one wants to seize the synergies that exist between individuals' creativity and their shared ecosystem. With a living and working ecosystem in place, innovators from many different disciplines and backgrounds can produce new ideas and turn them into commercial benefits, with all of the diverse functions and processes in the organization contributing to the various links of the chain from the raw idea to the commercial product (participation, team management, business development, IP protection, finance management, controlling, marketing, and so on).

All of these processes and functions resemble an administrative machine, but the effective management of this ecosystem means more than forming a network between its actors. An innovation strategy only ever makes sense if it proves its ability to function under "open innovation" circumstances. For an innovation to produce real commercial benefits, it needs to initiate a momentum that is carried forward by all of the links along the process chain until it becomes a (commercial) success.

As managers of innovating ecosystems, IT service organizations need to focus on the interfaces and inter-dependencies between the actors in the system. They need to know which actor has the greatest leverage on the new technology. Managing the ecosystem means navigating through this multifaceted system and getting more value out of the sum of its parts. This makes "ecosystem relationship management" the counterpart to usual organizational functions, such as customer relationship management. It becomes the means to tie all of the strings together and operate the system from a central vantage point.

It has been stated many times that the time it takes to implement an innovation will determine the competitive success of any IT service organization. The same goes for the integration of new partners into the ecosystem. The ability to do so at high speed is the result of knowing the system and its actors, while delays are usually caused by external forces, such as being dependent on other actors or working with cautious investors controlling the purse strings.

The war for talent mentioned in the previous chapter describes a situation in which the organization is not able to create or sustain this system or when creative minds and their ideas begin to abandon the organization—whether mentally or physically. In such cases, the levers are to be found in close cooperation with HR management: An innovative culture needs to get many HR-related aspects right, including flexi-time models or the availability of training and travel opportunities. Executives also need the HR department to offer them specific development opportunities: They should be put into a place where they can recognize innovation when they see it, promote it, and take it further to become part of the innovating ecosystem. Innovation needs versatile integration skills, not specialist expertise in narrowly limited areas. This means that companies need to continue to invest in the development of their executives to make sure that these skills are present.

One aspect should be remembered when engaging in the war for new-generation talent: Talent does not have to come from the inside. The key is that the right talent acts as part of the ecosystem, and not that the company offers a constant stream of incentives to retain the talent for the company. Talented minds with creative ideas can hail from other companies or other external organizations, such as research institutes: What matters is that they contribute their innovative potential as part of the ecosystem. IT service organizations should therefore consider the entire ecosystem as its talent pool. This means that it needs to integrate and look after all of the actors in it, be they within or without the organization. A rethink is in order, away from the old belief that innovation should belong only within one's own organization and that all of its resources should be kept within it. Opening up to the world in this sense allows real "open innovation". Add this to a sustainably managed ecosystem, and innovation begins to produce real competitive advantages.

26.4 Innovation as an Opportunity for Employees

Innovation is far more than mere new products or services. Seen in terms of the inner workings of the innovating organization, it becomes an important lever for more efficiency, and an opportunity for the organization's people. In IT service organizations, innovation is an integral part of everyday work and a means for keeping the company and its people ready for the future. At the same time, innovative ideas often act faster than people's sense for the changes that are under way. Companies can help their people develop the right awareness for changes by enabling them to get involved with new developments.

Innovation happens, anywhere and anytime. Every member of staff has the ideas and creativity to make him or her a potential source for innovation. How should an innovative culture be shaped to help tap into this potential? For IT service organizations, an awareness of the problems and original thinking seem to be the prime aspects. If they want to be aware of and understand their client's needs, expectations, and benefits, reaching out to the customer is still the way to go. This cannot be replaced by simple market research, because it lives off the creativity, experience, and mutual interaction that happens when employees engage with clients or cooperation partners.

Another important lever is an inspiring and engaging working atmosphere that encourages people to innovate. This includes opportunities for participating and for expressing constructive criticism. IT service organizations should try to be active, not passive in the growth of innovation. This means listening to the customer, but it also means listening to the many ideas about how to use innovative solutions that are already there in the workforce. In current ICT organizations in particular, many, if not most working ideas are the product of the innovative input coming from within.

How can one integrate such innovative input into the innovation process? User-friendly, straightforward tools like databases need the right software to be in active use. Another way of generating ideas and also a great medium for larger companies in particular is the "idea storm". An idea storm is a form of collective brainstorming, made possible with a medium that everybody can access. The principle is that a platform is created to promote communication and cooperation at the company. Such a platform can become the perfect medium for seizing the combined creativity and mental potential of all of the organization's people. Many well-known names in the ICT sector have already come to recognize the advantages of the system and conduct their own idea storms regularly—often in many different forms and modes, but always with a huge response from their people.

The platform for an idea storm can be a website on which employees can post, comment on, discuss, and rate ideas and innovative concepts. It can also become a forum with which specific areas or the executive management of the company can address their specific concerns and listen to people's input and innovative contributions. The key is to review the many contributions that are posted and bring the most promising ones to fruition. Special events, such as live debates with top management representatives, are another very popular approach.

People's creative potential is the fuel that powers constant modernization in businesses operating in competitive markets. A positive culture of innovation can encourage people to see their ideas as the opportunities they are. Continuous innovation in this sense teaches employees to see change not as a threat, but as an opportunity. Engaging with new technologies means creating new vistas for development, as well as constant professional and personal growth. With managers and employees communicating and sharing their know-how, innovation processes are stimulated that help people identify with the organization around them—the seedbed for more participation and engagement in large and potentially anonymous organizations.

Part VI

En Route to the IT Factory

Conclusions and a Look Ahead 27

Ferri Abolhassan

The survey of "The Road to a Modern IT Factory" has cast a wide net. It has taken a look at the key aspects of IT industrialization and introduced models that IT units and entire IT service organizations will find useful in their practical work. To name but a few selected aspects, these have included ways to reduce costs, increase efficiency, and improve quality over the short, medium, and long term. At the same time, the exploration has shown that standardization and automation are not making equal progress in all cases, with obvious differences coming to light in processes, infrastructures, and services. For IT professionals, the next challenge will therefore be to level these differences as soon as possible and better align the advances being made in technology and processes. This is nonetheless another key conclusion from the present work: The advancing industrialization of technologies needs to keep in step with the development of processes, and vice versa. This is easier said than done, as innovation never rests and the competition never sleeps. How to master this challenge will be one of the most exciting questions for businesses in the future.

27.1 Keeping Technological and Process Industrialization in Pace

The recent study on "IT Trends 2013" by Capgemini (cf. http://www.de.capgemini.com) suggests that CIOs are beginning to shift their interest from matters of technical innovation to the optimization of their businesses processes—with the new ratio falling somewhere in the 60/40 range. Asked to envision their IT departments in the year 2023, a third of the CIOs could even imagine a direct split of responsibilities, distinguishing between technology and business processes. It remains to be seen whether this trend would indeed lead to better efficiency or, above all, better quality and lower costs, as it would result in the loss of invaluable

F. Abolhassan (✉)
T-Systems International GmbH, Mecklenburgring 25, 66121 Saarbrücken, Germany
e-mail: Ferri.Abolhassan@t-systems.com

F. Abolhassan (ed.), *The Road to a Modern IT Factory*, Management for Professionals,
DOI 10.1007/978-3-642-40219-7_27, © Springer-Verlag Berlin Heidelberg 2014

synergies and create obstacles such as additional coordination effort. For all that, a majority of the CIOs surveyed by Capgemini suggested no such split in responsibilities. Instead, almost every second respondent was in fact of the opinion that the majority of IT services would be sourced from external providers, with internal IT teams in charge of their integration.

27.2 Focusing on Core Competencies

To avoid friction in operations and in the efficient design of business processes, the people in charge of IT need to be aware of their key competencies and learn to focus on them. The expert voices we have heard in "The Road to a Modern IT Factory" agree in this respect. Services that are not part of these actual core competencies should be outsourced in full. Now, in the "age of the customer", it is up to the IT service providers to get behind their clients and support them as best they can—and as equal partners—in the pursuit of their goals. The evolutionary leap from "cottage industry" IT to true industrialized IT will only be possible within the coming decade if this is achieved. After all: IT industrialization has no lesser goal in mind than establishing IT as a long-term business enabler and offering clients "IT on tap".

27.3 Embedding IT Industrialization in the Corporate Culture

We are only witnessing the first steps of this sea change—That much we know. But where to go from here? Including key factors like cost optimization or higher efficiency in all decisions, actions, and projects must be the first and foremost goal for all businesses and IT service providers—pursued with singlemindedness to perfection. By giving standardization, automation, and constant quality improvement a lasting place in the corporate culture, the risk of human error is reduced automatically. Processes become more efficient, costs are reined in, and performance improves. However, just as lasting success does not happen overnight, IT industrialization cannot be done as an afterthought. Rather, IT organizations need to be injected with a climate that favors innovation, in which the evolution of the IT factory has a permanent, culturally internalized role and is promoted at all times. One means of doing so can be found in decision trees with repeating paths. Such tools can help IT organizations check which standardized or automated solutions could be transferred from one business unit to another, or which services should be relocated somewhere else or outsourced to a partner. The role of pilot projects or isolated solutions is now taken by replicable processes that help promote the industrialization of IT down to the level of clients and suppliers.

27.4 The Duty to Engage with Current Trends

While logic might suggest it should be second nature to the IT industry, it is unfortunately still far from standard practice: engaging with new trends from all areas and staying in a productive dialogue with research and practitioners as a means of finding ways to optimize one's work. Many IT managers have a blinkered vision of their work. Why move beyond tried and tested solutions if they are enough to get where one wants to go? The answer is perfectly simple: Because it can always be more efficient, less wasteful, and more economical. In the age of the internet, specialist forums, and partner networks, there is no excuse for the old attitude, not to mention the need to work with the institutions that set domestic and international standards or the end users whose needs deserve to be listened to in full. IT service providers play a key role in communication and in the sharing of experience and innovations between the various actors in this equation.

The need to engage and comply with norms and legal requirements is obvious. Engaging with new trends is a different matter. Despite all forecasts and analyses, any judgment about the future direction of technology still has an element of soothsaying about it. However: Anybody who does not get fully engaged with trends and shapes their strategy in response to them will lose market share over time. This book has therefore cast a light on some of the most important and most likely developments that will shape many companies' core business in the foreseeable future. It has shown how business processes, production, and infrastructures will change in response. Across the economy, the efficient use of resources is key—not only with a view to the ambitions of Green IT, but also in terms of the access to well-qualified, talented, and experienced specialists. Another continuing trend is the increasing role of communication via social media to pursue new ideas or avenues for professionalization. One comparatively new trend for the coming years will be the so-called "brokerage of services". Its potential promise can be seen in the case of "cloud services brokerage": Specialized service providers, tailoring standardized cloud services packs to match the individual needs of their clients, allow other IT service providers and their clients to concentrate fully on their core business. The end product: a customized solution based on accepted standards.

27.5 Living up to IT's Role as Business Enabler

Over the next months and years, people will judge the success of IT industrialization depending on how efficiently and economically the products and processes of IT service organizations are designed and marketed. Time will also tell whether the next phases of innovation will be used effectively in that they lead to solutions that actually offer added value for the end user. Innovation management is again called for—both internally and externally. The IT departments and IT service providers of companies need to establish themselves as the engines of innovation and, specifically, develop durable and flexible structures and processes on the basis of standardization and automation. Only then can they hope to make real use of future innovation and come out stronger and more successful after the next cycles of evolution and innovation. With advancing IT industrialization, the people in charge might have to move beyond the established models of industrial production and develop their own best-practice models. Not least because the challenges of the future will be ever more specific and less and less susceptible to the generic solutions of the past.

This book considers itself to be a first step along the road ahead of us. We will continue to guide and power the transformation to industrial IT production in the twenty-first century. In an ideal world, research on the topic will also progress, with other companies taking the lead and sharing their experiences. We encourage businesses from all sectors of industry and the institutions engaged in research and development to contribute their insights and their know-how. It remains for us to say: Let us set to work!

Reference

Capgemini. (2013). *IT-Trends 2013*. Retrieved January 31, 2013, from http://www.de.capgemini.com

Glossary

Apache Hadoop Java-based technology for the distributed storage and processing of extremely large data sets on the basis of highly standardized computing and network infrastructures.

Automation Introduction, harmonization, and standardization of recurrent processes and workflows (cf. Standardization).

Big Data The increasing volume and complexity of business data that needs to be stored, structured, and retrieved for analysis efficiently and immediately—e.g. for real-time risk assessments in the finance or energy industry (e.g. smart metering).

Bring Your Own Device (BYOD) The trend towards allowing employees to use their private (usually mobile) devices, such as smartphones and tablets in their work environment. The precondition is a comprehensive concept for integrating such hardware with corporate IT.

Broad Network Access A term from cloud computing that refers to all services being accessible via the network without reliance on a single client.

Build-to-Order (BTO) Production after an order has been received (and not preemptively); a project-oriented approach. Can lead to major process complexity in IT organizations.

Business Process Outsourcing (BPO) The outsourcing of entire business processes, such as bookkeeping or call center operation.

Carry-Over Effect A delayed influence (up to years later) of an activity on product sales (cf. Spill-Over Effect).

Central Change Advisory Board (CCAB) Responsible for reviewing, monitoring, and approving all important and critical changes in the IT landscape and acting as part of global de-escalation management.

Cloud Computing Provision of IT infrastructures or applications (such as software or storage capacities) from a network, usually operated by a service provider. The data is not kept on local storage, but in the data centers of the provider. Users receive dynamic and scalable IT resources, that can be adjusted flexibly to their needs; generally priced by actual capacities used (cf. Private Cloud and Public Cloud).

Commodity Business Increasingly easily interchangeable services in the market.

Configuration Management Database (CMDB) Within Configuration Management, a database for IT infrastructure and configuration management; helps

F. Abolhassan (ed.), *The Road to a Modern IT Factory*, Management for Professionals, DOI 10.1007/978-3-642-40219-7,

companies assess risks and their implications and reduce the number of adverse incidents.

Consumerization of IT The merging of the private and professional use of IT; solutions from the consumer market, such as smartphones, are used increasingly for professional purposes (cf. BYOD), while employees are using the cloud to access job-related data from home.

Critical Landscape Overview of business-critical IT systems of the client; relevant e.g. for incident management (cf. Major Incidents).

Crowd Sourcing Outsourcing of formerly internal functions to external users (via the internet at large or in a defined ecosystem) to be completed on a voluntary basis, e.g. for app testing. Business receive an insight into real-life practices for their product developers.

Customer Business Impact (CBI) Systematic evaluation of the effects of an IT outage on the customer's business processes. Among other uses, helps to classify changes or incidents by their potential or actual impact on the customer.

Defragmenting In this book, refers to a periodic process used to optimize the service volume covered in a location or reduce the number of operational units acting for a client.

Embedded Systems Computers or IT technologies integrated in machines or other equipment (e.g. in the automotive industry).

Fire Drill In IT: The simulation of system crashes to test troubleshooting processes.

Fix Phase Second phase of a quality initiative, aimed at the introduction of lasting changes in the sense of structural improvements (cf. Quick-Fix Phase and Stabilization Phase).

Follow-the-Sun Concept Enabling 24/7 support; services, such as call center operations, delivered non-stop by relying on locations in partner countries in other time zones.

Global Delivery Model (GDM) Sales model using globally distributed internal or external partners of an IT organization, including onshore, offshore, and near-shore activities (cf. Nearshore, Offshore and Onshore).

Infrastructure as a Service (IaaS) Provisioning or outsourcing of infrastructure resources (such as server capacities) to match demand (cf. Platform as a Service and Software as a Service).

IT Industrialization Here referring to the transformation of IT service organizations into factory-type structures by means of standardization and automation. Applying industrial methods and processes to IT to increase efficiency and effectiveness.

Kaizen "Change for the better"; a concept of Japanese origins, perfected at Toyota, for the permanent improvement of process and product quality.

Key Performance Indicator (KPI) A monitoring or performance indicator used to track defined targets.

Lean Management Ways to achieve better, "leaner" processes.

M2M (Machine-to-Machine) Concept for the increasing integration of machines for sharing operating data.

Major Incidents (MI) Major disruption—e.g. crash—of an IT system that causes a serious interruption to business activities and demands an urgent response to avoid considerable damages (e.g. loss of reputation or financial damage).

Make-or-Buy Business-related check to see whether a service (e.g. an IT service) should be produced in-house or bought from an external provider.

Mean Time to Repair (MTTR) Average time need to recover IT system operations after a crash.

Multi-Tenancy Architecture enabling multiple "tenants" (i.e. customers) to be served by the same infrastructure without these customers also gaining access to each other's data, user administration systems, etc.

Nearshore Outsourcing of services to neighboring countries (cf. Offshore and Onshore).

Offshore Global outsourcing of services (cf. Nearshore and Onshore).

Onshore Outsourcing of services within one's own country (cf. Nearshore and Offshore).

Onsite Similar to local onshore services, but local employees are used instead. With onshoring, services are provided locally by near/offshore employees (cf. Onshore).

Outsourcing Handing over of services or parts of the business to third parties.

Platform as a Service (PaaS) Use of a development and operating environment, such as databases, in the cloud. (cf. Infrastructure as a Service and Software as a Service).

Private Cloud The non-public variant of cloud computing. The cloud infrastructure is operated specifically for one organization or defined user group, either by the organization itself or an outside provider (cf. Cloud Computing and Public Cloud).

Provider Lock-In Commitment to or dependence on a specific provider.

Public Cloud The public variant of cloud computing. The cloud is available to a broad user group or freely accessible via the internet (e.g. the Telekom media center) (cf. Cloud Computing and Private Cloud).

Quick-Fix Phase First phase of a quality initiative with quick-action interventions for improving quality and efficiency (cf. Fix-Phase and Stabilization Phase).

Rapid Elasticity Quick and dynamic delivery of services (via the cloud), also during demand peaks.

Resource Pooling Resources combined in the cloud for use by multiple users (cf. Multi-Tenancy).

Root Cause Rate/Root Cause Rate in Time Indicator of whether the root cause for an incident is identified immediately or within a defined timeframe.

Service Level Agreement (SLA) Agreement between clients and providers to make the quality of a service measurable (e.g. bandwidths, response times, availability etc.).

Software as a Service (SaaS) Use of software solutions in accordance with current demand, without purchasing a license (cf. Infrastructure as a Service, Platform as a Service).

Spill-Over Effect A situation where one activity impacts others, such as where actions taken for one product have an effect on other products (cf. Carry-Over Effect).

Stabilization Phase Integration of measures introduced as part of a quality initiative; continuation and expansion of tried and tested activities for lasting quality improvements (cf. Quick-Fix Phase and Fix Phase).

Standardization Means to creates shared parameters; referring in IT to the harmonization of processes, products, and services based on experience to make them more efficient (in terms of cost and productivity) and offer clients top-quality and top-profitability services.

Total Workforce Management (TWM) Focused and needs-oriented allocation of personnel resources for greater transparency e.g. about costs or skills.

Trading-Up Opposite of trading-down; strategy for optimizing service offerings in the market or reaching out to new target groups.

Unified Communication & Collaboration (UCC) Integrating communication on a single platform to offer the opportunity to collaborate and communicate in real-time across geographic boundaries.

Utilization Defines the degree to which IT resources (e.g. server systems) are being used.

Zero Outage Program In this book: a program for the comprehensive, long-term improvement of quality. It refers to all of the most important KPIs for operations (including 99.99 % availability), for service requests and projects, and for customer interfaces.